Peterson's
PSAT*
success
2005

Byron Demmer
Shirley Tarbell

Includes a vocabulary-building chapter
by Merriam-Webster—with Greek and
Latin roots, quizzes, and a practice exam

Merriam-
Webster

THOMSON
*
PETERSON'S

Australia • Canada • Mexico • Singapore • Spain • United Kingdom • United States

About The Thomson Corporation and Peterson's

The Thomson Corporation, with 2002 revenues of US$7.8 billion, is a global leader in providing integrated information solutions to business and professional customers. The Corporation's common shares are listed on the Toronto and New York stock exchanges (TSX: TOC; NYSE: TOC). Its learning businesses and brands serve the needs of individuals, learning institutions, corporations, and government agencies with products and services for both traditional and distributed learning. Peterson's (www.petersons.com) is a leading provider of education information and advice, with books and online resources focusing on education search, test preparation, and financial aid. Its Web site offers searchable databases and interactive tools for contacting educational institutions, online practice tests and instruction, and planning tools for securing financial aid. Peterson's serves 110 million education consumers annually.

Petersons.com/publishing

Check out our Web site at www.petersons.com/publishing to see if there is any new information regarding the test and any revisions or corrections to the content of this book. We've made sure the information in this book is accurate and up-to-date; however, the test format or content may have changed since the time of publication.

For more information, contact Peterson's, 2000 Lenox Drive, Lawrenceville, NJ 08648; 800-338-3282; or find us on the World Wide Web at www.petersons.com/about.

Editor: Joe Ziegler; Production Editor: Megan Hellerman; Manufacturing Manager: Ray Golaszewski; Composition Manager: Gary Rozmierski; Interior and Cover Design: Allison Sullivan.

ISBN 0-7689-1443-4

Printed in the United States of America

10 9 8 7 6 5 4 3 2 1   06 05 04

Fourth Edition

Contents

PETERSON'S
getting you there

The New PSAT

As you have probably heard by now, the Preliminary SAT National Merit Scholarship Qualifying Test—usually referred to simply as the PSAT—has changed. The new PSAT/NMSQT will be administered for the first time in October 2004. Many of the changes to the new PSAT mirror the changes to the new SAT. However, the new PSAT and the new SAT are not identical. The following is a summary of the changes to the PSAT:

Total Testing Time

What Has Changed
- The new PSAT/NMSQT is 2 hours and 5 minutes. This is 5 minutes less than the old PSAT/NMSQT.

Critical Reading (formerly called Verbal)

What Has Changed
- Analogies have been eliminated.
- Short reading passages (75–125 words) with critical reading questions have been added.

What Has Remained the Same
- The critical reading section still consists of two 25-minute sections.
- Sentence completion questions are still on the test.
- Long reading passages (500 to 800 words) with critical reading questions remain a part of the test.

Mathematics

What Has Changed

- Quantitative comparisons have been eliminated.
- Two student-produced response questions have been added for a total of 10 questions.
- Higher level math content has been added, including the following new or expanded topics:

  - Number and Operations
  - Sequences and series involving exponential growth
  - Sets (union, intersection, elements)
  - Algebra and Functions
  - Operation on algebraic expressions
  - Absolute value
  - Rational equations and inequalities
  - Radical equations
  - Manipulation with integer and rational exponents
  - Direct and inverse variation
  - Functions as models
  - Linear functions (equations and graphs)
  - Geometry and Measurement
  - Geometric notation for length, segments, lines, rays, and congruence
  - Triangles (nonspecial)
  - Properties of tangent lines
  - Coordinate geometry
  - Data Analysis, Statistics, and Probability
  - Data interpretation, including scatter plots
  - Geometric probability
  - Median and mode

What Has Remained the Same

- The math section still consists of two 25-minute sections.

Writing

What Has Changed

- The new writing portion of the test consists of one 25-minute section—5 minutes less than the old writing section.

What Has Remained the Same

- The multiple-choice questions in this section still test students' ability to identify sentence errors, improve sentences, and improve paragraphs.

- There is still no official essay included, but schools will be offered options, such as ScoreWrite™, for practice

Why the Changes Were Made

The changes to both the PSAT and the SAT came on the heels of complaints by educators about the current exam. They asserted that the old tests were not an accurate enough indicator of the content taught in high school classrooms. The test had also been accused of being too susceptible to tricks and coaching techniques and biased against less affluent students.

The College Board has stated that it has three goals in revising the SAT:

- To better align it with high school study programs and college requirements

- To provide college admissions officers with a measure of a student's writing skills

- To emphasize how crucial writing is to success in college and beyond

How to Prepare for the New Test

You won't have to change your study methods so much for the PSAT because you won't have to write an essay, and the math won't include Algebra II. But it is never too early to prepare for the actual SAT. Also you should read a *lot*. And during high school you should *take challenging courses*—not only in English and math, but in other subjects as well. The more you challenge yourself, the better you'll do on the test.

About the PSAT/NMSQT

The Preliminary SAT National Merit Scholarship Qualifying Test (PSAT/NMSQT—usually referred to simply as the Preliminary SAT or the PSAT) is a standardized test designed to be one measure of your ability to do college work. It offers advantages of its own (some of which are described in this section), but its most important function is to provide practice for the SAT. The PSAT is shorter, but the questions are of the same difficulty as those on the SAT.

Overview of the PSAT/NMSQT Content

The PSAT/NMSQT measures reasoning, reading, and math skills, based on what you've learned so far in school. However, *you will NOT have to recall facts or dates, define grammatical terms, or provide math formulas, nor will you have to write an essay.* Rather, you will be asked to use the skills you've acquired in your years of schooling to solve problems—verbal, math, and reasoning—using materials that are given to you on the test.

Here are the sections you'll encounter on the test; they will be described in more detail later in the book.

Sections 1 and 3—Critical Reading (formerly called Verbal)

(25 minutes each, approximately 52 questions altogether.) These sections will include:

- Sentence Completions questions

- Reading Skills questions—passages of 500 to 800 words, followed by several multiple-choice questions each

- Reading Skills questions—paragraph-length passages of about 100 words, followed by 2 or 3 multiple-choice questions each (These short passages are a new addition to the PSAT.)

Sections 2 and 4—Math

(25 minutes each, approximately 40 questions altogether.) These sections will include:

- Multiple-choice questions with five choices

- Student-Produced Response questions

4

Section 5—Writing Skills

(25 minutes, approximately 39 multiple-choice questions altogether.) This section will include:

- Identifying Sentence Errors questions

- Improving Sentences questions

- Improving Paragraphs questions

Further Explanation of the Changes to the Math Section of the New PSAT

The new PSAT will test your skills in arithmetic reasoning, algebra, and geometry. Although the new PSAT will not test you on Algebra II-level material, it will have some harder questions and expanded coverage of several topics. According to the College Board, topics in four categories will be new or have expanded coverage on the new PSAT:

1. Number and Operations
    - Sequences and series involving exponential growth
    - Sets (union, intersection, elements)

2. Algebra and Functions
    - Operation on algebraic expressions
    - Absolute value
    - Rational equations and inequalities
    - Radical equations
    - Manipulation with integer and rational exponents
    - Direct and inverse variation
    - Functions as models
    - Linear functions (equations and graphs)

3. Geometry and Measurement
    - Geometric notation for length, segments, lines, rays, and congruence
    - Triangles (nonspecial)
    - Properties of tangent lines
    - Coordinate geometry

4. Data Analysis, Statistics, and Probability
    - Data interpretation (including scatter plots and matrices)
    - Median and mode
    - Geometric probability

Details of the Changes

Let's look at this material in greater detail so you will know what to expect.

1. Number and Operations

Sequences and series involving exponential growth

A list of numbers related to each other by a rule is called a **sequence**. The nth term, or **general term**, is usually denoted a_n. The sequence itself is represented by $\{a_n\}$.

In an **arithmetic sequence**, each term after the first differs from the preceding term by a constant amount, the **common difference** (d). For example, in the arithmetic sequence 5, 7, 9, 11, the common difference is 2. The formula for the general term of an arithmetic sequence is: $a_n = a_1 + (n - 1)d$ where d is the common difference. An arithmetic sequence is a linear function whose domain is the set of positive integers.

In contrast, a **geometric sequence** is an exponential function whose domain is the set of positive integers. Each term after the first is obtained by multiplying the preceding term by a fixed nonzero constant called the **common ratio** (r). To find the common ratio, divide any term after the first term by the term that directly precedes it. For example, in the geometric sequence 1, 4, 16, 64, the common ratio is: $16 \div 4 = 4$. The formula for the general term of a geometric sequence is: $a_n = a_1 r^{n-1}$.

Population growth is an important example of a geometric sequence. It can be tricky to set up correctly because the general term may have a rational exponent instead of an integer exponent. Consider these examples:

A geometrically increasing population that triples **every year** has this general term:

$$p_n = p_1 3^{n-1}$$

A geometrically increasing population that triples **every nine years** has this general term:

$$p_n = p_1 3^{\frac{n-1}{9}}$$

6

Sets (union, intersection, elements)

A **set** is a collection of things called **elements**, or members, of the set. The **union** of two sets, denoted ∪, is the set containing elements that are in both sets or either set. The **intersection** of two sets, denoted ∩, is the set containing elements that both sets have in common.

Consider the set of real numbers. It has two important **subsets**, the set of rational numbers and the set of irrational numbers. The set of rational numbers also has a subset, the set of integers. The set of integers has a subset called whole numbers. The set of whole numbers has a subset called the natural numbers. Each subset of the rational number set is nested inside the next larger set, like this diagram for the set of real numbers:

The Set of Real Numbers

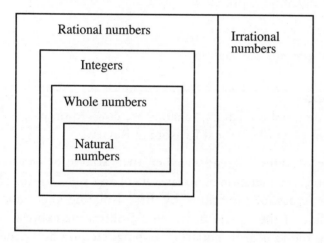

To understand the relationship:

- Begin with the set of counting numbers or **natural numbers:**

    {1, 2, 3, . . .}

- Add zero to the set of natural numbers to create the set of **whole numbers:**

    {0, 1, 2, 3, . . .}

- Add the negatives of whole numbers to create the set of **integers:**

    {. . ., −3, −2, −1, 0, 1, 2, 3, . . .}

- Divide one integer by another nonzero integer, $\frac{a}{b}$, to create the set of **rational numbers:**

$$\left\{ \ldots -\frac{3}{1}, \ldots -\frac{3}{2}, \ldots -\frac{3}{2}, \ldots 0 \ldots, \frac{3}{3}, \ldots \frac{3}{2}, \ldots \frac{3}{1}, \ldots \right\}$$

Rational numbers can be expressed either as repeating decimals or terminating decimals.

In contrast, **irrational numbers** have decimal representations that neither repeat nor terminate. Because of this, irrational numbers cannot be expressed as the quotient of two integers. The symbol $\approx$ is often used when working with irrational numbers. It means "approximately equal to." An example is the irrational number pi, $\pi \approx 3.1416$.

2. Algebra and Functions

The following topics are covered on pages 198–212 in the Algebra section of Mathematical Reasoning Review:

- Operation on algebraic expressions
- Absolute value
- Rational equations and inequalities

Radical equations

The properties of individual radical expressions are covered on page 210 in the Algebra section of Mathematical Reasoning Review.

An equation is called a radical equation when the variable occurs in a square root, cube root, or a higher root; for instance, $3\sqrt{y} + 50 = 65$. In general, solve these types of equations by first isolating the radical expression on one side of the equation, which simplifies the expression, and then eliminating the radical by squaring, cubing, etc., on both sides. For example, solve for y in the equation given above:

$$3\sqrt{y} + 50 = 65$$
$$3\sqrt{y} = 65 - 50 \quad \text{Isolate.}$$
$$\sqrt{y} = \frac{15}{3} = 5 \quad \text{Simplify.}$$
$$(\sqrt{y})^2 = (5)^2 \quad \text{Eliminate radical.}$$
$$y = 25$$

8

Manipulation with integer and rational exponents

The properties of positive integer exponents are covered on pages 208–209 in the Algebra section of Mathematical Reasoning Review.

The new PSAT will be enhanced to test you on your knowledge of rational and negative integer exponents in addition to positive integer exponents. For example, the new test may ask you about expressions like these:

$$x^{\frac{1}{3}} \text{ or } x^{-\frac{2}{3}}$$

Be sure you are comfortable with these kinds of expressions. Here is a brief review of some important information about integer and rational exponents.

Definition of exponent

If b is a real number and n is a natural number, $b^n = b \cdot b \cdot b \cdot \ldots \cdot b$, where b is a factor n times, b is called the base, and n is called the exponent. For example,

$$7^3 = 7 \cdot 7 \cdot 7 = 343$$

Negative exponent rule

If b is any nonzero real number and n is a natural number, then $b^{-n} = \dfrac{1}{b^n}$.

For example, $3^{-2} = \dfrac{1}{3^2} = \dfrac{1}{9}$

Definition of rational exponent

If $\sqrt[n]{a}$ is a real number and n is an integer where $n \geq 2$, then $a^{\frac{1}{n}} = \sqrt[n]{a}$. Stated more generally, if $\dfrac{m}{n}$ is a rational number that has been reduced to its lowest terms, then $a^{\frac{m}{n}} = \left(\sqrt[n]{a}\right)^m = \sqrt[n]{a^m}$ and $a^{-\frac{m}{n}} = \dfrac{1}{a^{\frac{m}{n}}}$.

Here are two examples:

Simplify: $9^{\frac{3}{2}} = \left(\sqrt{9}\right)^3 = 3^3 = 27$

Simplify: $32^{-\frac{3}{5}} = \dfrac{1}{\left(\sqrt[5]{32}\right)^3} = \dfrac{1}{2^3} = \dfrac{1}{8}$

Direct and inverse variation

Have you ever noticed how interrelated things are? How the condition of one thing often depends upon the condition of some other thing? For

instance, the time it takes for light from a star to reach Earth depends upon the star's distance from Earth; the time it takes varies directly with the star's distance from Earth.

Sometimes, the condition of one thing will change in the opposite direction in response to changes in something else; it may decrease if the other condition increases, or increase if the other condition decreases. For example, the time it takes to get to a friend's house depends upon how fast you are traveling. Increase your traveling speed and you decrease the time it takes to get there.

Here is a more rigorous way to describe direct and inverse variation, one you will need to know for the new PSAT:

- A quantity (y) that **varies directly** with another quantity (x) is directly proportional to that quantity and takes the general form $y = kx$ where k is a constant.

- A quantity (y) that **varies inversely** with another quantity (x) is inversely proportional to that quantity and takes the general form $y = \dfrac{k}{x}$ or $y = k \cdot \dfrac{1}{x}$ where k is a constant.

Functions as models

When you buy oranges at the grocery store, the amount charged is based on the weight and price per pound of the oranges. The probability that a dart will land within a circle in the center of a square target depends upon the relative size of the circle to the square. In each case there is a relationship between variables that can be turned into a mathematical relationship, or model. For instance, a model for the cost of oranges could be:

$c = w \times p$ or *cost = (weight) × (price per pound)*

A mathematical model is often a function. A function is defined as an association between two sets, X and Y, that assigns to each element (x) in set X one and only one element (y) in set Y.

Recall that a **relation** is a set of ordered pairs, like (x,y). The set that contains all of the first components of the ordered pairs is called the **domain** of the relation; the set that contains all of the second components of the ordered pair is called the **range** of the relation.

A relation in which each element of the domain corresponds to one and only one element of the range is called a **function**, usually denoted $f(x)$. It is a relation in which no two ordered pairs have the same first component but different second components.

Think of a function as a machine that has an input x and an output y, or $f(x)$. The domain of the function is the set of its inputs, and the range is the set of its outputs, or values. The function's output, y, depends upon its input, x, so we call y the dependent variable and x the independent variable.

Linear functions (equations and graphs)

Do you remember that a polynomial is a term, or the sum of several terms, with whole number exponents? A polynomial with one term is called a monomial, a polynomial with two terms is a binomial, and so in. In the standard form of a polynomial, the terms are written in descending order of their powers. Considering only polynomials with one variable, for the expression ax^n, if $a \neq 0$, the degree of the expression is n. So, the degree of a polynomial is the degree of the highest term in that polynomial. For example, the polynomial function $f(x) = x^7 - 5x^3 + 8$ is a degree 7 polynomial.

A linear function is a polynomial function of degree 1. Its graph is a straight line.

The **general form** of the equation of a line is: $Ax + By + C = 0$, where A, B, and C are real numbers and A and B are not both zero.

Usually, you will find it easier to work with a linear equation by expressing it in the **slope-intercept form** of the equation of a line:

$$y = mx + b$$

In this form, **m**, the coefficient of x, is the **slope** of the line and **b**, the constant, is the **y-intercept** of the line.

There are four possibilities for the slope of a line:

Positive slope, $m > 0$; the line rises from left to right.

Negative slope, $m < 0$; the line falls from left to right.

Zero slope, $m = 0$; the line is horizontal.

11

Undefined slope; m is undefined.

There are two special cases for the equation of a line:

First, if the slope, m, is zero, the equation reduces to: $y = b$, where b is the y-intercept.

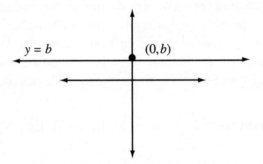

Second, if the slope, m, is undefined, the equation reduces to: $x = a$, where a is the x-intercept.

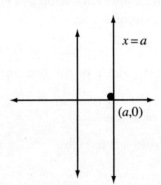

To find the slope of a line when you are given two points, use this formula:

$$m = \frac{y_2 - y_1}{x_2 - x_1} = \frac{\text{Change in } y}{\text{Change in } x}$$

When you know the coordinates for one point and the slope, you can use the **point-slope form** of the equation of a line:

$$y - y_1 = m(x - x_1)$$

Substitute the coordinates of the known point and the value of the slope, m, into the formula to get the equation of the line.

Let's work an example problem:

What is the slope-intercept form of the equation for the line shown in this graph?

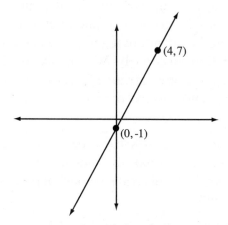

Solution:

First, let's find the slope using the slope formula:

$$m = \frac{y_2 - y_1}{x_2 - x_1} = \frac{7 - (-1)}{4 - 0} = \frac{8}{4} = 2$$

Now, use the point-slope formula to find the equation of the line:

$$y - y_1 = m(x - x_1)$$
$$y - 7 = 2(x - 4)$$
$$y = 2x - 8 + 7$$
$$y = 2x - 1$$

The answer, $y = 2x - 1$, is in the slope-intercept form of the equation of a line.

3. Geometry and Measurement

These topics are covered on pages 215–236 in the Geometry section of Mathematical Reasoning Review:

- Geometric notation for length, segments, lines, rays, and congruence

- Triangles (nonspecial)

- Properties of tangent lines

- Coordinate geometry

4. Data Analysis, Statistics, and Probability

Data interpretation (including scatter plots)

The ability to correctly interpret information is a very important skill—not only to do well on the PSAT but also to do well in life. It is just as important to see mathematical relationships accurately. Since mathematics is a symbolic representation of our world and our thoughts, we want to be able to understand these representations accurately. We can do this by correctly interpreting data. To be well prepared for the PSAT, be sure you can work comfortably with the common forms of data presentation: charts, tables, and graphs.

One way that data is presented for interpretation is in the form of a **scatter plot,** which is a set of points plotted on a graph. By finding a line that passes through, or close to, these points, we can create a model of the data to use in interpretation and prediction.

Here is an example of a scatter plot and its mathematical model:

$$y = -\frac{1}{2}x + 3$$

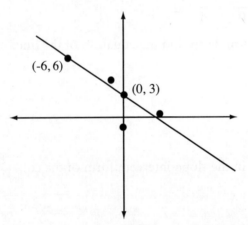

This example is an easy one, a linear equation where (1) two points are known, and (2) all the points are in near perfect alignment, or collinear.

You may be shown a scatter plot without a line and asked to find the properties of a line that best fits these points. You won't be asked to use formal methods to find the line of best fit but you should be able to make general observations about the line.

14

For instance, in the scatter plot shown below, it is clear the slope of the line will be positive and greater than 1. (A slope of 1 is equal to 45° from the *x*-axis.) We can also see the *y*-intercept will be very close to, or possibly pass through, the origin.

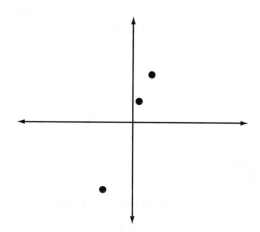

Median and mode

This topic is covered on page 194 in the Arithmetic section of Mathematical Reasoning Review.

Geometric probability

Geometric probability combines geometry and probability. It uses geometric forms to evaluate the probability of a successful outcome for an event. For example, suppose you have two target areas, a circular target area located in the exact center of a larger square target area, as in the diagram below:

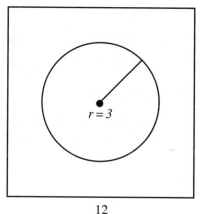

12

Note: Figure not drawn to scale.

Question: What is the probability that a dart, thrown in such a way that it is equally likely to hit any point on the target, will land inside the circle?

Answer: The probability that a dart will land inside the circle is the same as the proportion of circle area to square area. The area of the square is $s^2 = 144$ units. The area of the circle is $A = \pi r^2 = \pi 3^2 = 9\pi \approx 28.3$ units. Divide the circle area by the square area to get the answer:

$$\frac{28.3}{144} \approx .197$$

The geometric probability that a dart will land in the circle is .197, or about 20%.

Why Should I Take the PSAT?

Just how much taking the PSAT will help ease your transition from high school to college depends largely on your attitude toward it. First of all, it should NOT be regarded as a measure of your total worth—if you look at it that way, you'll freeze up. Remember: You'll grow and change a great deal during the year (or two or three) that lies between you and college, and college administrators know that. What colleges look for, as much as good scores, is potential, along with *improvement* as you proceed through high school.

So the best way to look at the PSAT is as an opportunity, as a way to get feedback on your college preparedness at this point, and as an aid to mapping out the best course to follow through the rest of your high school career. Perhaps you'll find you stack up pretty well when measured against other college applicants. Or perhaps you'll realize you'd better hustle! Whichever is the case, taking the test will help you plan additional classes you may need, as well as a course of independent study, so you can overcome your weaknesses and fortify your strengths.

That's not to say that taking the PSAT lacks immediate practical value, both in terms of getting into the college of your choice and in terms of financing your education. In addition to acting as a yardstick to measure your readiness for college, the test will do the following:

- It will help you prepare for the SAT, which you'll take in the spring. The PSAT includes most—but not all—of the content tested by the SAT.

16

- It can qualify you to receive information from colleges via the College Board's Student Search Service, a free information service for students who take the PSAT, the SAT I, and Advanced Placement tests. You can sign up for this service at the time you register for the PSAT. By participating in the Student Search Service, you can alert colleges, universities, and scholarship programs that you are interested in hearing from them and in receiving educational and financial aid information.

- It will place you in the National Merit Scholarship competition and in competition for other prestigious scholarships and special promotions.

What Are Some of These Scholarships and Programs?

Among the many scholarships and programs open to students who do well on the PSAT are:

The National Merit Scholarship

The PSAT, which is given in the fall each year, is also used as a qualifying test for the National Merit Scholarship Program, thus the official name PSAT/NMSQT. The National Merit Program consists of five steps. The first step is program entry; students must take the PSAT and meet other eligibility requirements to enter the Merit Program (discussed in more detail below).

This scholarship is sponsored by the National Merit Scholarship Corporation (NMSC), which is a privately financed, not-for-profit organization. The corporation co-sponsors the PSAT and will receive your scores and other information you may choose to provide on your answer sheet. If you qualify for recognition by the NMSC, you will be notified through your high school. For more information on the National Merit Scholarship, you may contact:

National Merit Scholarship Corporation
1560 Sherman Avenue, Suite 200
Evanston, IL 60201-4897
847-866-5100
www.nationalmerit.org

The National Hispanic Scholar Recognition Program

If you identify yourself as Hispanic or Latino on your PSAT, you may qualify for help from this program, which sends the names of academically talented students to various colleges for recruitment and offer of financial aid. (If you qualify but fail to identify yourself, your counselor can place you in competition anyway.) For more information, write to:

> The College Board
> National Recognitions Program
> 11911 Freedom Drive, Suite 300
> Reston, VA 20190-5602
> 703-464-8410

National Scholarship Service and Fund for Negro Students (NSSFNS)

If you are a junior, plan to attend a two-year or four-year college, and identify yourself as African American, you may qualify for this program. The NSSFNS offers a college advisory and referral service at no charge. For more information, write to:

> National Scholarship Service and Fund for Negro Students
> 2001 Martin Luther King Drive, Suite 501
> PO Box 11409
> Atlanta, GA 30310
> 404-752-7277
> www.nssfns.com

The Telluride Association

This association has scholarships available to academically talented juniors for summer seminars in the humanities and social sciences. For more information, write to:

> Telluride Association
> 217 West Avenue
> Ithaca, NY 14850
> 607-273-5011

Other Programs

A good score on the PSAT may help you qualify for many other programs. Valuable sources of information on these programs are:

- The *PSAT/NMSQT Student Bulletin* (a MUST—if you haven't already done so, you should pick one up at your school's guidance office NOW).

18

- Your school's guidance office.

- The library—your school's and the public library.

- The Internet—where you'll find many good sites, including the official College Board site at www.collegeboard.com.

How Does the PSAT Work?

Here are some common questions students ask about the mechanics of taking the PSAT.

When Should I Take the PSAT?

Most students attend high school for four years and take the PSAT in Grade 11, their junior year. If you plan to graduate early or to take college courses while still in high school, consult your school counselor and the *PSAT/NMSQT Student Bulletin*, discussed in the previous section. (See your school's guidance office for the most up-to-date information on registration.)

The test is given once a year, in mid-October.

You may also take the test for practice as early as your freshman or sophomore year, and this is a good idea, as long as you keep in mind that you will be learning and growing a great deal between your sophomore and junior year and, as emphasized above, this is by no means your last chance for anything.

If you elect to take the test in your sophomore year, however, *you must still take it in your junior year* in order to be eligible for all the perks it offers.

Where and on What Date May I Take the PSAT?

Again, be sure to consult your school's guidance office and the *PSAT/NMSQT Student Bulletin* for the most recent information; the particulars do change from year to year. As of this writing, the following applies:

- You will sign up for the test at your high school. Online registration for the PSAT is not available.

- The fee is generally $10 (some schools add an extra charge to cover administrative costs), but fee waivers are available from the College Board for juniors whose families cannot afford the fee.

- To learn registration procedures, as well as the correct date, time, and location of the PSAT, you must consult your school's guidance office or the principal of your school.

How Is the Test Scored?

After you work through the sample tests in this book, you will probably want to know how you did.

Here is the way to estimate your scores on the sample tests.

First, find the **Raw Score**. Begin by determining how many answers you got right and how many you got wrong. To do this, use the Quick Score answers on pages 63, 299, and 358. Now fill in the blanks below, then do the computations as indicated. Do NOT count the questions you omitted.

Critical Reading Sections

Questions 1–52

Number of correct answers: _____ = C

Number of incorrect answers: _____ $\times \dfrac{1}{4}$ = I

Now subtract: C − I = _____ (Critical Reading Raw Score)

Math Sections

Questions 1–20

Number of correct answers: _____ = C

Number of incorrect answers: _____ $\times \dfrac{1}{4}$ = I

Now subtract: C − I = _____ (Math Raw Score #1)

Questions 21–32

Number of correct answers: _____ = C

Number of incorrect answers: _____ $\times \dfrac{1}{3}$ = I

Now subtract: C − I = _____ (Math Raw Score #2)

Questions 33–40

Number of correct answers: _____ = C (Math Raw Score #3)

Now add:

Math Raw Score #1 _____

Math Raw Score #2 _____

Math Raw Score #3 _____

= _____ (Total Math Raw Score)

Writing Section

Questions 1–39

Number of correct answers: _____ = C

Number of incorrect answers: _____ $\times \frac{1}{4} = I$

Now subtract: C − I = _____ (Writing Raw Score)

Now use the table below to convert your **Raw Score** into your **SCORE** on each of the three sections.

CRITICAL READING		MATH		WRITING	
RAW SCORE	SCORE	RAW SCORE	SCORE	RAW SCORE	SCORE
52	80	40	80	39	80
47	74	35	69	34	75
42	68	30	63	29	67
37	62	25	57	24	60
32	57	20	51	19	54
27	52	15	45	14	49
22	47	10	39	9	43
17	42	5	33	4	37
12	37	2	28	2	34
7	31	0	24	0	31
2	24	−1	22	−1	30
0	21	−2	20	−5	24
−1	20			−9	20

A score of approximately 50 is considered average (the actual "average" score varies each year by a few points). To estimate the score you might receive on the SAT I, add a zero to your PSAT Critical Reading and Math scores. Add a zero to your Writing score to estimate your SAT II Writing score.

What can the scores be used for?

Your PSAT score report—which will be mailed to your high school principal and be available to you after Thanksgiving—will indicate how ready you are academically for college-level work as well as provide valuable information about your test-taking skills. It will give you question-by-question feedback so that you can discover the test questions you missed. That way you will know your strong areas and be able to work on your weak ones.

The score report will help you prepare for the SAT—the really important test and your "second chance," so to speak—by including your estimated SAT I scores (critical reading and math) and your estimated SAT II writing score.

In addition, as noted above, the score report will tell you if you are eligible for a National Merit Scholarship.

Once again, be sure you pick up a copy of the *PSAT/NMSQT Student Bulletin* when your test-taking period rolls around. It will give you complete and up-to-date official information on registration; time, date, and location; and scoring of the PSAT.

About This Book

Let's face it—taking the PSAT is no picnic. It's hard, and the stakes are high. And if you're one of those people who believes they're simply "no good at taking tests," the process can fill you with dread.

However, you should be aware that there are a lot of reasons why people feel they're no good at taking tests that have little to do with actually taking tests. And a good many of those reasons can be remedied. In fact, that's what this book is all about.

To combat fear, learn all you can about the test—the knowledge will calm you down because you'll feel more grounded, more in control. *PSAT Success* will help on that front by telling you what you need to know about the mechanics of the test and by offering you plenty of material to practice on. Never quite ready on test day? Make a vow right NOW to *plan ahead* this time. Make lists of things to do. Make a schedule of when to do them.

The most important thing of all to remember, however, is this: the PSAT is important, yes, but *no standardized test is a measure of who you are, how basically smart you are, or even how well you'll do on the next test.* So relax a little, okay?

Of course, it's entirely possible that you're one of the lucky people who are good at taking standardized tests. If that's the case, though, don't be lulled into false confidence—you'll still need to work hard and limber up your test-taking muscles for the big event.

Working your way through this book will be an excellent start.

Optimize Your Study Environment

To get the most out of *PSAT Success*, begin by taking these steps.

Find a quiet, uncluttered place to work. Remember, one of the most important skills you can develop for test-taking preparation is concentration. You may tell yourself that you work best with your cat draped across your books, sticky candy wrappers decorating your desk, and the CD player blasting like the takeoff of a 747. But trust us, you're telling yourself a big, fat lie.

In your quiet place, gather together the following:

- This book, along with the *PSAT/NMSQT Student Bulletin* (a nifty little newspaper-type document that you'll find in your school's guidance office, which contains official information about the test as well as a practice test to add to the ones you'll find here in *PSAT Success*).

- Pencils, scratch paper, and the calculator that you'll be using during the actual PSAT (don't buy a new calculator a week before the test—become thoroughly familiar with the one that you'll be taking with you by working with it in your practice sessions).

- A kitchen timer (not a clock or stop watch) to use when you do the practice tests.

Set aside a specific time each day to work on preparation for the PSAT. An hour a day is probably best, but it's up to you. The important thing is to make a daily appointment with yourself and *keep* it.

During your scheduled time, discourage your friends from calling or coming over. Discourage the people you live with from asking you to do stuff.

Make a Study Plan

Follow one of the suggested Study Plans on pages 24–28—or devise a study plan of your own—so you can keep your studying on track.

Work your way through this book from beginning to end. *Don't skip* anything just because you think you already know it. Thoroughly study *all* the sections and—most importantly—do *all* the practice questions.

23

Practice, Practice, Practice

You've heard this before, but it bears repeating: In order to do anything well—from playing the guitar to baking prize-winning muffins to skateboarding—you have to work at it. That goes for the PSAT, too. Much of the work consists of plain, grueling drill, doing whatever it is over and over and over.

There's an old joke that illustrates the point: A couple of baseball fans, Katie and Mike, are tourists in Cooperstown, New York, a town that houses a famous baseball museum. They stop a man on the street and ask, "How do we get to the Baseball Hall of Fame?" The man answers, "Practice, practice, practice."

This book will provide you with ample material to do just that.

Study Plans

The Nine-Week Study Plan

The study plan below isn't set in granite, but it will provide a general guideline for your next nine weeks of preparation. Plan to devote at least 5 or 6 hours per week to preparing for the PSAT—more if your schedule permits. This plan assumes you're equally skilled in all areas. You aren't, of course, so you'll want to play with the schedule a little, giving more emphasis to your weaker areas, less to your stronger ones. Take a little extra time in Week 1 to tailor the schedule to your particular needs.

REMEMBER: The test is important, but it is by no means your last chance at anything! So relax. And good luck!

WEEK 1	READ
Prepare yourself psychologically. Make a commitment of 5 or 6 hours a week for the next nine weeks.	"About This Book" (p. 22).
Prepare yourself physically. Make a commitment to eat well (this includes breakfast) and get some exercise every day.	Book chapters or articles on health and fitness. (You'll need to **read widely** over the next nine weeks. Might as well start with these!)
Set up your study area.	Reread "Optimize Your Study Environment" (p. 23).
Learn the basics about the test.	"About the PSAT/NMSQT" (p. 4).

24

Do the Diagnostic Test. Score your test. Pay special attention to the answer explanations that come after it. Identify your strengths and weaknesses—tailor your study plan accordingly.	"How Is the Test Scored?" (pp. 20–21). This "Nine-Week Study Plan" (pp. 24–27).
Critical Reading—Vocabulary.	"Merriam-Webster's Roots to Word Mastery" (pp. 113–179).
WEEK 2	**READ**
Critical Reading—Sentence Completion. Memorize the instructions for the Sentence Completion portion. Do the Sentence Completion practice exercises (pp. 90–92). Be sure to study the answer explanations.	"Sentence Completion" (pp.83–89). Magazine articles or book chapters—try *Time*, *Newsweek*, *Sports Illustrated*, or *Discover*.
Math—Mathematical Reasoning and Arithmetic. Memorize the instructions for the Multiple-Choice, and Grid-in sections. Review basic arithmetic. Do the Arithmetic practice exercises (p. 196). Study the answer explanations carefully.	"Mathematical Reasoning Review" (pp. 181–184). "Arithmetic" (pp. 184–195).
WEEK 3	**READ**
Math—Algebra and Word Problems. Review the instructions for the math portions. Continue to memorize these! Do the Algebra practice exercises (p. 213). Study the answer explanations carefully.	"Algebra" (pp. 198–212).

WEEK 4	READ
Critical Reading—Reading Skills. Memorize the instructions for the Reading Skills portion. Do the Reading Skills exercises (pp. 102–108). Again, study the answer explanations.	"Reading Skills" (pp. 92–101). Do a LOT of reading. Try the *New York Times*, *Smithsonian Magazine*, or *Scientific American*. Try novels and short stories.
Math—Continue your algebra review. Concentrate on your weakest areas.	Review "Algebra" (pp. 198–212).

WEEK 5	READ
Writing—Identifying Sentence Errors and Improving Sentences. Memorize the instructions for the Identifying Sentence Errors and Improving Sentences portions. Do the Identifying Sentence Errors and the Improving Sentences practice exercises (pp. 250–256). Study the answer explanations with care.	"Identifying Sentence Errors" (pp. 239–242). "Improving Sentences" (pp. 242–245). WRITE this week—letters, journal entries, or reflections on something you enjoy or believe in strongly.
Math—Geometry. Review the instructions for the math portions. Have a friend test you on these. Do the Geometry practice exercises (pp. 237–237). Study the answer explanations with care.	Review "Geometry" (pp. 215–236).

WEEK 6	READ
Writing—Improving Paragraphs. Memorize the instructions for the Improving Paragraphs portions. Do the Improving Paragraphs practice exercises (pp. 256–258). Don't forget to pay special attention to the answer explanations.	"Improving Paragraphs" (pp. 245–250). Write a LOT. Try imitating the writing style of a magazine article or book chapter of interest. Don't forget to continue your reading!
Math—Continue your Geometry review. Concentrate on the areas that you've identified as your weakest.	Review "Geometry" (pp. 215–236).

WEEK 7	READ
Do Practice Test 1. Score the test. For the rest of the week, go back and review your weakest areas. Study the answer explanations. You'll learn a great deal from these.	Review the critical reading, writing, and math chapters that deal with your weakest areas. Continue to read widely. Try *Harper's*, *National Geographic*, or the *New Yorker*.
WEEK 8	**READ**
Do Practice Test 2. Again, score the test. Continue reviewing your weakest areas. Study the answer explanations for all they're worth!	Review the critical reading, writing, and math chapters that deal with your weakest areas. Continue to read widely. Try reading fiction this week: *Lord of the Flies* (William Golding), *Song of Solomon* (Toni Morrison), the stories of Ernest Hemingway, Joyce Carol Oates, or Stephen King.
WEEK 9	**READ**
REVIEW, both your weak areas AND your strong ones. Be good to yourself. See a movie. Go to a ball game. Have dinner out.	Read challenging material related to a field you think you'd like to study in college.

The Eighteen-Week Study Plan

Most schools prefer this plan to the nine-week schedule. So if you're one of those organized, on-top-of-things people, go for it! Double the time you spend on each of the nine weeks, above. (Plan to spend at least 3 hours a week—or more if you can manage it.)

The Panic Plan

Too frightened (or busy) to even THINK about the test until two weeks before zero hour? Join the club, taking comfort in the fact that you're not alone! This isn't the optimal schedule, because you'll have to lock yourself in your room and have somebody deliver your food. But you can still succeed! Try this:

WEEK 1	READ
Critical Reading. Memorize the instructions for the Verbal portions. Do the Critical Reading practice exercises. Check your answers and carefully read the answer explanations. You'll learn more from these than you thought possible!	All Critical Reading "Review" sections. As many magazine articles as you can before drifting off to sleep—try *Time, Newsweek, Sports Illustrated,* or *Discover.*
Math. Memorize the instructions for the Math portions. Do the Math practice problems.	All the math "Review" sections.

WEEK 2	READ
Do Practice Test 1. Identify your strengths and weaknesses. Carefully study the answer explanations to those questions you missed. If you have time, do the same for Practice Test 2.	Read articles about important political figures, the space program, or exotic plants and animals. Do this instead of watching TV, going out, or daydreaming. Remember: it's just for two weeks!
Math. Continue to memorize the instructions for the math portions. Have a friend test you. If you have time, do Practice Test 2 and study the answer explanations.	All the math "Review" sections.

Answer Sheet

SECTION 1 — Critical Reading

1 Ⓐ Ⓑ Ⓒ Ⓓ Ⓔ
2 Ⓐ Ⓑ Ⓒ Ⓓ Ⓔ
3 Ⓐ Ⓑ Ⓒ Ⓓ Ⓔ
4 Ⓐ Ⓑ Ⓒ Ⓓ Ⓔ
5 Ⓐ Ⓑ Ⓒ Ⓓ Ⓔ
6 Ⓐ Ⓑ Ⓒ Ⓓ Ⓔ
7 Ⓐ Ⓑ Ⓒ Ⓓ Ⓔ

8 Ⓐ Ⓑ Ⓒ Ⓓ Ⓔ
9 Ⓐ Ⓑ Ⓒ Ⓓ Ⓔ
10 Ⓐ Ⓑ Ⓒ Ⓓ Ⓔ
11 Ⓐ Ⓑ Ⓒ Ⓓ Ⓔ
12 Ⓐ Ⓑ Ⓒ Ⓓ Ⓔ
13 Ⓐ Ⓑ Ⓒ Ⓓ Ⓔ
14 Ⓐ Ⓑ Ⓒ Ⓓ Ⓔ

15 Ⓐ Ⓑ Ⓒ Ⓓ Ⓔ
16 Ⓐ Ⓑ Ⓒ Ⓓ Ⓔ
17 Ⓐ Ⓑ Ⓒ Ⓓ Ⓔ
18 Ⓐ Ⓑ Ⓒ Ⓓ Ⓔ
19 Ⓐ Ⓑ Ⓒ Ⓓ Ⓔ
20 Ⓐ Ⓑ Ⓒ Ⓓ Ⓔ
21 Ⓐ Ⓑ Ⓒ Ⓓ Ⓔ

22 Ⓐ Ⓑ Ⓒ Ⓓ Ⓔ
23 Ⓐ Ⓑ Ⓒ Ⓓ Ⓔ
24 Ⓐ Ⓑ Ⓒ Ⓓ Ⓔ
25 Ⓐ Ⓑ Ⓒ Ⓓ Ⓔ

SECTION 2 — Math

1 Ⓐ Ⓑ Ⓒ Ⓓ Ⓔ
2 Ⓐ Ⓑ Ⓒ Ⓓ Ⓔ
3 Ⓐ Ⓑ Ⓒ Ⓓ Ⓔ
4 Ⓐ Ⓑ Ⓒ Ⓓ Ⓔ
5 Ⓐ Ⓑ Ⓒ Ⓓ Ⓔ
6 Ⓐ Ⓑ Ⓒ Ⓓ Ⓔ
7 Ⓐ Ⓑ Ⓒ Ⓓ Ⓔ

8 Ⓐ Ⓑ Ⓒ Ⓓ Ⓔ
9 Ⓐ Ⓑ Ⓒ Ⓓ Ⓔ
10 Ⓐ Ⓑ Ⓒ Ⓓ Ⓔ
11 Ⓐ Ⓑ Ⓒ Ⓓ Ⓔ
12 Ⓐ Ⓑ Ⓒ Ⓓ Ⓔ
13 Ⓐ Ⓑ Ⓒ Ⓓ Ⓔ
14 Ⓐ Ⓑ Ⓒ Ⓓ Ⓔ

15 Ⓐ Ⓑ Ⓒ Ⓓ Ⓔ
16 Ⓐ Ⓑ Ⓒ Ⓓ Ⓔ
17 Ⓐ Ⓑ Ⓒ Ⓓ Ⓔ
18 Ⓐ Ⓑ Ⓒ Ⓓ Ⓔ
19 Ⓐ Ⓑ Ⓒ Ⓓ Ⓔ
20 Ⓐ Ⓑ Ⓒ Ⓓ Ⓔ

SECTION 3 — Critical Reading

1 Ⓐ Ⓑ Ⓒ Ⓓ Ⓔ
2 Ⓐ Ⓑ Ⓒ Ⓓ Ⓔ
3 Ⓐ Ⓑ Ⓒ Ⓓ Ⓔ
4 Ⓐ Ⓑ Ⓒ Ⓓ Ⓔ
5 Ⓐ Ⓑ Ⓒ Ⓓ Ⓔ
6 Ⓐ Ⓑ Ⓒ Ⓓ Ⓔ
7 Ⓐ Ⓑ Ⓒ Ⓓ Ⓔ
8 Ⓐ Ⓑ Ⓒ Ⓓ Ⓔ

9 Ⓐ Ⓑ Ⓒ Ⓓ Ⓔ
10 Ⓐ Ⓑ Ⓒ Ⓓ Ⓔ
11 Ⓐ Ⓑ Ⓒ Ⓓ Ⓔ
12 Ⓐ Ⓑ Ⓒ Ⓓ Ⓔ
13 Ⓐ Ⓑ Ⓒ Ⓓ Ⓔ
14 Ⓐ Ⓑ Ⓒ Ⓓ Ⓔ
15 Ⓐ Ⓑ Ⓒ Ⓓ Ⓔ
16 Ⓐ Ⓑ Ⓒ Ⓓ Ⓔ

17 Ⓐ Ⓑ Ⓒ Ⓓ Ⓔ
18 Ⓐ Ⓑ Ⓒ Ⓓ Ⓔ
19 Ⓐ Ⓑ Ⓒ Ⓓ Ⓔ
20 Ⓐ Ⓑ Ⓒ Ⓓ Ⓔ
21 Ⓐ Ⓑ Ⓒ Ⓓ Ⓔ
22 Ⓐ Ⓑ Ⓒ Ⓓ Ⓔ
23 Ⓐ Ⓑ Ⓒ Ⓓ Ⓔ
24 Ⓐ Ⓑ Ⓒ Ⓓ Ⓔ

25 Ⓐ Ⓑ Ⓒ Ⓓ Ⓔ
26 Ⓐ Ⓑ Ⓒ Ⓓ Ⓔ
27 Ⓐ Ⓑ Ⓒ Ⓓ Ⓔ

PETERSON'S
getting you there

SECTION 4

Math

1. Ⓐ Ⓑ Ⓒ Ⓓ Ⓔ
2. Ⓐ Ⓑ Ⓒ Ⓓ Ⓔ
3. Ⓐ Ⓑ Ⓒ Ⓓ Ⓔ
4. Ⓐ Ⓑ Ⓒ Ⓓ Ⓔ

5. Ⓐ Ⓑ Ⓒ Ⓓ Ⓔ
6. Ⓐ Ⓑ Ⓒ Ⓓ Ⓔ
7. Ⓐ Ⓑ Ⓒ Ⓓ Ⓔ

8. Ⓐ Ⓑ Ⓒ Ⓓ Ⓔ
9. Ⓐ Ⓑ Ⓒ Ⓓ Ⓔ
10. Ⓐ Ⓑ Ⓒ Ⓓ Ⓔ

Grid-in answer boxes (numbers 11–20), each with digits 0–9.

11. 12. 13. 14. 15.
16. 17. 18. 19. 20.

SECTION 5

Writing Skills

1. Ⓐ Ⓑ Ⓒ Ⓓ Ⓔ
2. Ⓐ Ⓑ Ⓒ Ⓓ Ⓔ
3. Ⓐ Ⓑ Ⓒ Ⓓ Ⓔ
4. Ⓐ Ⓑ Ⓒ Ⓓ Ⓔ
5. Ⓐ Ⓑ Ⓒ Ⓓ Ⓔ
6. Ⓐ Ⓑ Ⓒ Ⓓ Ⓔ
7. Ⓐ Ⓑ Ⓒ Ⓓ Ⓔ
8. Ⓐ Ⓑ Ⓒ Ⓓ Ⓔ
9. Ⓐ Ⓑ Ⓒ Ⓓ Ⓔ
10. Ⓐ Ⓑ Ⓒ Ⓓ Ⓔ

11. Ⓐ Ⓑ Ⓒ Ⓓ Ⓔ
12. Ⓐ Ⓑ Ⓒ Ⓓ Ⓔ
13. Ⓐ Ⓑ Ⓒ Ⓓ Ⓔ
14. Ⓐ Ⓑ Ⓒ Ⓓ Ⓔ
15. Ⓐ Ⓑ Ⓒ Ⓓ Ⓔ
16. Ⓐ Ⓑ Ⓒ Ⓓ Ⓔ
17. Ⓐ Ⓑ Ⓒ Ⓓ Ⓔ
18. Ⓐ Ⓑ Ⓒ Ⓓ Ⓔ
19. Ⓐ Ⓑ Ⓒ Ⓓ Ⓔ
20. Ⓐ Ⓑ Ⓒ Ⓓ Ⓔ

21. Ⓐ Ⓑ Ⓒ Ⓓ Ⓔ
22. Ⓐ Ⓑ Ⓒ Ⓓ Ⓔ
23. Ⓐ Ⓑ Ⓒ Ⓓ Ⓔ
24. Ⓐ Ⓑ Ⓒ Ⓓ Ⓔ
25. Ⓐ Ⓑ Ⓒ Ⓓ Ⓔ
26. Ⓐ Ⓑ Ⓒ Ⓓ Ⓔ
27. Ⓐ Ⓑ Ⓒ Ⓓ Ⓔ
28. Ⓐ Ⓑ Ⓒ Ⓓ Ⓔ
29. Ⓐ Ⓑ Ⓒ Ⓓ Ⓔ
30. Ⓐ Ⓑ Ⓒ Ⓓ Ⓔ

31. Ⓐ Ⓑ Ⓒ Ⓓ Ⓔ
32. Ⓐ Ⓑ Ⓒ Ⓓ Ⓔ
33. Ⓐ Ⓑ Ⓒ Ⓓ Ⓔ
34. Ⓐ Ⓑ Ⓒ Ⓓ Ⓔ
35. Ⓐ Ⓑ Ⓒ Ⓓ Ⓔ
36. Ⓐ Ⓑ Ⓒ Ⓓ Ⓔ
37. Ⓐ Ⓑ Ⓒ Ⓓ Ⓔ
38. Ⓐ Ⓑ Ⓒ Ⓓ Ⓔ
39. Ⓐ Ⓑ Ⓒ Ⓓ Ⓔ

Diagnostic Test

Section 1—Critical Reading

Time—25 Minutes • 25 Questions

For each question below, choose the best answer from the choices given and fill in the corresponding oval on the answer sheet.

> **Directions:** Each sentence below has either one or two blanks in it and is followed by five choices, labeled (A) through (E). These choices represent words or phrases that have been left out. Choose the word or phrase that, if inserted into the sentence, would best fit the meaning of the sentence as a whole.
>
> **Example:**
>
> Canine massage is a veterinary technique for calming dogs that are extremely _____.
>
> (A) inept
> (B) disciplined
> (C) controlled
> (D) stressed
> (E) restrained

1. Paradoxically, science demands of its practitioners both _____ and _____.

    (A) a controlled intellect..a free imagination
    (B) dedication..hard work
    (C) meticulousness..good math skills
    (D) skepticism..an inquiring mind
    (E) ambition..creativity

2. Bubonic plague, which once _____ Europe, killing millions, is now easily _____ by modern antibiotics.

    (A) devastated..contracted
    (B) sickened..concealed
    (C) shocked..obscured
    (D) captivated..routed
    (E) ravaged..halted

GO ON TO THE NEXT PAGE

PETERSON'S
getting you there

3. Because she had refined, gourmet tastes, Brenda was _____ when Trent served greasy sausage stew for lunch—she simply could not force down a bite.

   (A) distraught
   (B) scandalized
   (C) revolted
   (D) perplexed
   (E) ecstatic

4. _____, Sir Edward grew up to be exactly like his father, whom he hated.

   (A) Obviously
   (B) Arrogantly
   (C) Ominously
   (D) Perilously
   (E) Ironically

5. Corey was the most notorious bully in the school—both _____ and _____.

   (A) paltry..stingy
   (B) ungainly..crude
   (C) domineering..cruel
   (D) ugly..selfish
   (E) vigorous..demanding

Directions: Read each of the passages carefully, then answer the questions that come after them. The answer to each question may be stated overtly or only implied. You will not have to use outside knowledge to answer the questions—all the material you will need will be in the passage itself. In some cases, you will be asked to read two related passages and answer questions about their relationship to one another.

Questions 6–7 are based on the following passage.

The passage is an excerpt from a short story by Edith Wharton, "The Lady's Maid's Bell."

Line   I had been [employed] near a week at Brympton before I saw my master. Word came that he was arriving one afternoon, and a change passed over the whole
(5)   household. It was plain that nobody loved him below stairs. Mrs. Blinder took uncommon care with the dinner that night, but she snapped at the kitchen-maid in a way quite unusual with her;
(10)   and Mr. Wace, the butler, . . . went about his duties as if he'd been getting ready for a funeral. He was a great Bible-reader, Mr. Wace was[,] . . . but that day he used such dreadful language that I was about
(15)   to leave the table, when he assured me it was all out of Isaiah; and I noticed that whenever the master came Mr. Wace took to the prophets.

6. The phrase, "took to the prophets" (line 18), most likely means

(A) prayed.
(B) wept.
(C) swore.
(D) read the Bible aloud.
(E) lectured the other staff.

7. Based on the passage, Mrs. Blinder most likely took uncommon care with the dinner that night because the master would be present, and Mrs. Blinder

(A) knew he would be hungry.
(B) took pride in her work.
(C) was meeting him for the first time.
(D) feared his criticism.
(E) was resigned to having a bad boss.

Questions 8–9 are based on the following passage.

This excerpt is from a 1993 government document, posted on the NASA Internet site.

Line All visible celestial objects known today account for only 10 percent of the mass in the universe. The rest of this "missing mass," also known as "dark matter," is
(5) presumably invisible . . . Since all visible matter is only a small fraction of the total mass in the universe, the amount of dark mass that is present will determine the evolutionary future of the universe. If
(10) there is not enough dark matter to gravitationally bind the universe together, it could continue expanding forever. If there is enough mass in the universe to gravitationally hold it together, the
(15) universe may slow down its expansion, come to a halt, and begin to contract and eventually collapse.

8. The main purpose of the passage is to speculate on the

(A) composition of "dark matter."
(B) composition of "celestial objects."
(C) validity of the theory of evolution.
(D) reason for the existence of the universe.
(E) ultimate fate of the universe.

9. Which of the following is the best example of a "visible celestial object" (line 1), based on inference from the information in the passage?

(A) A clump of dark matter
(B) The pull of gravity
(C) A planet or galaxy
(D) A collapsed star
(E) A black hole

Questions 10–11 are based on the following passage.

This passage is based on "Theories of the North American Trickster," by Ake Hultkrantz.

Line The figure of Trickster, found in myth and folklore around the world, is usually male and depicted as an animal, a spirit, or a god. He is a rule-breaker and a thief,
(5) but he is also of great benefit to human-kind—both the Native American Coyote and the Greek god Prometheus, for example, are tricksters who stole fire and presented it as a gift to human beings. (In
(10) one story, however, after the humans had cooked their first meal, Coyote stole the food and ate it.) Trickster has been called a thief and gift-giver, a liar and a teller of the most uncomfortable truths; a wily
(15) mischief-maker, and creator and de-stroyer of worlds.

GO ON TO THE NEXT PAGE

PETERSON'S
getting you there

10. Which adjective best sums up all the character traits of Trickster as described in the passage?

(A) Deceitful
(B) Paradoxical
(C) Beneficial
(D) Mythological
(E) Mysterious

11. The examples of Coyote and Prometheus primarily serve to

(A) support the author's statements about the Trickster figure.
(B) lighten the tone of the passage.
(C) demonstrate that the Trickster is a comic figure in mythology.
(D) provide a vivid visual image of the Trickster.
(E) compare Native American myths to Greek myths.

Questions 12–17 are based on the following passage.

This passage is part of an essay written in the 1990s about the author's grandmother.

Line   From an early age, I knew that my grandma was different from other kids' grandmas. She was a preacher, for one thing, back in the days when there were
(5)   hardly any women preachers. Also, she was less enthusiastic about me than other kids' grandmas were about them. Whenever she was preaching a revival near the town of Crossland where we
(10)   lived, she'd always stay with us. When she arrived, she'd hug me, and tell me I'd grown, and ask me if I said my prayers and if I read my Bible, but her mind always seemed to be someplace else when
(15)   I answered. Even when I recited all the books of the Old Testament for her, or

said a poem such as "Richard Cory" or "The Highwayman," the best I could get out of her was a sharp "Well, listen at
(20)   that. Don't *that* beat all?"

When the week of revival was over, she'd leave, going back to St. Louis where she ran a mission for the lost and destitute. Crossland's over a hundred
(25)   miles from St. Louis, and Dad would offer to drive her back, but she'd always answer the same thing. "There isn't any use of that, Clyde. The bus is just as good."
(30)   So we'd take her down to the Greyhound station and watch her hand her ticket to the uniformed driver, disappear inside and reappear to wave good-bye, her expression obscured by the
(35)   bus's grimy window. Then, even before the bus got moving, she'd look away, ahead toward her real life. Leaving us behind in a bitter cloud of exhaust, the bus would cough and jolt down the
(40)   narrow main street of Crossland. But I could always imagine the way it would be once it got out on the highway, gathering speed as if the wind had caught its sails, bearing Grandma back to a life
(45)   as exotic to me as the deserts of Egypt.

She lived in two rooms up over the mission. When Grandpa died, she had sold their home and furniture, and her only possessions were a single bed with a
(50)   black iron bedstead, a shabby, faded-green, overstuffed chair, a rickety drop-leaf table, a kerosene stove, and rag rugs on the floor. It was a men's mission, and downstairs there were always five or
(55)   six old men, coughing and drinking coffee, talking to each other or to themselves, and although Grandma kept it spotless, the mission always had a sour smell. Mama and Dad would go to visit

(60) her every month, and once in a long while, if it was a holiday or Grandma's birthday, they'd take me, but they didn't very often. They didn't think it was a fit place for a child.

(65)   So Grandma wasn't the pink-cheeked, twinkly-eyed grandma I read about in books, and her visits weren't festooned with presents, or trips to the zoo, or jaunts down to the ice cream

(70) parlor, but when she came to visit she did always trail a little glamor and glory. Still, we'd all breathe a sigh of relief when she left, even Mama, whose chicken was always "a little dry, Kate,

(75) why don't you try the oven at a slower heat? Seems like gas stoves don't cook chicken like wood stoves used to."

    Dad would be the most relieved of all to see her go, although I didn't know it

(80) then. It was after I was grown up that he confided in me that he never had liked Grandma very much. She was too strict with Mama and made her do all the work, cooking and cleaning and keeping

(85) house for Grandpa, while she was off preaching revivals. It was the reason Mama was thirty before she got married. "She never gave Kate a bit of credit," he said.

(90)   The thing I remember most vividly about Grandma (oddly, because she wasn't given to physical vanity at all) is her shining hair, which was white shot through with silver. She wore it up in

(95) braids during the day, but at night sometimes I was allowed to help Mama take the pins and small tortoiseshell combs out and brush it. It tumbled to her waist, and I remember thinking she had

(100) the most beautiful hair in the world. It was a task I took seriously, even though I almost always came up against a tangle,

and she'd snap at me, "You're just like Kate was when she was your age, you

(105) just have to yank and pull. You never can remember I'm tender-headed."

12. Of the following choices, which best describes the grandmother's emotional relationship with her family?

(A) Distant
(B) Timid
(C) Hateful
(D) Folksy
(E) Devoted

13. The reader can deduce from the passage that the grandmother's attitude toward the narrator's mother was characterized by

(A) ridicule.
(B) repugnance.
(C) puzzlement.
(D) disapproval.
(E) alarm.

14. As it is used in line 45, the word "exotic" most nearly means

(A) dangerous.
(B) mysterious.
(C) outlandish.
(D) ridiculous.
(E) tedious.

15. Which of the following does the narrator remember most vividly about her grandmother?

(A) A visit to her grandmother's mission
(B) Her grandmother's spirituality
(C) Her grandmother's meanness
(D) A physical feature her grandmother had
(E) Her grandmother's strictness

35

16. In the sentence "It was the reason Mama was thirty before she got married" (lines 86–87), to what does "it" refer?

(A) The grandmother's fundamentalist religion

(B) The mother's fear of the grandmother

(C) The mother's overwork in service of the grandmother

(D) The father's dislike of the grandmother

(E) The mother's choosing the grandmother's well-being over her husband's

17. What do the words "shot through" mean in the context of lines 93–94?

(A) Separated from

(B) Intermingled with

(C) Concealed by

(D) Inseparable from

(E) Alongside

Questions 18–25 are based on the following passage.

This passage is adapted from The Myth of Culture *by Jo Lynn Southard, J.D., LL.M.*

Line　Oppression of women is embedded in most, if not all, societies, its message usually couched in terms of the protection and promotion of traditional
(5)　cultural practices. These practices are presented as natural and unremarkable, inherently beneficial to society by virtue simply of their connection with the past, with tradition. The call to preserve
(10)　traditional cultural practices can wield enormous power, and it can be easily manipulated by those in power.

　　In 1963, in the United States, Betty Friedan wrote of what she called the
(15)　"feminine mystique," which referred to the tradition (at that time pretty much unexamined—in fact, Friedan called it "the problem that has no name")—that being a wife and mother was a woman's
(20)　highest and only calling. It is a message still alive today, one that dies hard and severely limits women's life choices. In other cultures the message is much the same, sometimes going so far as to
(25)　harshly limit what a woman can wear in public, where she can travel, whether she can receive an education, whether she can work outside the home, and even whether she is to be allowed to learn to
(30)　read and write.

　　Time and again, in wars and revolutions, women are welcomed into the struggle for freedom from oppression, only to be forced back into the private
(35)　realm when freedom is attained. In the midst of a struggle or immediately after a change in power in a country, women are told that their particular issues must wait while the more pressing, "larger" issues
(40)　are addressed. Meanwhile, women are urged to return to the home to fulfill their traditional roles, one of which is to replenish a population decimated by the struggle itself. As a result, women's
(45)　issues—issues that affect half the population—never really become a priority.

　　International human rights law itself does far too little to respond to the needs
(50)　particular to women. Until very recently, virtually all precepts of international law ignored the concept of gender discrimination. Genocide, persecution, torture, and refugee status are still mostly defined by
(55)　race, religion, nationality, ethnicity, or membership in a particular social or political group. While all women fit into

one or more of those groups, by definition these human rights abuses cannot be
(60) said to be committed against women
because of their gender, but rather are
committed against all people. Human
rights abuses against women *as women*
(from denial of basic education or the
(65) right to travel up to, until very recently,
such heinous abuses as rape and mutila-
tion) are pretty much ignored. In fact,
even the Convention on the Elimination
of All Forms of Discrimination Against
(70) Women did not mandate the inclusion of
women in the process of implementing
the treaty. Decision-making, even when it
comes to decisions about ending their
own oppression, is simply not viewed as
(75) a woman's "place." The decisions for
ending discrimination under the treaty
were and are made, in the main, by those
who created and perpetuated the cultural
traditions that enabled discrimination
(80) and abuse to happen in the first place.

The traditions of the culture into
which we are born have great influence
over how we live our lives. Traditionally,
most, if not all, cultures have defined
(85) themselves from the point of view of the
males in power. And it is natural for
those who have power—even if they are
kindly and well-meaning in other
ways—to want to keep that power.
(90) Patriarchy is the general rule in the public
realm of government and religion, as well
as in the private realm of the home. All
of us receive messages about how we are
to fit into our worlds—and, if we are
(95) women, the traditional fit may be in
serious need of alteration.

18. Which of the following best expresses the
main idea of the passage?

(A) In virtually all cultures, and even in
the realm of international human
rights law itself, women are excluded
by tradition from decision-making
about their own lives.

(B) All over the world, women are being
raped and mutilated, practices to
which the males in power, and even
international human rights law itself,
turn a blind eye.

(C) Cultural traditions hold society
together and have powerful influence
over the lives and well-being of
women, overriding even the sphere of
international human rights law.

(D) Oppression of women is common-
place, and until those in power are
willing to do something about it,
women will be abused and consequently suffer greatly.

(E) During wars and revolutions women
are valued, but afterward they are
not, a tradition that should be
addressed by international human
rights law.

19. In the context of the passage, which of the following best explains Friedan's term, "the problem that has no name"?

(A) In Friedan's time, the problems specific to wives and mothers were kept secret.

(B) At the time Friedan wrote, problems specific to women were ridiculed, so women were embarrassed to speak of them.

(C) At the time the phrase was coined, the problem of the severe limitations placed on women's lives was not generally recognized.

(D) In Friedan's time, women's problems were not spoken of for fear that the men in power would retaliate.

(E) In Friedan's time, women were more satisfied with their lot than they are today and so did not speak out about their problems.

20. What is the meaning of the phrase "embedded in" as it is used in the first paragraph?

(A) An integral part of
(B) An acknowledged part of
(C) A shameful part of
(D) Written into the laws of
(E) Kept a secret from

21. In the context of the passage, the phrase "abuses against women *as women*" (line 63) most nearly means

(A) sexual abuse.
(B) abuse that can happen to both men and women.
(C) domestic abuse.
(D) abuse that, for the most part, happens only to women.
(E) abuse that is not taken seriously by men.

22. The author suggests that males in power tend to be

(A) affluent.
(B) insolent.
(C) brutal.
(D) passive.
(E) self-serving.

23. Why has the author put quotation marks around the word "place" in line 75?

(A) The usage of the word in this sentence is ungrammatical.
(B) The word is from another source.
(C) The usage of the word in this sentence is faintly mocking.
(D) The word is used in this sentence for a humorous effect.
(E) The usage in this sentence is trite.

24. In line 3, the word "couched" most nearly means

(A) revised.
(B) illustrated.
(C) negated.
(D) denied.
(E) framed.

25. Reference to the Convention on the Elimination of All Forms of Discrimination Against Women (lines 68–70) primarily serves to

(A) make the writing style of the essay more appealing.

(B) achieve better overall organization of ideas in the essay.

(C) provide a concrete example to support the main point of the essay.

(D) cause the essay to seem more scholarly by appealing to authority.

(E) end the essay on a more optimistic note.

STOP If you finish before time is called, you may check your work on this section only. Do not turn to any other section in the test.

Section 2—Math

Time—25 Minutes • 20 Questions

Solve problems 1–20, then select the best of the choices given for each one and fill in the corresponding oval on the answer sheet. You may use available space on the page for scratchwork.

Notes:

1. You may use a calculator. All of the numbers used are real numbers.

2. You may use the figures that accompany the problems to help you find the solution. Unless the instructions say that a figure is not drawn to scale, assume that it has been drawn accurately. Each figure lies in a plane unless the instructions say otherwise.

Reference Information

$A = \pi r^2$
$C = 2\pi r$ $A = \ell w$ $A = \frac{1}{2}bh$ $V = \ell wh$ $V = \pi r^2 h$ $c^2 = a^2 + b^2$ Special Right Triangles

The number of degrees of arc in a circle is 360.
The measure in degrees of a straight angle is 180.
The sum of the measures in degrees of the angles of a triangle is 180.

---

1. $\frac{1}{3} \times \frac{3}{5} \times \frac{5}{7} \times \frac{7}{9} =$

(A) $\frac{1}{9}$

(B) $\frac{3}{15}$

(C) $\frac{35}{63}$

(D) $\frac{3}{63}$

(E) $\frac{35}{945}$

2. What is the value of $\left(\frac{1}{3}\right)c$ if $\left(\frac{5}{3}\right)c = 25$?

(A) 2
(B) 3
(C) 4
(D) 5
(E) 6

3. What is 732,471 rounded to the nearest thousand?

(A) 730,000
(B) 732,000
(C) 732,500
(D) 733,000
(E) 740,000

4. If Sally walks at an average speed of c miles per hour, how many miles does she walk in 4 hours?

   (A) $\dfrac{4}{c}$

   (B) $\dfrac{c}{4}$

   (C) $4c$

   (D) $4 - c$

   (E) $4 + c$

5. If a hiker can travel at a steady rate of 15 minutes per $\dfrac{3}{4}$ mile, how many hours would it take to walk 9 miles?

   (A) 1.8
   (B) 2
   (C) 3
   (D) 4
   (E) 6.75

6. When a positive number is added to the square of that number, the result is 42. What is the number?

   (A) 2
   (B) 3
   (C) 4
   (D) 5
   (E) 6

7. What is the least positive integer x, such that $|3 - x| \geq 4$?

   (A) 6
   (B) 7
   (C) 8
   (D) 9
   (E) 10

8. A rectangle is 3 inches wide and 4 inches long. Find the length of the diagonal of this rectangle.

   (A) 4.25
   (B) 5
   (C) 6
   (D) 7
   (E) 7.5

9. In the following figure, line c intersects the parallel lines a and b. What is the measure of angle β?

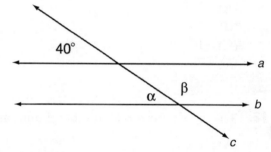

   (A) 110°
   (B) 120°
   (C) 130°
   (D) 140°
   (E) 150°

10. Which of the following is a simplified form of $\dfrac{5x^2 + 12x + 4}{x^2 - 4}$?

    (A) $\dfrac{5x + 2}{x - 2}$

    (B) $\dfrac{5(x^2 + 2)}{x + 2}$

    (C) $\dfrac{(5x + 2)(x + 6)}{x^2 - 2}$

    (D) $5x + 2$

    (E) $x + 2$

41

11. If one of the angles of an isosceles triangle is 18°, which of the following could be another angle of the triangle?

(A) 72°
(B) 78°
(C) 81°
(D) 108°
(E) 162°

12. The perimeter of a circular building measures 158 feet. What is the approximate radius of the building's outer wall?

(A) 7
(B) 25
(C) 50
(D) 76
(E) 101

13. The $\sqrt{x-7}$ is a real number if and only if

(A) $x \geq 7$
(B) $x = 0$
(C) $-7 < x < 7$
(D) $-7 < x < 0$
(E) $x \leq -7$

14. What is 7% of 60?

(A) .42
(B) 4.2
(C) 8.57
(D) 11.67
(E) 42

15. Which of the following are solutions to the equation $(x - a)(x - b) = 0$?

(A) $x = -a$ and $x = -b$
(B) $x = a$ and $x = b$
(C) $x = ab$
(D) $x = (-a)(-b)$
(E) $x = 2a + 2b$

16. If a circle has a diameter of 10 inches, how many square inches is the area of the circle?

(A) 5π
(B) 12π
(C) 25π
(D) 50π
(E) 100π

17. If $x + y = 4$, then $y^2 =$

(A) $16 - x^2$
(B) $x^2 - 16$
(C) $x^2 + 8x + 16$
(D) $16 - 8x + x^2$
(E) $16 + 8x - x^2$

18. If $-7 < x < -4$, which of the following could be a value of $5x$?

(A) -5.50
(B) -6.25
(C) -12.75
(D) -19
(E) -21.50

19. Which of the following numbers is greatest?

(A) .04
(B) .17
(C) .179
(D) .192
(E) .1912

20. If three different numbers are chosen, one from each of the following sets, what is the least sum these numbers could have?

C = {2,4,6}

D = {5,6,7}

E = {2,5,9}

(A)   9

(B)   11

(C)   13

(D)   15

(E)   16

STOP   If you finish before time is called, you may check your work on this section only. Do not turn to any other section in the test.

Section 3—Critical Reading

Time—25 Minutes • 27 Questions

For each question below, choose the best answer from the choices given and fill in the corresponding oval on the answer sheet.

Directions: Each sentence below has either one or two blanks in it and is followed by five choices, labeled (A) through (E). These choices represent words or phrases that have been left out. Choose the word or phrase that, if inserted into the sentence, would best fit the meaning of the sentence as a whole.

Example:

Canine massage is a veterinary technique for calming dogs that are extremely _____.

(A) inept
(B) disciplined
(C) controlled
(D) stressed
(E) restrained

---

1. Because the brain tends to play tricks on us, sometimes we cannot tell whether what we see is _____ or _____.

    (A) perceived..received
    (B) fanciful..imaginary
    (C) disguised..credible
    (D) reliable..stable
    (E) substantial..illusory

2. The rapid, _____ pace of the modern world has affected people so _____ that many seek chemical antidotes in order to achieve a sense of well-being and peace.

    (A) fast-paced..definitely
    (B) upbeat..powerfully
    (C) energetic..negatively
    (D) manic..vigorously
    (E) frenzied..adversely

3. In some corporations today, the Chief Executive Officer earns more than 400 times as much as the typical production worker—a practice that some find flagrantly unfair, in fact downright _____.

    (A) snobbish
    (B) deranged
    (C) marginal
    (D) prosperous
    (E) egregious

4. Humankind has evolved to the point where 3 billion people are interconnected—by newspaper, telephone, television, computer, satellite systems—leading one to believe that we have an inborn need to exchange information, to _____.

(A) transmit
(B) announce
(C) communicate
(D) dominate
(E) reflect

5. Because Armand found his book so _____, he did not see the oncoming train.

(A) inspiring
(B) engrossing
(C) boring
(D) entertaining
(E) educational

6. Although psychics, mediums, and other believers in the occult sometimes quote psychoanalyst Carl Jung to _____ their claims, in reality many of his theories work to _____ them.

(A) refute..support
(B) bolster..debunk
(C) enhance..surpass
(D) embellish..answer
(E) fulfill..execute

7. Formerly _____ as a heretic, Galileo is now _____ as a great man of science.

(A) imprisoned..surpassed
(B) hailed..decried
(C) scorned..derided
(D) persecuted..revered
(E) recognized..acclaimed

8. Optical illusions _____ our senses.

(A) disengage
(B) infuriate
(C) confound
(D) embody
(E) elucidate

Directions: Read each of the passages carefully, and answer the questions that come after them. Base your answers on what is stated or implied, as well as any introductory material provided.

Questions 9–10 are based on the following passage.

This passage is from an excerpt of UN Secretary-General Kofi Annan's Nobel Peace Prize lecture on December 10, 2001.

Line Today's real borders are not between nations, but between powerful and powerless, free and fettered, privileged and humiliated. Today, no walls can
(5) separate . . . human rights crises in one part of the world from national security crises in another. . . . Scientists tell us that the world of nature is so small and interdependent that a butterfly flapping
(10) its wings in the Amazon rain forest can generate a violent storm on the other side of the earth. This principle is known as the "Butterfly Effect." Today we realize, perhaps more than ever, that the world of
(15) human activity also has its own "Butterfly Effect"—for better or worse.

GO ON TO THE NEXT PAGE

9. Which best illustrates the main idea of the passage?

   (A) The fate of human beings is inseparable from the fate of nature.
   (B) Global weather patterns are sensitive to very small changes.
   (C) The most significant division in the world is between the powerful and the powerless.
   (D) Injustice in a distant part of the world can bring insecurity to our own.
   (E) National borders are no longer important.

10. The tone of the passage can best be described as

   (A) stunned.
   (B) irritable.
   (C) impassive.
   (D) sincere.
   (E) jubilant.

Questions 11–12 are based on the following passage.

This passage is adapted from an entry in the online encyclopedia Wikipedia.

Line   Graffiti is subject to different societal pressures than are popularly recognized art forms, since graffiti appears on walls, freeways, buildings, trains or any
(5)   accessible surfaces that are not owned by, or under the control of, the person who applies the graffiti. . . . Spray paint and broad permanent markers are commonly used, and the organizational structure of
(10)   the art is sometimes influenced by the need to apply the art quickly before it is noticed by authorities. In an effort to reduce vandalism, many cities have designated walls or areas exclusively for

(15)   use by graffiti artists. This . . . encourages artists to take their time and produce great art, without worry of being caught or arrested.

11. Based on the tone and content of the passage, which is most likely the author's attitude toward graffiti artists?

   (A) Disapproving
   (B) Respectful
   (C) Indifferent
   (D) Reverent
   (E) Puzzled

12. The passage suggests that, because of "societal pressures," graffiti art tends to be

   (A) permanent.
   (B) rushed.
   (C) ugly.
   (D) great.
   (E) inferior.

Questions 13–15 are based on the following passage.

This passage is an excerpt from an essay by Max Beerbohm, "In Homes Unblest" (1919).

Line   Nothing is more pleasant than to see suddenly endowed with motion a thing stagnant by nature. The hat that on the head of the man in the street is nothing
(5)   to us, how much it is if it be animated by a gust of wind! . . . Conversely, nothing is more dismal than to see set in permanent rigidness a thing whose aspect is linked for us with the idea of great mobility.
(10)   Even the blithest of us and least easily depressed would make a long detour to avoid a stuffed squirrel or a case of pinned butterflies. And you can well imagine with what a sinking of the heart

(15) I beheld, this morning, on a road near the coast of Norfolk, a railway-car without wheels.

13. What is the meaning of the word "stagnant," as used in the passage (line 3)?

- (A) Stale
- (B) Inert
- (C) Silent
- (D) Heavy
- (E) Numb

14. Which is the main reason the author finds the railway car depressing?

- (A) It is ugly, shabby, and broken.
- (B) It is ancient and entirely useless.
- (C) It was designed for motion but cannot move.
- (D) It can no longer carry passengers as it used to.
- (E) It reminds him of bygone days.

15. As described in the passage, the *hat* and the *squirrel* are similar in that each is

- (A) made animate by an outside force.
- (B) immobilized by an outside force.
- (C) changed in some permanent way.
- (D) mobile in its natural state.
- (E) in a state unnatural to it.

Passage 1

From Steep Trails *by John Muir.*

Line   Nature is a good mother, and sees well to the clothing of her many bairns—birds with smoothly imbricated feathers, beetles with shining jackets, and bears
(5)   with shaggy furs. In the tropical south, where the sun warms like a fire, they are allowed to go thinly clad; but in the snowy northland she takes care to clothe warmly. The squirrel has socks and

(10) mittens, and a tail broad enough for a blanket; the grouse is densely feathered down to the ends of his toes; and the wild sheep, besides his undergarment of fine wool, has a thick overcoat of hair
(15) that sheds off both the snow and the rain. Other provisions and adaptations in the dresses of animals, relating less to climate than to the more mechanical circumstances of life, are made with the
(20) same consummate skill that characterizes all the love work of Nature. Land, water, and air, jagged rocks, muddy ground, sand beds, forests, underbrush, grassy plains, etc., are considered in all their
(25) possible combinations while the clothing of her beautiful wildlings is preparing. No matter what the circumstances of their lives may be, she never allows them to go dirty or ragged. The mole, living
(30) always in the dark and in the dirt, is yet as clean as the otter or the wave-washed seal; and our wild sheep, wading in snow, roaming through bushes, and leaping among jagged storm-beaten cliffs, wears
(35) a dress so exquisitely adapted to its mountain life that it is always found as unruffled and stainless as a bird.

Passage 2

From The Origins of Species *by Charles Darwin.*

Line   A struggle for existence inevitably follows from the high rate at which all organic beings tend to increase. Every being, which during its natural lifetime
(5)   produces several eggs or seeds, must suffer destruction during some period of its life, and during some season or occasional year, otherwise, on the principle of geometrical increase, its
(10)   numbers would quickly become so

inordinately great that no country could support the product. Hence, as more individuals are produced than can possibly survive, there must in every case (15) be a struggle for existence, either one individual with another of the same species, or with the individuals of distinct species, or with the physical conditions of life. It is the doctrine of Malthus applied (20) with manifold force to the whole animal and vegetable kingdoms; for in this case there can be no artificial increase of food, and no prudential restraint from marriage. Although some species may be now (25) increasing, more or less rapidly, in numbers, all cannot do so, for the world would not hold them. . . .

There is no exception to the rule that every organic being naturally increases at (30) so high a rate, that if not destroyed, the earth would soon be covered by the progeny of a single pair. Even slow-breeding man has doubled in twenty-five years, and at this rate, in a few thousand (35) years, there would literally not be standing room for his progeny. Linnaeus has calculated that if an annual plant produced only two seeds and there is no plant so unproductive as this and their (40) seedlings next year produced two, and so on, then in twenty years there would be a million plants. . . . Lighten any check, mitigate the destruction ever so little, and the number of the species will almost (45) instantaneously increase to any amount. The face of Nature may be compared to a yielding surface, with ten thousand sharp wedges packed close together and driven inwards by incessant blows, (50) sometimes one wedge being struck, and then another with greater force.

16. What is the meaning of the word "bairns" in line 2 of the first passage?

(A) Duties
(B) Loves
(C) Travels
(D) Children
(E) Apects

17. What is the main idea of Passage 1?

(A) A benevolent God watches over all things.
(B) All members of the wildlife kingdom are happy.
(C) Nature is beautiful in all seasons.
(D) Nature benevolently clothes all living things.
(E) All birds and animals adapt to the changing seasons.

18. In Passage 1, the phrase "Other provisions and adaptations" (line 16) refers to the fact that each animal

(A) is "clothed" so that it can endure, no matter how harsh the weather.
(B) is "clothed" with an eye to its specific habitat (forest, cliff, water, etc.).
(C) has enough provisions so it can be fed in all seasons.
(D) has a protective living space.
(E) has some camouflage to hide it from predators.

48

19. What is the main idea of Passage 2?

   (A) Evolution cannot take place without struggle between individuals.

   (B) Every organism on Earth must suffer and die.

   (C) Unless individuals are destroyed, whole species will perish from overabundance.

   (D) Nature is cruel and cares nothing for the individual.

   (E) Unless "slow breeding man" stops reproducing at such a rapid rate, the human species won't even have standing room on the earth.

20. If the author of Passage 2 were writing today, which of the following problems could he most effectively use to support the ideas in the first paragraph?

   (A) Violent crime

   (B) Terrorism

   (C) Overpopulation

   (D) Racial tension

   (E) Weakening of the family

21. Which of the following statements is most likely part of the "doctrine of Malthus" (line 19), as discussed in the context of Passage 2?

   (A) The concept of evolution is open to question.

   (B) Unchecked reproduction will lead to disaster.

   (C) Marriage imposes unnatural restraints on human reproduction.

   (D) Some species are increasing too rapidly, while others are dying off.

   (E) The animal and vegetable kingdoms are equally significant.

22. What is the meaning of the phrase "Lighten any check" as it is used in the second paragraph of Passage 2?

   (A) Remove any obstacle.

   (B) Alleviate any suffering.

   (C) Encourage any hope.

   (D) Take away any privilege.

   (E) Handicap any individual.

23. In the context of Passage 2, the phrase in lines 23–24, "no prudential restraint from marriage," means that, unlike humans, the lower animals

   (A) are completely amoral.

   (B) do not usually form bonds beyond the mother-offspring bond.

   (C) do not usually live in what humans would call a "family."

   (D) do not usually mate for life.

   (E) have no societal customs or mores against unlimited breeding.

24. Based on the content of both passages, on which of the following statements would the authors of Passage 1 and Passage 2 be most likely to disagree?

   (A) There is no God.

   (B) There should be a limit to the speed of human reproduction.

   (C) Science can remedy many of the ills of the world.

   (D) Human beings are more important than other species.

   (E) Nature cares about the individual.

GO ON TO THE NEXT PAGE

25. Based on his beliefs as expressed in the passage, the author of Passage 2 would most likely say that the author of Passage 1 is

(A) obsessive.
(B) infuriating.
(C) spiritual.
(D) pompous.
(E) sentimental.

26. Based on the content of the passages alone, the author of Passage 1 would most likely say that the attitude toward nature expressed in Passage 2 is

(A) remorseful.
(B) harsh.
(C) complacent.
(D) ironic.
(E) sophomoric.

27. Both authors would most likely say that the intensive study of nature is

(A) futile.
(B) worthwhile.
(C) arduous.
(D) effortless.
(E) irreligious.

S T O P If you finish before time is called, you may check your work on this section only. Do not turn to any other section in the test.

Section 4—Math

Time—25 Minutes • 20 Questions

This section is made up of two types of questions, multiple choice—10 questions—and Student-Produced Response—10 questions. You have 25 minutes to complete the section. You may use available space on the page for scratchwork.

Notes:

1. You may use a calculator. All of the numbers used are real numbers.

2. You may use the figures that accompany the problems to help you find the solution. Unless the instructions say that a figure is not drawn to scale, assume that it has been drawn accurately. Each figure lies in a plane unless the instructions say otherwise. .

Reference Information

      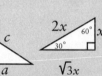

$A = \pi r^2$
$C = 2\pi r$ $A = \ell w$ $A = \dfrac{1}{2}bh$ $V = \ell w h$ $V = \pi r^2 h$ $c^2 = a^2 + b^2$ Special Right Triangles

The number of degrees of arc in a circle is 360.
The measure in degrees of a straight angle is 180.
The sum of the measures in degrees of the angles of a triangle is 180.

---

1. Given $3x - 4 = 8$, find $x + 1$.

(A) 3
(B) 4
(C) 5
(D) 6
(E) 7

2. Find $A \cap B$, given $A = \{0, 1, 2, 4\}$ and $B = \{0, 1, 3, 4\}$.

(A) $\{0, 1, 4\}$
(B) $\{0, 1\}$
(C) $\{2, 3\}$
(D) $\{0, 1, 2, 3, 4\}$
(E) $\{0\}$

3. Find the third term of the geometric sequence whose first two terms are 8, 2.

(A) $\dfrac{1}{2}$

(B) $\dfrac{1}{4}$

(C) $\dfrac{1}{8}$

(D) $\dfrac{1}{16}$

(E) $\dfrac{1}{32}$

4. Given $x + 2 = 3$ and $3y + 9 = 18$, find $x + y$.

(A) 3
(B) 4
(C) 5
(D) 6
(E) 7

5. Points C and D lie on a circle. Line segment $\overline{CD}$ passes through the center of the circle. The length of $\overline{CD}$ is 12. What is the area of the circle?

(A) 6π
(B) 12π
(C) 18π
(D) 36π
(E) 144π

6. Given the following diagram, find α.

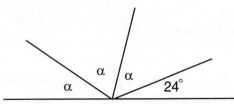

Note: Figure not drawn to scale.

(A) $45°$
(B) $52°$
(C) $53°$
(D) $63°$
(E) $66°$

7. Let z equal the sum of .4 and its reciprocal. Find z.

(A) 4.4
(B) 2.9
(C) 1.20
(D) 0.65
(E) 0.44

8. Let $x \ni y = (x^3)(y)$ for all real values of x and y. Find $y + (x \ni y)$, for $x = -1$.

(A) 6
(B) 2
(C) 1
(D) 0
(E) -1

9. Given the following figure, find x.

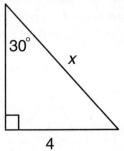

$30°$
x
4

Note: Figure not drawn to scale.

(A) 12
(B) 10
(C) 8
(D) 5
(E) 4

10. In the following diagram, find BC, given $AC = 12$, $AD = 18$, and $BD = 10$.

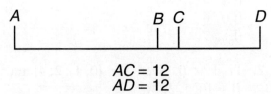

$AC = 12$
$AD = 12$

Note: Figure not drawn to scale.

(A) 4
(B) 5
(C) 6
(D) 7
(E) 8

Questions 11–20 require you to solve the problems, then enter your answers by marking ovals in the special grid, as shown in the examples below.

Directions for Student-Produced Response Questions

Each of the remaining 10 questions requires you to solve the problem and enter your answer by marking the ovals in the special grid, as shown in the examples below.

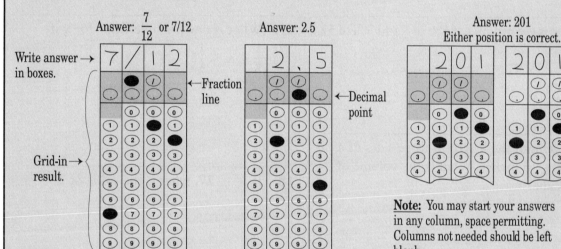

- Mark no more than one oval in any column.
- Because the answer sheet will be machine-scored, **you will receive credit only if the ovals are filled in correctly.**
- Although not required, it is suggested that you write your answer in the boxes at the top of the columns to help you fill in the ovals accurately.
- Some problems may have more than one correct answer. In such cases, grid only one answer.
- No question has a negative answer.
- **Mixed numbers** such as $2\frac{1}{2}$ must be gridded as 2.5 or 5/2. (If 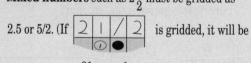 is gridded, it will be interpreted as $\frac{21}{2}$, not $2\frac{1}{2}$.)

- **Decimal Accuracy:** If you obtain a decimal answer, **enter the most accurate value the grid will accommodate.** For example, if you obtain an answer such as 0.6666 . . . , you should record the result as .666 or .667. **Less accurate values such as .66 or .67 are not acceptable.**

Acceptable ways to grid $\frac{2}{3}$ = .6666 . . .

GO ON TO THE NEXT PAGE

PETERSON'S
getting you there

11. Let function f be defined by $f(x) = x^2 + 6$. If n is a positive number such that $f(3n) = 3f(n)$, what is the value of n^2?

16. Sixty-five percent of a group of students pass their driving test. If 260 people pass this test, how many took the test?

12. What is the product of 5% of 7 and 7% of 5?

17. What is one possible value for x if $\frac{1}{8} < x < \frac{1}{5}$?

13. The sum of the length of three sides of a cube is 15 inches. What is the volume of the cube?

18. If $3^x = 27$, what is the value of 2^{x+1}?

14. The average of 4 numbers is 8.5. Three of the numbers are 3, 7, and 9. What is the fourth number?

19. .003 is the same as the ratio of 3 to what number?

15. A container of apples sells for $6, which is $\frac{4}{5}$ of the original asking price. What was the original price?

20. The area of square $ABCD$ is equal to the area of rectangle $EFGH$. If $CD = 4$ feet and $EF = 2$ feet, what is the length of the rectangle's perimeter, in feet?

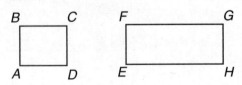

Note: Figures not drawn to scale.

S T O P   If you finish before time is called, you may check your work on this section only. Do not turn to any other section in the test.

54

Section 5—Writing Skills

Time—25 Minutes • 39 Questions

For each question below, select the best answer from the choices given and fill in the corresponding oval on the answer sheet.

Directions: The following questions will test your knowledge of grammar, usage, diction, and idiom.

Some sentences are correct.

No sentence contains multiple errors.

In each sentence below, five elements, labeled (A) through (E), are underlined and lettered. One (and ONLY one) of the underlined elements may contain an error. In choosing your answer, be sure to follow the rules of standard written English. You can assume that the parts of the sentences not underlined are correct.

If the sentence has no error, choose Ⓔ , "No error."

Example:

My dog Sally and my cat Buster

<u>gets along well</u> with each <u>other, eating</u>
      A   B

and sleeping <u>together, playing</u> quietly,
             C

and <u>sharing</u> their food and treats.
     D

<u>No error.</u>
 E

Sample Answer:

1. The cuttlefish, <u>which</u> looks <u>something like</u>
            A   B
a large squid, is highly intelligent <u>and, like</u>
                               C
the octopus, <u>was</u> a member of the order of
           D
cephalopods. <u>No error.</u>
               E

2. <u>Dashing out of the chapel,</u> the rain fell
                     A
<u>lightly on our heads,</u> so
            B
<u>we hastened to the car</u> to be whisked
               C
<u>away to our honeymoon cottage.</u>
               D
<u>No error.</u>
 E

GO ON TO THE NEXT PAGE

PETERSON'S
getting you there

3. There will be a full moon on Halloween
    <u>A</u>
   night, <u>according with</u> the almanac,
           <u>B</u>
   so werewolves and vampires <u>will be out in</u>
                          <u>C</u>   <u>D</u>
   force. <u>No error.</u>
          <u>E</u>

4. Baxter <u>screamed when</u> he saw the snake
              <u>A</u>
   <u>in his footlocker,</u> <u>as he was opening it</u>
      <u>B</u>   <u>C</u>
   <u>to get out</u> his pajamas. <u>No error.</u>
      <u>D</u>   <u>E</u>

5. Frederich Nietzsche wrote <u>his famous</u>
                              <u>A</u>
   book <u>about Richard Wagner</u> <u>some years</u>
              <u>B</u>   <u>C</u>
   <u>before he descended</u> into madness.
          <u>D</u>
   <u>No error.</u>
   <u>E</u>

6. General Colin Powell and

   <u>Superman, though</u> one is real and one
       <u>A</u>
   fictional, <u>are both</u> a <u>superhero</u> in many
              <u>B</u>   <u>C</u>
   <u>people's eyes.</u> <u>No error.</u>
      <u>D</u>   <u>E</u>

7. Dr. Martin stood <u>accused with</u> malpractice
                       <u>A</u>
   when he <u>accidentally</u> cut off <u>a patient's</u>
           <u>B</u>   <u>C</u>
   nose <u>during surgery.</u> <u>No error.</u>
           <u>D</u>   <u>E</u>

8. My dog <u>Zelda's</u> tricks are <u>far more</u>
            <u>A</u>   <u>B</u>
   dazzling and complicated

   than your dog Rex, <u>which proves that</u>
                         <u>C</u>
   Zelda is <u>the more clever</u> of the two.
               <u>D</u>
   <u>No error.</u>
   <u>E</u>

9. Bachelor <u>parties should</u> never be <u>held on</u>
                 <u>A</u>   <u>B</u>
   the night before the <u>wedding because the</u>
                             <u>C</u>
   <u>groom will need</u> time to rest up. <u>No error.</u>
      <u>D</u>   <u>E</u>

10. The three of them, Marge, Janelle, and

    Rosemary, <u>has dinner</u> once a <u>week, rain</u> or
                 <u>A</u>   <u>B</u>
    shine, <u>at</u> the Pizza Palace
           <u>C</u>
    over on Lafayette Street. <u>No error.</u>
             <u>D</u>   <u>E</u>

11. In medieval <u>fable,</u> the unicorn is some-
                  <u>A</u>
    times <u>described as</u> a white deer with a
             <u>B</u>
    horse's mane, cloven hooves, and a

    <u>single spiral horn</u> growing out of the
         <u>C</u>
    <u>middle of their foreheads.</u> <u>No error.</u>
             <u>D</u>   <u>E</u>

12. After <u>you</u> see the film *The Blair Witch*
           <u>A</u>
    Project, most people <u>don't want to walk</u>
                              <u>B</u>
    in the woods at <u>night for</u> awhile, <u>for fear</u>
                        <u>C</u>   <u>D</u>
    of evil forces. <u>No error.</u>
                       <u>E</u>

13. I informed the police that there were
   <u>   A   </u>
   <u>people living in</u> my attic, who
   <u>   B   </u>
   <u>rummaged around in</u> my refrigerator
   <u>   C   </u>
   during the night, but the police refused

   <u>to take action.</u> <u>No error.</u>
   <u>   D   </u>   <u>   E   </u>

14. The City has <u>distributed</u> standardized
   <u>   A   </u>
   recycling containers <u>with</u> all households,
   <u>   B   </u>
   along with <u>explicit</u> directions <u>for their use.</u>
   <u>   C   </u>   <u>   D   </u>
   <u>No error.</u>
   <u>   E   </u>

15. One of the <u>most</u> dangerous phenomena
   <u>   A   </u>
   <u>a firefighter will</u> ever face is the
   <u>   B   </u>
   <u>backdraft, which</u> can occur during the
   <u>   C   </u>
   smoldering phase of a fire after the

   <u>fire appeared</u> to be out. <u>No error.</u>
   <u>   D   </u>   <u>   E   </u>

16. <u>By their driving tests,</u> students <u>are to drive</u>
   <u>A</u>   <u>   B   </u>
   between two parallel rows of cones,

   <u>as shown in the diagram on page 5,</u>
   <u>   C   </u>
   <u>without knocking over</u> any of the cones.
   <u>   D   </u>
   <u>No error.</u>
   <u>   E   </u>

17. Workers cannot be <u>productive</u> or happy in
   <u>   A   </u>
   <u>their jobs if</u> they are in physical pain,
   <u>   B   </u>
   so progressive offices today
   <u>   C   </u>
   are <u>constructed</u> with an eye to ergonom-
   <u>   D   </u>
   ics. <u>No error.</u>
        <u>   E   </u>

18. According to some physicists, <u>approxi-</u>
   <u>   A   </u>
   mately 1 million years <u>after the</u> big bang,
   <u>   B   </u>
   the universe cooled to

   <u>about 3000° C (5000° F),</u> and protons
   <u>   C   </u>
   and electrons <u>combine</u> to make hydrogen
   <u>   D   </u>
   atoms. <u>No error.</u>
          <u>   E   </u>

19. <u>Of metabolism,</u> the body uses oxygen and
   <u>   A   </u>
   produces carbon dioxide, and

   <u>it is important</u> that these
   <u>   B   </u>
   two gases <u>maintain</u> a normal state
   <u>   C   </u>
   <u>of equilibrium.</u> <u>No error.</u>
   <u>   D   </u> <u>   E   </u>

GO ON TO THE NEXT PAGE

Directions: The sentences below test correctness and effectiveness of expression. When you choose your answers, select the sentence or sentence part that is most clear and correct and that conforms best to the requirements of standard written English.

Each of the following sentences is either underlined or contains an underlined part. Under each sentence, there are five ways of phrasing the underlined portion. Choice (A) repeats the original; the other four options are different. You can assume that the elements that are not underlined are correct.

Choose the answer that best expresses the meaning of the original sentence. If in your opinion the original sentence is the best option, choose it. Your choice should produce the most effective sentence.

<table>
<tr><td>

Example:

I am going to the store to <u>buy a food item, which is bread.</u>

</td><td>

Sample Answer:

</td></tr>
</table>

(A) buy a food item, which is bread
(B) buy a food item, bread
(C) buy bread
(D) buy a food item, which is called bread
(E) buy what is called bread

---

20. <u>At this point in time, dogs are not allowed anywhere within the confines of Higgins Beach.</u>

(A) At this point in time, dogs are not allowed anywhere within the confines of Higgins Beach.
(B) At this point in time, dogs are not allowed on Higgins Beach.
(C) Dogs are not allowed on Higgins Beach.
(D) Dogs are not allowed within the confines of Higgins Beach.
(E) On Higgins Beach, dogs are not allowed within the confines.

21. To celebrate winning the big game, <u>a wild party, that got out of hand, was thrown by Bad Bob Bellows, the team manager.</u>

(A) a wild party, that got out of hand, was thrown by Bad Bob Bellows, the team manager.
(B) a wild party was thrown by Bad Bob Bellows, the team manager, that got out of hand.
(C) an out of hand, wild party was thrown by Bad Bob Bellows, the team manager.
(D) Bad Bob Bellows, the team manager, threw a wild party that got out of hand.
(E) Bad Bob Bellows, the team manager, threw a wild party (it got out of hand).

22. Too much credence was given by the police to Lefty's statement.

(A) Too much credence was given by the police to Lefty's statement.

(B) Lefty's statement, by the police, was given too much credence.

(C) The police gave Lefty's statement too much credence.

(D) Too much credence, by the police, was given to Lefty's statement.

(E) Lefty's statement was given, by the police, too much credence.

23. Two great rationalist mathematicians, Descartes and Leibniz, believed the world could be fully explained by use of reason alone.

(A) Two great rationalist mathematicians, Descartes and Leibniz, believed the world could be fully explained by use of reason alone.

(B) Two great rationalist mathematicians believed they and others could fully explain the world by use of reason alone—Descartes and Leibniz.

(C) That the world could be fully explained by use of reason alone were two rationalist mathematicians, Descartes and Leibniz, who were both great.

(D) Two great rationalist mathematicians, believing that the world could be fully explained by use of reason alone, were Descartes and Leibniz.

(E) By reason alone, two great rationalists, Descartes and Leibniz, could understand the world, so they thought.

24. Some physicists believe that the Universe will end "not with a bang but a whimper"; however, I don't buy it.

(A) I don't buy it.

(B) I reject the notion out of hand in its entirety.

(C) I oppugn that presumption.

(D) I disagree.

(E) I am not of that precise persuasion.

25. In John Milton's epic poem, "Paradise Lost," Satan declares that it is preferable to rule in Hell than go to Heaven as a loser.

(A) it is preferable to rule in Hell than go to Heaven as a loser

(B) it is better to reign in Hell than serve in Heaven

(C) to lead in Hell is better than to be a heavenly servant

(D) it is better to dominate in Hell than be a follower in Heaven

(E) to enforce the rules in Hell is good, unlike being a follower in Heaven

26. People constantly deny responsibility, even though they profess belief in freedom of the will.

(A) responsibility, even though

(B) responsibility; even though

(C) responsibility! Even though

(D) responsibility. Even though

(E) responsibility? Even though

27. The amusement park's Wild Earthworm ride was dangerous over the Spitting Frog.

(A) dangerous over

(B) more dangerous than

(C) dangerouser than

(D) dangerous beyond

(E) dangerous above

GO ON TO THE NEXT PAGE

28. Throughout history, the idea that each of us has a phantom <u>double or *doppelganger*,</u> <u>has</u> persisted.

    (A) double or *doppelganger*, has
    (B) double, or *doppelganger* has
    (C) double, or *doppelganger*. Has
    (D) double or *doppelganger* has
    (E) double, or *doppelganger*, has

29. Nigerian poet Chinua Achebe maintains that the colonial regime in Africa was not a democratic system <u>and</u> the most extreme form of totalitarianism.

    (A) and
    (B) so
    (C) but
    (D) yet
    (E) nor

30. If Shakespeare had lived in the present day, he <u>loved</u> the movies, especially the special effects.

    (A) loved
    (B) loves
    (C) will love
    (D) would be loving
    (E) would have loved

31. <u>Why did you betray me and ruin my life</u> <u>and my career?</u>

    (A) Why did you betray me and ruin my life and my career?
    (B) Did you betray me and ruin my life and my career, why?
    (C) Why did you betray me and ruin my life, to say nothing of my career?
    (D) My life and my career have been ruined by you, and why?
    (E) Why, did you betray me and ruin my life and my career?

32. Consciousness is one of the most baffling of the brain's mysteries <u>and it may well</u> never be fully explained.

    (A) and it may well
    (B) and may
    (C) and it may
    (D) and it also may
    (E) but may

33. <u>Why did Weldon, wear that</u> hideous suit to the swearing-in ceremony?

    (A) Why did Weldon, wear that
    (B) Why did, Weldon, wear that
    (C) Why did Weldon wear, that
    (D) Why did Weldon wear that
    (E) Why did, Weldon wear that

Directions: The following passage is from an essay in its early stages. Some of it may need revision. Read the passage below and answer the questions that come after it. Some of the questions will ask you to improve sentence structure and word choice. Other questions will refer to parts of the essay or to the entire essay and ask you to improve organization and development. Base your decisions on the rules of standard written English, and mark your answer in the corresponding oval on the answer sheet.

Questions 34–39 are based on the following passage.

(1) *Many early fans of jazz musician Miles Davis became aggravated and upset as they watched their hero change through the years.* (2) *The change involved not only the type of music he played but the way he behaved on-stage.*

(3) *Miles Dewey Davis was born May 25, 1926, in Alton, Illinois.* (4) *He grew up in East St. Louis.* (5) *He was given his first trumpet at the age of 13, and, in 1945, enrolled in the Juilliard School of Music.* (6) *Once in New York, Miles, in his own words, "followed [jazz great Charlie Parker] around down to 52nd Street," every night.* (7) *New York night life was interesting to the young jazz musician.* (8) *He'd write down Parker's chords and the next day play them in the practice rooms at Juilliard, instead of going to classes.*

(9) *Miles gradually, however, completely and finally broke away from the hard, aggressive temperament of the former bebop tradition.* (10) *He moved to a more subtle, cool, sometimes even gentle, kind of jazz, characterized by his* Birth of the Cool *album in 1949–50.* (11) *Later works, such as "Stella by Starlight," "Round About Midnight," his* Kind of Blue *album in 1959, and his* Sketches of Spain *album in 1960, continued to reveal a more gentle, open, and melodic musical style.*

(12) *In his early days, Miles's behavior was reserved.* (13) *He avoided interviews where he could and did not even respond to applause, remaining off stage unless he was playing.* (14) *By the late 1970s, however, when he had attained what some have termed a cult following of younger fans, he became more unguarded in manner, smiling and shaking hands with fans nearest the stage, waving to the audience, and giving generous, genial interviews.* (15) *Even the way he behaved in public changed over the years.*

34. Logically, the final sentence should be placed before

(A) sentence 8.
(B) sentence 9.
(C) sentence 10.
(D) sentence 11.
(E) sentence 12.

35. To improve unity, which of the following sentences would be the best one to delete from the second paragraph?

(A) Sentence 3
(B) Sentence 4
(C) Sentence 5
(D) Sentence 6
(E) Sentence 7

GO ON TO THE NEXT PAGE

36. Which of the following best spells out the writer's purpose in the final paragraph?

    (A) Miles Davis is an important figure in the history of music, equal in rank to Charlie Parker and other jazz greats.

    (B) Over the course of his career, Miles Davis changed, in both his musical and his personal style.

    (C) Miles Davis's music was at first hard and aggressive, influenced by the early bebop tradition.

    (D) Miles Davis's later music was subtle and gentle, as exemplified by his albums *Birth of the Cool* and *Sketches of Spain*.

    (E) Miles Davis was changeable throughout his lifetime, his behavior on stage constantly surprising and upsetting.

37. Which of the following is the best revision of Sentence 9?

    (A) As it is now

    (B) Gradually, however, Miles broke away from the hard, aggressive temperament of the bebop tradition.

    (C) Miles gradually broke away and distanced himself from the hard, aggressive temperament of the bebop tradition.

    (D) The hard, aggressive temperament of the bebop tradition, however, Miles gradually broke away from.

    (E) The hard, aggressive temperament of the bebop tradition, however, was finally broken away from by Miles.

38. Which of the following sentences, if added, would most logically conclude the final paragraph?

    (A) Even though Miles's music departed from its traditions, bebop continued to be a driving force in jazz and remains so to this day.

    (B) Charlie Parker's influence on Miles Davis is emphasized in most of the biographies Miles's life has inspired.

    (C) It was Miles's father who bought him his first trumpet and who enabled him to attend Juilliard.

    (D) In spite of the changes that upset many of his early fans, Miles remained a formidable creative force in jazz throughout his career.

    (E) Moving from East St. Louis to New York City must have been a shock to the young Miles.

39. In the context of the passage, which of the following is the best way to combine sentences 3 and 4?

    (A) Miles Dewey Davis was born May 25, 1926 and, being born in Alton, Illinois, grew up in East St. Louis.

    (B) Miles Dewey Davis grew up in East St. Louis and was born May 25, 1926 in Alton, Illinois.

    (C) Growing up in East St. Louis, Miles Dewey Davis was born May 25, 1926 in Alton, Illinois.

    (D) Born May 25, 1926 in Alton, Illinois, Miles Dewey Davis grew up in East St. Louis.

    (E) Miles Dewey Davis: Born May 25, 1926 in Alton, Illinois; grew up in East St. Louis.

S T O P If you finish before time is called, you may check your work on this section only. Do not turn to any other section in the test.

NOTES • ЗАПИСКИ

Section 3 Reading	Section 4 Math	Section 5 Writing Skills
E	1. C	1. D
E	2. A	2. A
E	3. A	3. B
C	4. B	4. E
B	5. D	5. D
B	6. B	6. C
D	7. B	7. A
C	8. D	8. C
D	9. C	9. E
D	10. A	10. A
B	11. $n^2 = 2$	11. D
B	12. 0.1225	12. A
B	13. 125 cubic inches	13. E
C	14. 15	14. B
E	15. $7.50	15. D
D	16. 400	16. A
D	17. Any number in the range $.125 < x < .200$.	17. E
B		18. D
C		19. A
20. A 20. B 20. C	18. 16	20. C
21. D 21. B	19. 1000	21. D
22. E 22. A	20. 20 feet	22. C
23. C 23. E		23. A
24. E 24. E		24. D
25. C 25. E		25. B
26. B		26. A
27. B		27. B
		28. E
		29. C
		30. E
		31. A
		32. B
		33. D
		34. E
		35. E
		36. B
		37. B
		38. D
		39. D

Explanatory Answers

Section 1—Critical Reading

1. **The correct answer is (A).** The word *paradoxically* is a signal that the first phrase must contrast to the second. Only choice (A) contains truly contrasting elements—the words *controlled* and *free* are opposites.

2. **The correct answer is (E).** The key words here are *once* and *now*, which hint that there are contrasting elements in the sentence. Ask yourself: What is the difference between bubonic plague then and now? Note that the first word in all the choices, except for (D), fits the sentence, so you have to move on to the second word to get the answer.

3. **The correct answer is (C).** The first word *because* is, of course, a clue that you are dealing with cause and effect. Ask yourself: What would the serving of greasy sausage stew most likely *cause* Brenda to be? Keep in mind that you are to choose not just a possible answer, but the BEST answer. (Brenda might <u>possibly</u> be distraught by the meal, but the word *greasy* points more logically to the word *revolted*.)

4. **The correct answer is (E).** What will help you most here is a good vocabulary, so that you'll know that the word *ironically* describes a situation in which what is expected and what actually occurs are incongruous or do not seem to fit.

5. **The correct answer is (C).** This is a definition question, and again you'll need a wide vocabulary. A bully, of course, is the mean guy at school who beats you up and steals your lunch money. The other choices may describe the <u>person</u> Corey, but only choice (C) describes a bully.

6. **The correct answer is (C).** The phrase is a joke, based on Mr. Wace's excusing his *dreadful language* (actually caused by his dislike of the master) by saying he was only quoting the prophet Isaiah.

7. **The correct answer is (D).** The arrival of the master causes in Mrs. Blinder such distress that there seems little reason, other than fear, for her to take special care with the dinner. The passage says that *nobody loved* the master, so it's unlikely Mrs. Blinder would care if he were hungry, choice (A). The passage does not mention how Mrs. Blinder feels about her work, choice (B). It is the narrator, not Mrs. Blinder, who is meeting the master for the first time, choice (C). Mrs. Blinder's unusual irritation at the kitchen-maid implies she is on edge, not resigned, choice (E).

64

8. **The correct answer is (E).** The entire second paragraph discusses the question of whether the universe will continue to expand or eventually collapse. The other choices are not discussed.

9. **The correct answer is (C).** Planets and galaxies are visible. Choice (A) is contradicted by the passage, which states that dark matter is invisible. Choice (B) is illogical because gravity is not an object, but a force. Choices (D) and (E) are incorrect because neither collapsed stars nor black holes are mentioned in the passage.

10. **The correct answer is (B).** The Trickster performs paradoxical actions, such as giving the gift of fire and then stealing the meal that the gift receivers cooked using the fire. Choices (A) and (C) are each only partial qualities of the Trickster, and do not sum up all of the charter's traits. Choice (D) is incorrect because *mythological* is not a character trait. Choice (E) is incorrect because the passage does not describe the Trickster as mysterious.

11. **The correct answer is (A).** In the passage, the author states that the Trickster is *of great benefit to humankind*, and supports this statement by explaining that Coyote and Prometheus stole fire and gave it to humans. Choices (B) and (C) are incorrect because there is nothing funny about this part of the passage and so there is no reason to think the author was trying to lighten the tone or demonstate the Trickster's sense of humor. Choice (D) is incorrect because the author does not provide a picture or even a vivid description of Coyote or Prometheus. Choice (E) is incorrect because it is not what the discussion of Coyote and Prometheus primarily serves to do in the passage.

12. **The correct answer is (A).** This is supported by lines 10–15, which express the grandmother's lack of interest in her grandchild; lines 28–29, in which she refuses her son-in-law's offer of a ride by saying "the bus is just as good"; and lines 36–37, in which, once on the bus, the grandmother looks *away, ahead toward her real life*.

13. **The correct answer is (D).** This is indicated by the grandmother's criticism of the mother's cooking in lines 68–69 and by lines 95–98, in which she criticizes the narrator's method of combing her hair, then says, *You're just like [your mother]*.

14. **The correct answer is (B).** The overall thrust of the passage reveals that the narrator regarded her grandmother with some wonder. There is no indication that she felt endangered in her grandmother's presence, choice (A), and her feelings for her grandmother are not shown to be completely negative, which rules out the other choices.

65

15. **The correct answer is (D).** This is explicitly stated in lines 90–94: *The thing I remember most vividly about Grandma . . . is her shining hair . . .*

16. **The correct answer is (C).** Immediately prior to the word *it*, the father has described how the mother was left to do all the work while the grandmother went out to preach.

17. **The correct answer is (B).** The other choices are illogical.

18. **The correct answer is (A).** Choice (A) addresses the three main points in the passage, having to do with culture, human rights law, and the exclusion of women from decision-making. Choice (B) is too narrow to be the main idea. Choice (C) is wrong because the passage does not discuss tradition overriding human rights law. Choice (D) might be deduced from the passage, but it is not really in the passage. Choice (E) is too narrow to be the main idea.

19. **The correct answer is (C).** The other choices are not in the passage.

20. **The correct answer is (A).** This is the dictionary meaning of the word *embedded*.

21. **The correct answer is (D).** Choices (A) and (C) may seem attractive at first, but sexual abuse and domestic abuse can happen to both men and women. Choice (B) is illogical. Choice (E) is possible, but it is not the best answer.

22. **The correct answer is (E).** Lines 87–89 contain the phrase *even if they are kindly and well-meaning in other ways*, implying that some males are well-meaning, thus ruling out choices (B) and (C). Choices (A) and (D) are not in the passage.

23. **The correct answer is (C).** From the tone of the essay, the writer clearly believes that a woman's position in society should not be prescribed by others.

24. **The correct answer is (E).** To *frame* an argument in a certain way is to arrange it or adjust it for a purpose (in this case, to convince women that their oppression exists for a reason that is beneficial to society). The other choices do not really make sense.

25. **The correct answer is (C).** The example of the Convention supports the author's argument that women are excluded from important decision-making about their own treatment. The addition of the reference to the Convention does not make the essay more appealing, choice (A), or enhance organization of ideas, choice (B). The author is criticizing the Convention, not appealing to its authority, thus refuting choice (D), and her observations about the Convention are pessimistic, not optimistic, refuting choice (E).

Section 2—Math

1. **The correct answer is (A).** The 3, 5, and 7 in both the numerator and denominator divide each other out, leaving a value of $\frac{1}{9}$.

2. **The correct answer is (D).** The quick method of solution is to divide both sides of the equation by 5. This leaves $\frac{1}{3}c = 5$. Another method is to solve for c first:

$$\frac{5}{3}c = 25$$

$$\left(\frac{3}{5}\right)\left(\frac{5}{3}\right)c = \left(\frac{3}{5}\right)(25)$$

$$c = \frac{75}{5} = 15$$

$$\frac{1}{3}c = 5$$

3. **The correct answer is (B).** Rounding to the nearest thousand means just dealing with the 2,471 part of the number. Since 471 is less than 500, round down to 2,000. This makes the rounded number equal to 732,000.

4. **The correct answer is (C).** The distance Sally walks is equal to the rate she walks multiplied by the time she walks, or $D = RT$. In this case, c = the rate she walks and 4 = the time she walks, which makes the answer $4c$.

5. **The correct answer is (C).** First, convert 15 minutes to hours to make the units of measurement match, 15 minutes = .25 hour. In this case, it is easier to work with decimals, so convert also $\frac{3}{4}$ mile = .75 mile. Now set up the following proportion and solve for x:

$$\frac{.25\text{hr}}{.75\text{mi}} = \frac{x\text{hr}}{9\text{mi}}$$

$$(.75)x = (.25)(9)$$

$$x = (.25)(9) \div (.75)$$

$$x = 3\text{hr}$$

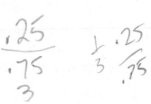
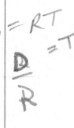

67

6. **The correct answer is (E).** First, translate the words into an equation:

A positive number (x) is added $(+)$ to the square of that number (x^2) becomes: $x + x^2$. The "result is 42" becomes: $= 42$. So, the translation into an algebraic equation is:

$x + x^2 = 42$

In this case, it is fastest to just plug in the numbers until you find the correct answer, $6 + 6^2 = 6 + 36 = 42$.

An alternate solution is to solve the quadratic equation for x.

$$x^2 + x - 42 = 0$$
$$(x - 6)(x + 7) = 0$$
$$\Rightarrow x = 6 \text{ or } x = -7$$

Since x must be positive, $x = 6$.

7. **The correct answer is (B).** Solve this one by setting $|3 - x| = 4$. The choice that fulfills this condition is $x = 7$. Thus, we have $|3 - 7| = |-4| = 4$.

8. **The correct answer is (B).** If you recognized the diagonal as the hypotenuse of a 3-4-5 triangle, you will know immediately that the length of the diagonal is 5. Otherwise, you can solve this problem by using the **Pythagorean Theorem**, which states: *the sum of the squares of each leg of a right triangle is equal to the square of the hypotenuse,* or $a^2 + b^2 = c^2$, where a and b are the sides of a right triangle and c is the hypotenuse. Using this formula, we have:

$$3^2 + 4^2 = c^2$$
$$9 + 16 = c^2$$

or

$$c^2 = 25$$
$$c = 5$$

9. **The correct answer is (D).** We know that, when a line intersects two parallel lines, both angle α and the 40° angle must be equal. We know that $\alpha + \beta = 180°$, and since $\alpha = 40°$, we have:

$40° + \beta = 180°$

or

$$\beta = 180° - 40°$$
$$\beta = 140°$$

10. The correct answer is (**A**). The expression can be factored to:

$$\frac{(5x + 2)(x + 2)}{(x + 2)(x - 2)}$$

The expression $(x + 2)$ can be divided in both the numerator and the denominator, leaving the answer:

$$\frac{5x + 2}{x - 2}$$

11. The correct answer is (**C**). We know one angle of the isosceles triangle and we know that two angles of the triangle must be equal to each other. Since all three angles added together must equal 180°, we have the following relations:

$$18° + 2\alpha = 180°$$
$$2\alpha = 162°$$
$$\alpha = 81°$$

or

$$18° + c + b = 180°$$
$$18° + 18° + b = 180°$$
$$36° + b = 180°$$
$$b = 144°$$

Thus, there are three possible answers (18°, 81°, or 144°). Only 81° is an answer choice.

12. The correct answer is (**B**). The circumference of a circle is $C = 2\pi r$. We are given $C = 158$, so we have:

$$158 = 2\pi r$$

or

$$r = 158 \div 2\pi$$
$$r \approx 25$$

13. The correct answer is (**A**). $\sqrt{x}$ cannot be a negative number, so the only possible choice is the one for which $x \geq 7$.

14. The correct answer is (**B**). First translate the English into algebra:

What is 7% of 60

becomes $x = \left(\frac{7}{100}\right)(60)$

$$x = 4.2$$

15. **The correct answer is (B).** To find the solutions to the equation, set $x - a = 0$ and $x - b = 0$. Solving for x yields the solutions, $x = a$ and $x = b$.

16. **The correct answer is (C).** The formula for the area of a circle is $A = \pi r^2$. Since the radius of a circle is $\frac{1}{2}$ the diameter, $r = 5$. By plugging 5 into the formula, the answer is obtained, $A = \pi 5^2 = 25\pi$.

17. **The correct answer is (D).** Solving for y:

$y = 4 - x$.

Squaring both sides:
$$y^2 = (4 - x)^2$$
$$= (4 - x)(4 - x)$$
$$= 16 - 8x + x^2$$

18. **The correct answer is (E).** Solve this one by multiplying through by 5. This yields: $-35 < 5x < -20$. The only choice that satisfies this condition is -21.50.

19. **The correct answer is (D).** It is easy to compare the numbers without getting mixed up if you make all the choices the same number of decimal places. Since .1912 has four decimal places, put zeroes in the other choices to make them all read four decimal places. It's faster to just do this mentally, but you are less likely to make a mistake if you can quickly write them in. Now it is easy to see that .1920 is the greatest number.

20. **The correct answer is (B).** The combination with the least sum will have the three least **different** numbers. To satisfy this condition, choose:

$C = \{4\}$
$D = \{5\}$
$E = \{2\}$

This makes the sum $= 11$.

Section 3—Critical Reading

1. **The correct answer is (E).** The word *or* will alert you that you are dealing with two contrasting elements, so look among the choices for antonyms (opposites). Choice (A) makes no sense. Choices (B) and (D) are composed of synonyms. Choice (C) may seem closer, since at first glance they have an opposite "feel"; however, *disguised* and *credible* really are not antonyms. Only choice (E) is comprised of true antonyms.

2. **The correct answer is (E).** The gist of the sentence tells you that you are dealing with cause and effect. Why would a person seek a chemical antidote (cure or remedy) for something? Probably because that something is negative or troubling. Now look among the choices for words that connote trouble. The only choice comprised of <u>two</u> such words is (E).

3. **The correct answer is (E).** This is a definition question. Except for choice (E), none of the adjectives would necessarily apply to something flagrantly unfair. (Look up the word *egregious* in your dictionary and add it to your vocabulary.)

4. **The correct answer is (C).** This question involves cause and effect, but it is also a definition question. To *exchange information* is to *communicate*.

5. **The correct answer is (B).** The sentence implies that poor Armand was actually hit by the train. Since the word *because* is at the beginning of the sentence, you can ask yourself: Why would a person not notice a train coming? Being completely absorbed—or *engrossed*—is the best answer.

6. **The correct answer is (B).** The words *although* and *in reality* will alert you that you are dealing with two contrasting elements, so look for opposites, then fit them into the sentence to see if they make sense. Only choices (A) and (B) contain antonyms. Choice (A) is illogical, because people do not usually seek out authorities to refute their own claims. That leaves only choice (B).

7. **The correct answer is (D).** Again, the sentence alerts you that you are dealing with contrasting elements through the use of the words *formerly* and *now*. Only choices (B) and (D) contain opposites, so you can disregard the other choices. In choice (B), the words are in the wrong order—a person probably would not be *hailed* (or lauded) as a heretic, which leaves choice (D) as your answer. Do not be misled by choice (A) just because you may have outside knowledge that Galileo was once imprisoned. The questions will never ask for outside knowledge, and in this context the second word, *surpassed*, makes no sense.

8. **The correct answer is (C).** This is a definition question. In order to know that the word *confound* is the best answer, you will have to be aware that it means *to confuse* or *bewilder*.

9. **The correct answer is (D).** The passage suggests that there is a relationship between injustice in one part of the world and the loss of national security in another. Choices (A) and (B) are incorrect, because they focus on nature and weather instead of human beings' treatment of one another. Choices (C) and (E) are incorrect because they are too narrow to be the main idea of the passage.

10. **The correct answer is (D).** The speaker's style is elegant, and his words carefully chosen. Choices (A), (B), and (E) are incorrect because they would cause the style to be overtly emotional. Choice (C) is incorrect.

11. **The correct answer is (B).** Choices (A) and (C) are contradicted by the author's suggestion that it is possible for graffiti artists to produce *great art*, which denotes approval and interest. Choice (D) is wrong because no words in the passage denote awe. Choice (E) is wrong because the author writes straightforwardly and knowledgeably on the subject.

12. **The correct answer is (B).** The passage speaks of the *need to apply the art quickly* (line 11).

13. **The correct choice is (B).** A thing that is *inert* is motionless, the opposite of a thing *endowed with motion*. The other choices are less closely related to the idea of motionlessness.

14. **The correct answer is (C).** The passage introduces the railway car by saying how *dismal* it is to see a thing set in rigidness *whose aspect is linked . . . with . . . mobility*. The other choices are not in the passage.

15. **The correct answer is (E).** Motion is unnatural for a hat; being stuffed and immobile is unnatural for a squirrel. Choice (A) is wrong because the squirrel is not animate. Choice (B) is wrong because the hat is not immobilized. Choice (C) is wrong because the hat is not permanently changed. Choice (D) is wrong because the hat is not mobile in its natural state.

16. **The correct answer is (D).** In the same sentence, the author speaks of Nature as a *good mother*.

17. **The correct answer is (D).** The whole passage deals with the tenderness and care with which nature appropriately dresses each of her *wildlings*. The other choices are implied by the passage—except for choice (A) since the author does not mention God—but they are not its focus.

18. **The correct answer is (B).** The author states that these other provisions relate *less to climate*, ruling out choice (A), *than to the more mechanical circumstances of life*—and goes on to give examples of the "clothing" of the mole living *in the dark and . . . dirt*; the *wave-washed seal*; and the *wild sheep . . . leaping among jagged storm-beaten cliffs*. The other choices are not in the passage.

19. **The correct answer is (C).** See the second sentence of the passage. The essay does not mention evolution, choice (A). The author does not pass judgment on nature, choice (D), but merely states the way things are as he sees them. Choices (B) and (E) are each too narrow to be the main idea of the passage.

20. **The correct answer is (C).** The danger of overpopulation in the animal kingdom is the topic of the first paragraph, in which the author states that if reproduction of species were to proceed unchecked, *the world would not hold them*.

21. **The correct answer is (B).** The essay deals almost entirely with the fact that disaster would result from unchecked population growth of any species. Note that you do not have to know who Thomas Malthus was to answer this question—all answers are stated or implied in the passage itself.

22. **The correct answer is (A).** In this paragraph, the author is talking about the necessity of obstacles to reproduction, because, if breeding is allowed to go unchecked in any species, that species will increase to the point where the earth cannot support it. The other choices would not make sense in the context of the passage.

23. **The correct answer is (E).** The word *restraint* here means abstinence. Not being married is (in Darwin's view) the human societal custom that would place an obstacle in the way of breeding.

24. **The correct answer is (E).** The author of Passage 1 speaks about *the love work of nature* (line 21). The author of Passage 2 states at the very beginning that each individual in a species is engaged in a *struggle for existence* and will inevitably be destroyed (line 1).

73

25. **The correct answer is (E).** Since the author of Passage 2 so clearly believes that hard evidence points to the routine destruction of the individual in the natural world, he would most likely see Passage 1 as based on emotion (or sentiment), rather than on fact. The other choices indicate attitudes for which there is no evidence in Passage 2.

26. **The correct answer is (B).** It is logical to believe that an author who speaks of nature as *a good mother* would find the idea that unmitigated destruction is nature's norm a harsh one. He *might* find it sophomoric, too, but *harsh* is a better answer based on the content of both passages.

27. **The correct answer is (B).** Since both authors cared enough to write serious essays on the subject, they evidently think it's worthwhile. There is no evidence in the passage for the other choices.

Section 4—Math

1. **The correct answer is (C).** Begin the solution by solving for x:

   $3x - 4 = 8$
   $3x = 8 + 4$
   $3x = 12$
   $x = 4$

   Careful, the questions asks us to find $x + 1$, not x, so $x + 1 = 4 + 1 = 5$.

2. **The correct answer is (A).** The intersection of sets A and B, denoted $A \cap B$, is the set containing all elements that both sets have in common: 0, 1, and 4.

3. **The correct answer is (A).** Each term of a geometric sequence is found by multiplying the preceding term by a constant, called the common ratio. The common ratio is found by dividing the second term by the first term, $\frac{2}{8} = \frac{1}{4}$. Thus, the third term in the geometric sequence is $2 \cdot \frac{1}{4} = \frac{1}{2}$.

4. **The correct answer is (B).** You can figure this one out by solving for x and y.

$$x + 2 = 3 \qquad\qquad 3y + 9 = 18$$
$$x = 3 - 2 \qquad\qquad 3y = 18 - 9$$
$$x = 1 \qquad\qquad\quad 3y = 9$$
$$y = 3$$

Now $x + y = 1 + 3 = 4$.

5. **The correct answer is (D).** The key to solving this problem is to realize that a line segment between two points on a circle that passes through the center of the circle must be a diameter. This means the radius of the circle is 6. Now it is a simple matter to calculate the area of the circle: $A = \pi r^2 = \pi 6^2 = 36\pi$.

6. **The correct answer is (B).** Since you know that the sum of the angles must equal 180°, it is just a matter of setting up an equation and solving for α.

$$3\alpha + 24° = 180°$$
$$3\alpha = 180° - 24°$$
$$3\alpha = 156°$$
$$\alpha = 52°$$

7. **The correct answer is (B).** Stated algebraically, the sum of .4 and its reciprocal is:

$$z = .4 + \left(\frac{1}{.4} \right)$$
$$z = .4 + 2.5$$
$$z = 2.9$$

8. **The correct answer is (D).** This one is easier than it looks. Simply substituting -1 for x gives us $x \ni y = (x^3)(y) = (-1)^3(y) = -y$, or $x \ni y = -y$. Now substitute $-y$ for $x \ni y$, and we are left with $y + (-y) = y - y = 0$.

9. **The correct answer is (C).** You should have immediately recognized this triangle as a 30°-60°-90° right triangle. By the definition of 30°-60°-90° right triangles, the hypotenuse (x) is twice the length of the short leg (4). This means that $x = 8$.

75

10. **The correct answer is (A).** To solve this problem, set up the algebraic relationships, then plug in known quantities. From the diagram, we can see that $BC + CD = BD$ or $BC = BD - CD$. We can also see that $CD = AD - AC$. Substituting $AD - AC$ for CD in the first relationship gives us: $BC = BD - (AD - AC)$. Now plug in the given values to yield: $BC = 10 - (18 - 12)$, or $BC = 4$.

11. **The correct answer is $n^2 = 2$.** Substituting $3n$ then n into $f(x) = x^2 + 6$ yields $f(3n) = (3n)^2 + 6 = 9n^2 + 6$ and $3f(n) = 3(n^2 + 6) = 3n^2 + 18$. Since we are given that $f(3n) = 3f(n)$, we know that $9n^2 + 6 = 3n^2 + 18$. Simplifying this expression gives us $9n^2 - 3n^2 = 18 - 6$ or $6n^2 = 12$, which is equivalent to $n^2 = \dfrac{12}{6}$ or $n^2 = 2$.

12. **The correct answer is 0.1225.** In order to get the relationships right in this problem, separate the problem into two components x and y. Let $x = 5\%$ of 7 and $y = 7\%$ of 5. Now you have simplified the problem to: what is xy. Just solve for x and y, then multiply them together to get the answer:

$$x = (0.05)(7) = 0.35$$
$$y = (0.07)(5) = 0.35$$
$$xy = (0.35)(0.35)$$
$$xy = 0.1225$$

13. **The correct answer is 125 cubic inches.** In a cube, all sides are of equal length. This means that each side has length $\dfrac{15}{3} = 5$. Now, just plug 5 into the formula for the volume of a cube (s^3) to get the answer:

$$V = s^3$$
$$= 5^3$$
$$= 125$$

14. **The correct answer is 15.** Solve this problem by setting up an equation, letting x be the unknown fourth number, then solving for x.

$$\frac{(3 + 7 + 9 + x)}{4} = 8.5$$
$$3 + 7 + 9 + x = (4)(8.5)$$
$$19 + x = 34$$
$$x = 34 - 19$$
$$x = 15$$

15. **The correct answer is $7.50.** To get this answer, translate the words into an equation, let x stand for the unknown original price, then solve for x.

$$6 = \left(\frac{4}{5}\right)x$$

$$6 = .80x$$

$$x = \frac{6}{.80}$$

$$x = 7.50$$

16. **The correct answer is 400.** Find this answer by putting the words into algebraic form, letting x be the unknown total number of people taking the test, and solving for x.

$$260 = 65\% \text{ of } x$$

$$260 = (.65)(x)$$

$$x = \frac{260}{.65}$$

$$x = 400$$

17. **The correct answer may be any number in the range** $.125 < x < .200$.

18. **The correct answer is 16.** Since $3^3 = 27$, $x = 3$. Substituting 3 into the expression yields the answer $2^{(3 + 1)} = 2^4 = 16$. Remember that the question asks what the value of the expression $2^{(x + 1)}$ is, **not** what the value of x is. (The value of x is 3.)

19. **The correct answer is 1000.** Remember, a decimal is an integer divided by some unit of 10. In this case, the ratio is 3 to 1000, or $\frac{3}{1000} = .003$.

20. **The correct answer is 20 feet.** First find the area of the square. We know its side has length $s = 4$ feet.

$$A = s^2$$
$$= 4^2$$
$$= 16 \text{ feet}$$

Now use the area just calculated to find the length of the long side of the rectangle. We are given that the two figures have equal area, which means the area of the rectangle is also 16 feet. Now solve for the rectangle's long side using the formula for area of a rectangle.

$$A = L \times W$$

Substituting $\quad 16 = L \times 2$

$$L = \frac{16}{2}$$

$$L = 8 \text{ feet}$$

You didn't forget the question, did you? It asks you to find the perimeter of the rectangle, **not** its length. The perimeter of the rectangle is

$$P = 2(L) + 2(W)$$
$$= 2(8) + 2(2)$$
$$= 16 + 4$$
$$= 20 \text{ feet}$$

Section 5—Writing Skills

1. **The correct answer is (D).** There is a shift in tense from present (*is . . . intelligent*) to past (*was a member*).

2. **The correct answer is (A).** The word order in the sentence is illogical. The phrase *Dashing out of the chapel* is a misplaced modifier describing the married couple, not the rain.

3. **The correct answer is (B).** The phrase *according with* is the wrong form of the idiom *according to*.

4. **The correct answer is (E).** There is no error in the sentence. It is written correctly in standard English.

5. **The correct answer is (D).** The error is one of vague pronoun reference. It is impossible to tell which man *descended into madness*.

6. **The correct answer is (C).** Noun number agreement is faulty in this sentence. The subjects of the sentence are both *superheroes*, not *a superhero.*

7. **The correct answer is (A).** This is a faulty use of an idiomatic phrase. The correct idiom would be *accused of.*

8. **The correct answer is (C).** The error is one of faulty comparison, and it's easy to miss. Zelda's tricks are more complex than Rex's tricks (not than Rex himself).

9. **The correct answer is (E).** There are no errors. The sentence is written in correct standard English.

10. **The correct answer is (A).** This is faulty subject-verb agreement—the subject is plural and the verb is singular.

11. **The correct answer is (D).** The error is one of shift in number from singular (*the unicorn*) to plural (*their foreheads*).

12. **The correct answer is (A).** The error here is a shift in person from second person (*you*) to third person (*most people*).

13. **The correct answer is (E).** There are no errors in the sentence—it is written in correct standard English.

14. **The correct answer is (B).** The preposition *with* is misused—the correct preposition is *to.*

15. **The correct answer is (D).** This is a shift in tense from present (*can occur*) to past (*appeared*).

16. **The correct answer is (A).** This is an error of faulty preposition. *By their driving tests . . .* should be changed to *On their driving tests . . .*

17. **The correct answer is (E).** The sentence is written in correct standard English.

18. **The correct answer is (D).** This is a shift in tense from past (*cooled*) to present (*combine*).

19. **The correct answer is (A).** This is a faulty use of the preposition *of.* The beginning of the sentence should read *In metabolism.*

20. **The correct answer is (C).** It is clear, to the point, and says all it needs to say. The cliché at the beginning of the original sentence, *At this point in time*, is a sign that choice (A) is not the answer. Clichés often make a sentence wordy. Choice (B) also contains the cliché and is wordy. Choice (D) has dropped the cliché, so it is better but still wordy. Choice (E) is vague and implies that the word *confines* refers to only a small area of Higgins Beach.

79

21. **The correct answer is (D).** It is grammatically accurate and the least awkward of all the sentences. In the original sentence and in choices (B) and (C), the wild party, not the people, seems to be celebrating; also, both versions lack "punch," since they make ineffective use of the passive voice (the actor, Bad Bob, is not active in the sentence). In choice (E), an important part of the sentence has been put in parentheses, making it seem a minor point.

22. **The correct answer is (C).** It is grammatically correct and the clearest version of the sentence. Choice (A) makes ineffective use of the passive voice, as does choice (B). In both cases, the people committing the action (the police) are not in the subject (or active) position, making the sentences sound insipid. Choices (D) and (E) are awkward and convoluted.

23. **The correct answer is (A).** The sentence is correct and rhythmical. Speak the others silently to yourself, and you'll find they sound convoluted, even clunky. In choice (C), the word *great* seems like slang, which would be incongruous in this rather formal sentence; also, the sentence makes ineffective use of the passive voice.

24. **The correct answer is (D).** Choice (A) is inappropriately informal for the formal writing in the rest of the sentence. Choice (B) is unnecessarily wordy. Choices (A) and (E) represent a shift in diction. Choice (C) seems pompous because of the use of the verb *oppugn*.

25. **The correct answer is (B).** The sentence makes effective use of parallelism. The other choices, though technically correct, do not. Choice (A) uses the slang term *loser*, which is inappropriately informal in style.

26. **The correct answer is (A).** It is correctly punctuated. In choice (B), the semicolon is misused. Used correctly, the semicolon separates two independent clauses. The phrase *even though* is a subordinator, denoting that the second half of this sentence is a dependent clause. Choices (C), (D), and (E) are incorrect because they turn the dependent clause into a sentence fragment.

27. **The correct answer is (B).** The other choices are unidiomatic; also *dangerouser,* choice (C), is not a word—the correct intensifier is *more dangerous*.

28. **The correct answer is (E).** The punctuation is incorrect in the other choices: Commas should be used on either side of a parenthetical phrase such as *or doppelganger*. Choice (A) omits the first comma (causing the comma that is in the sentence to incorrectly separate subject and verb), choice (B) omits the second, and choice (D) omits both. Choice (C) makes a sentence fragment after the second part of the sentence.

29. **The correct answer is (C).** The coordinating conjunction *but* correctly joins two contrasting elements, *democratic system* and *totalitarianism*. The other conjunctions create nonsense.

30. **The correct answer is (E).** The other choices represent shifts in tense.

31. **The correct answer is (A).** It is dramatic, straightforward, and correctly punctuated. Choice (B) makes no sense—if a person's life and career are ruined, surely that person would know it. In choice (C), the dramatic effect is ruined by wordiness. Choice (D) is unnecessarily convoluted. In choice (E), the comma is superfluous; also the meaning of the word *why* is ambiguous—here it could be an exclamation, as in "Why, you dog!"

32. **The correct answer is (B).** Except for choice (E), the choices are unnecessarily wordy. However, choice (E) represents a faulty conjunction. The word *but* should signal a contrast between two elements of a sentence, and there is no contrast between a thing being baffling and that same thing being unexplainable.

33. **The correct answer is (D).** The other choices have unnecessary commas.

34. **The correct answer is (E).** Choice (E) is correct because sentence 15 introduces the topic of the way Miles's behavior changed over the years, which is described in sentence 12.

35. **The correct answer is (E).** It is not a particularly interesting thought, as it is too obvious; also it interrupts the flow of the sentences about Miles's admiration of Charlie Parker.

36. **The correct answer is (B).** The paragraph emphasizes the change that took place in Miles's musical and personal style. Neither choice (A) nor choice (E) is in the paragraph. Choices (C) and (D) are each too narrow to be the main idea.

37. The correct answer is (B). It is clear and efficient. Examples of wordiness and redundancy in the other sentences are the phrase *completely and finally* in choice (A) and the phrase *and distanced himself* in choice (C). Choice (D) is convoluted and confusing. Choice (E) makes ineffective use of the passive voice.

38. The correct answer is (D). This is a logical conclusion to the discussion of the way Miles and his music changed over the years. The other sentences would be jarring, as they introduce new subjects.

39. The correct answer is (D). Choice (A) is unnecessarily complicated. Choices (B) and (C) sound strange because Miles's birth and his growing up are in reverse chronological order. Choice (E) does not fit the style of the rest of the passage, consisting of choppy phrases instead of full sentences.

Chapter
2

Critical Reading Review

Sentence Completion

What to Expect

Sentence completion questions are designed to measure:

- The strength of your vocabulary

- Your ability to read closely and carefully

- Your capacity to understand the logic of sentences

One of the most important things to do, well in advance of the test, is to acquaint yourself with the directions for each type of question. That way, you won't have to waste precious moments figuring out what's expected of you.

For sentence completion questions, you will be instructed as follows:

Directions: Each sentence below has either one or two blanks in it and is followed by five choices, labeled (A) through (E). These choices represent words or phrases that have been left out. Choose the word or phrase that, if inserted into the sentence, would <u>best</u> fit the meaning of the sentence as a whole.

Example:

Canine massage is a veterinary technique for calming dogs that are extremely _____.

(A) inept
(B) disciplined
(C) controlled
(D) stressed
(E) restrained   

How to Approach Sentence Completion Sentences

Following are pointers on how to prepare for and deal with these kinds of sentences.

Read Widely

The best way to prepare for the sentence completion portion of the PSAT—indeed for the entire test—is to read widely. Read books, magazines, and newspapers. Read literary fiction and fiction written for pure entertainment. Read a variety of nonfiction—everything from computer manuals, to sports magazines, to books on the habits of birds. If you don't feel like reading a whole work, read a few pages. When you run into a word you don't know, look it up. Nothing will improve your vocabulary and your ability to reason with words as much as reading will.

Practice

The practice tests in this book are designed to help you improve your verbal ability and optimize your chances of getting a good score on the PSAT. Do ALL the practice tests—don't skip any. The answer explanations that come at the end of the tests are particularly important. The explanations are every bit as important as the tests themselves. If you miss a question, the answer explanation will help you see the reason for your mistake, so you can avoid making the same mistake in the future.

Try These Strategies

Below are some tactics you can use in approaching the sentence completion portion of the test.

Read the initial sentence carefully. You'll need to get a sense of its *internal logic* before looking at the choices. This will make picking out the answer easier. Look for *key words and phrases*, especially for ones that contrast with one another. Suppose you are confronted with the following sentence:

> The world of quantum mechanics is a strange one, in which the _____ laws of physics, known to us in the everyday world, no longer work.
>
> (A) unusual
> (B) explicit
> (C) familiar
> (D) eccentric
> (E) fallible

The correct answer is (C). In this sentence, the word *strange* may catch your eye, followed by a contrasting phrase, *known to us in the everyday world*. Many times, as in this instance, another phrase in the sentence will be a synonym or near-synonym for what should go in the blank. A synonym for the word *known* is the word *familiar*, choice (C), which is the correct choice here. A quick survey of the other choices will show that none of them fit so well.

Read all the choices. Once in awhile, the best answer will seem to spring off the page at you, especially in the case of sentences with only one blank. Be sure, though, no matter how certain you feel that you know the answer, to read *all* the choices. For one thing, many words look alike at a quick glance. Consider this sentence, for example:

> Although my mom doesn't believe it, the CD player does not _____ me when I'm studying—I can concentrate just fine.
>
> (A) detract
> (B) remand
> (C) distress
> (D) motivate
> (E) distract

The correct answer is (E). To *distract* is to *divert attention*. It would be very easy to choose choice (A) in haste—*detract*, which means *to take away a desirable part of* or *to diminish*.

Remember also that the directions will ask you to pick the *best* answer, not simply a possible answer.

Check the initial blank first by itself. When you're faced with a sentence that has two blanks, check the initial blank; if it does not fit the logic of the sentence, discard the whole choice. Don't mull it over; just throw it out. If the first word *does* fit, then you have to go on to the second. Close reading is particularly important when you are faced with a two-blank sentence, because frequently the first word will fit just fine, but the second will be way off. For example:

> Bertha's inheritance was all gone, and now she was _____ and utterly _____ and desperate.
>
> (A) impulsive..repentant
> (B) elucidated..bereft
> (C) destitute..ebullient
> (D) inextricable..vivacious
> (E) impoverished..disconsolate

The correct answer is (E). However, if you look only at the first word, you might well pick choice (C). But you would be wrong, because the second word, *ebullient*, means *enthusiastic and lively*, which Bertha, having lost all her money and being desperate besides, probably isn't.

Pay special attention to small, qualifying words. Don't read so quickly that you overlook the word *not*, a prefix such as *un*, or a qualifier such as *many, almost, few,* or *only*. These tiny elements can change the meaning of the entire sentence. For example:

> He was not an outlaw but a good husband and father.
> He was not only an outlaw but a good husband and father.

Small words that come at the beginning of the sentence or that link the parts together are crucial clues to the internal logic of the sentence. Some examples are: *since, because, however, for example, similarly,* and *therefore.*

Know your prefixes. Be familiar with the meaning of certain important prefixes. A prefix (or suffix)—a small element added to the root, or base, of a word—can change the meaning of a word entirely. Some important prefixes (there are many) are:

- **dis-**, meaning not (*dis*agree, *dis*similar, *dis*comfort)
- **mis-**, meaning bad, badly, wrong, wrongly, failure, or lack (*mis*conduct, *mis*spent, *mis*fire)
- **re-**, meaning again or anew (*re*elect, *re*kindle)
- **un-**, meaning not (*un*happy, *un*usual)

Look at the following example:

> He had an _____ appearance, so you wouldn't notice him in a crowd.
>
> (A) uncanny
> (B) unusual
> (C) unarresting
> (D) unappealing
> (E) unprecedented

The correct answer is (C). All the other choices denote qualities that ARE noticeable in a crowd. Note also that the second half of this sentence defines the blank.

Eliminate as many obviously wrong choices as you can, right away. If the answer is not immediately apparent, begin by eliminating obviously wrong choices. Once you understand the gist of the sentence, you can usually throw out one or more of the choices. Take the following example:

The unicorn, being a/an _____ beast, exists only in legends and fairy tales.

(A) bizarre
(B) eccentric
(C) ribald
(D) mythical
(E) terrifying

The correct answer is (D). First, the phrase *being a _____ beast,* alerts you that you are looking for a *synonym* of one of the words at the end of the sentence to fill the blank. So you can eliminate choices (B), (C), and (E) as unlikely because you want a word that describes something that exists *only* in legends and fairy tales. Choice (A) is attractive, perhaps, but clearly choice (D), *mythical* (which means imaginary or fictitious), is the better of these last two choices. In some cases, if you're very lucky, you may be able to eliminate all the choices except one!

Simplify long, complex sentences. If faced with a long and complex sentence, cutting it down, making it simpler, or even making two sentences or more out of it is a good idea. Be careful, though: don't leave out anything important. Suppose you are given the following sentence:

Behaviorism is that branch of psychology that attempts to explain human behavior using purely objective, _____ data, with the theoretical goal of predicting and _____ that behavior, an approach some people find sinister.

(A) pristine..utilizing
(B) impartial..improving
(C) measurable..controlling
(D) biased..perverting
(E) limited..responding to

The correct answer is (C). This sentence probably seems pretty overwhelming at first, but there's a way to make it less so. After reading it once or twice closely, chop it into two, three, or even four segments. (You won't have to do this for all sentences—there won't be time—but for monsters like this, it's the best approach.)

Behaviorism is a branch of psychology.

It attempts to explain human behavior using purely objective, _____ data.

Its goal is predicting and _____ behavior.

[This is an approach] some people find sinister.

Now you can discern the overall logic of the sentence more easily and begin working on the first blank. The first blank, in combination with the word *objective*, modifies the word *data*, so the word in that blank will almost certainly be a synonym or near-synonym of the word *objective*.

Now eliminate the ones that are obviously wrong. One choice that can definitely be thrown out is the word *biased*, because it's the opposite of the word *objective*. The words *pristine* and *limited*, while possible, aren't particularly good bets either, so you can disregard them, at least for now.

The most likely choices, then, are the words *impartial* and *measurable*, with *impartial* momentarily having the edge, as it's most nearly synonymous with *objective*. When you move on to the second blank, however—looking now only at choices (B) and (C)—you find the words *improving* and *controlling*. Now you must ask yourself, which of these adjectives would more logically relate to the final part of the sentence—i.e., denote something *sinister*? *Improving* just doesn't fit the bill at all. Therefore, your second choice, (C), the word *controlling*, is the right answer.

Figure out the sentence type. Following are three main types of sentences that may be used on the PSAT.

1. The **cause-and-effect** sentence. Simply put, this is a sentence in which one element causes another.

   Because the scientific discovery of bacteria had not yet been made, people believed that disease had its source in the _____.

   (A) intrinsic
   (B) supernatural
   (C) egregious
   (D) tangible
   (E) outmoded

The correct answer is (B). The word *Because* at the beginning of the sentence speaks for itself. The first half of the sentence mentions *scientific discovery*, so you know that the correct choice will have to run counter to the objectivity of science.

2. The **comparison/contrast** sentence. This is a sentence that shows ways in which two things are similar to or different from one another.

   Unlike the usual half-hour television show, which resolves all its conflicts in the second 15-minute segment, the good short story often presents its audience with conflicts that are _____.

   (A) determinate
   (B) inevitable
   (C) demonstrable
   (D) mysterious
   (E) irreconcilable

The correct answer is (E). The word *Unlike* at the beginning of the sentence is a hint that you are dealing with *contrasting* elements in this sentence. Since the first half of the sentence speaks of conflicts that are quickly solved, you must look among the choices for a word that indicates the opposite.

3. The **definition** sentence. In this kind of sentence, one part defines another.

   Elke took a wrong turn, wandered into the boggy marshland, and sank into the _____.

   (A) current
   (B) quagmire
   (C) rivulet
   (D) estuary
   (E) copse

The correct answer is (B). Remember, always pay close attention to the words and phrases immediately preceding (and following) the blank. The second syllable of *quagmire* should help with this answer, also, even if you aren't sure what the definition of *quagmire* is. Choices (A), (C), and (D) indicate running water, not boggy land. A *copse* is a small thicket of trees.

Practice Exercises

Now is the time to apply what you've learned. Try your hand at the following sentence completion exercises. As you work on them, see if you can identify the sentence type. The answers appear on page 109.

1. Because it was winter, and because he loved his cat "Tinkerbell," Zelig fixed her a _____ basket in front of the fireplace.

   (A) cozy
   (B) soft
   (C) pleasant
   (D) charming
   (E) neat

2. We all stared in _____ as, _____, Mr. Peters snapped his suspenders, rose straight into the air, and was gone.

   (A) awe..understandably
   (B) admiration..repugnantly
   (C) indifference..miraculously
   (D) disbelief..incredibly
   (E) revulsion..courageously

3. Although it runs counter to what most of us believe, sometimes a flawlessly logical argument can lead to a/an _____ conclusion.

   (A) particular
   (B) predestined
   (C) inescapable
   (D) impeccable
   (E) erroneous

4. Arrested at the age of 70, the Greek philosopher Socrates was _____ to drink a deadly Hemlock potion, after being accused of the crime of _____ the youth of Athens.

   (A) required..tutoring
   (B) invited..impugning
   (C) condemned..corrupting
   (D) sentenced..eulogizing
   (E) accustomed..commending

5. Larry Furr was easily the most _____ person I ever met—he fell for every scam in the book.

   (A) entrepreneurial
   (B) gullible
   (C) savvy
   (D) vehement
   (E) innocuous

6. This communication channel is a public one; therefore, as an emergency medical technician, you should never transmit _____ information.

   (A) communicable
   (B) conventional
   (C) confidential
   (D) ceremonial
   (E) communal

7. That math problem had me completely _____; I knew I'd never be able to find the solution.

   (A) famished
   (B) finalized
   (C) fabricated
   (D) flummoxed
   (E) familiarized

8. Why did Gina betray me by _____ my secret desires?

   (A) revitalizing
   (B) divulging
   (C) alleviating
   (D) eluding
   (E) indulging

9. Although he never offended the non-Christians of his day by _____ the old pagan cults, at the end of his life the emperor Constantine _____ to Christianity and was baptized on his deathbed.

   (A) denying..reverted
   (B) disavowing..converted
   (C) accepting..deserted
   (D) repelling..matriculated
   (E) worshipping..adapted

10. My friend Abayomi's name means "brings joy," which is ironic, as he is always gloomy and _____.

    (A) pessimistic
    (B) optimistic
    (C) unkempt
    (D) repressed
    (E) orderly

11. Each word has a variety of connotations; similarly, many words have more than one _____, or dictionary meaning.

    (A) permutation
    (B) transposition
    (C) renovation
    (D) evocation
    (E) denotation

12. Science has found evidence that what we generally call "mind" resides in the organic structure of the brain; therefore, some scientists believe that when the body dies, the mind—and in some sense the soul—will likewise _____.

    (A) disintegrate
    (B) persevere
    (C) concede
    (D) conciliate
    (E) reassemble

Reading Skills

What to Expect

The Reading Skills section of the PSAT is crucial. Whether or not you do well in college depends very largely on your ability to read and understand what you've read. The Reading Skills section is designed to test your ability to do the following:

- Find the **main idea** of a reading passage.

- Make **inferences**—that is, recognize ideas that are not stated in the passage, but only implied.

- Figure out the **meaning of words or phrases** on the basis of their **context**.

- **Analyze and evaluate** the passage in terms of logic, implications, ideas, opinions, and arguments, including recognizing inconsistencies in arguments.

- Recognize **rhetorical techniques** that the author uses to advance the argument—consider the effects of **diction** (word choice), **style** (formal or informal; degree of detail used to support the argument), and **tone** (objective, passionate, sarcastic, etc.); consider the reasons behind what the author chose to include or leave out.

- **Compare and contrast** the central arguments of two separate blocks of text.

- Identify the **organizational techniques** used by the author—consider the **order** of the whole essay (chronological order, order of importance, order by comparison/contrast, order by cause-and-effect, etc.).

- Identify the author's **intent** in writing the passage and **attitude** toward the subject.

Reading Skills passages on the PSAT/NMSQT fall into two categories, based solely on length:

- Passages of approximately 100 words, followed by 1 to 3 questions.

- Passages that range from 500 to 850 words, followed by 6 to 12 questions.

You will prepare for both kinds of passage in the same way. For the Reading Skills questions, you will be instructed as follows:

> **Directions:** Read each of the passages carefully, then answer the questions that come after them. The answer to each question may be stated overtly or only implied. You will not have to use outside knowledge to answer the questions—all the material you will need will be in the passage itself. In some cases, you will be asked to read two related passages and answer questions about their relationship to one another.

How to Approach Reading Skills Questions

Below are pointers on how to prepare for and deal with Reading Skills questions.

Read! Read! Read!

Okay, okay, so you've heard it before. But it still bears repeating. The more you read, the better you'll do on the PSAT, as well as in college itself. Read material on a wide variety of subjects. Dip into popular magazines like *People* and *GQ*, and serious ones like the *New Yorker, Scientific American*, and *National Geographic*. Read your hometown newspaper—the news, the gossip column, and the business section. Read the *New York Times*. Don't be overwhelmed by what you read, though, or think that you have to remember it all. You're reading for the practice that it will give you at analyzing and evaluating written ideas, not for facts to regurgitate on the test. You won't be asked for facts. Everything you'll need will be in the passages themselves.

Maybe you watch a lot of TV. Most of us do, partly because it's entertaining and partly because it's easy. It's passive—you sit back with your pizza or popcorn and, too often, turn off your mind and even your curiosity, allowing yourself to be carried along by the flickering images on the screen. There's nothing wrong with that after a hard day.

But reading is—or should be—different, especially when you're boning up for the Reading Skills section of the PSAT. You'll be most successful on this part of the test if you work toward becoming an *active reader*. Don't allow your eyes to just slide over the words, or you're doomed. The important thing is to practice becoming *involved* in what you're reading, in looking for key words, phrases, and ideas to help you discern the overall meaning.

Practice

No need to be redundant, I suppose, but practice is the best way to develop your skill at anything, from scuba diving to shooting hoops to cooking gourmet meals. So do ALL the practice exercises in this book, and read the answer explanations at the end of the practice tests.

Employ These Strategies

One task you'll have to perform on the PSAT is to find the *main idea* of a reading passage. Main idea questions come in several guises. They may ask directly for the main idea, or they may ask for the *central concern*, or *theme*, or even the *author's intent or purpose* in writing the passage.

94

When asked for the main idea, look for a generalization. The main idea will be a generalization, rather than a specific fact that may only support the main idea. Beware of choosing answers that are too narrow and specific. Conversely, beware of answers that are so general that they leave out crucial information.

Passages will vary widely from one another, so finding main ideas is particularly challenging. Consider the following two, very different kinds of passages.

The first passage is based on a South Carolina Department of Health report. The second passage is an excerpt from a treatise on ghosts.

Passage 1

Line   *Cyclospora cayetanensis* is a recently characterized coccidian parasite. The first known cases of infection in humans were diagnosed in 1977. Before 1996, only three outbreaks of Cyclospora infection had been reported in the United States.

(5)   On June 14, 1996, the South Carolina Department of Health and Environmental Control (SCDHEC) was notified of digestive illness among persons who attended a luncheon near Charleston on May 23. All 64 attendees were interviewed. Of the 64 persons, 37 (58%) had Cyclospora infection, including

(10)   seven with laboratory-confirmed infection. The median incubation period was 7.5 days (range: 1–23 days).

      Based on analysis by the SCDHEC, food items associated with illness included raspberries, strawberries, and potato salad.

(15)   On May 23, a total of 95 persons attended a luncheon in an adjacent room and were served strawberries obtained from the same source, but they were not served raspberries; no cases were identified among these persons. One person who ate raspberries at the establishment that evening developed

(20)   laboratory-confirmed infection; she had not attended either luncheon or eaten strawberries.

Passage 2

Line   People often report sensing the presence of ghosts. Strange noises and smells, coldness, objects being moved about, but no mover seen—all these indicate that a ghost is nearby. Ghosts can also be present as a tactile sensation, the whisper of a

(5)   touch against the skin. Contrary to common belief, they are not usually corporeal—not at all like those sheets you wear at

Halloween—and when they are, they're usually ill-defined, transparent (although they may be luminous). Very rarely, though, they're as solid-seeming as a real person, can eat and

(10) drink and talk and even make love, fool people into thinking they're alive, then vanish. But more often they are only sounds, or smells, a coldness in the air or a felt Presence.

Ghosts can be either benevolent or malevolent. They can be comic and comfortable, like the old sea captain in *The*

(15) *Ghost and Mrs. Muir,* or horrific beyond belief like the ghosts of the revelers at the party in the Overlook Hotel, in Stephen King's *The Shining.* They can emerge from the afterlife to teach us lessons, like old Marley in *A Christmas Carol,* or come back moaning to be avenged, like the ghost in *Hamlet.*

(20) They cannot cross over running water, although they can definitely pass through solid objects. They cast shadows and can be reflected in mirrors. Invariably they are clothed!

You should not touch a ghost EVER.

No one knows for certain what they are. Most people

(25) think they are spirits of the dead. But they may be projections of the human unconscious. Or astral bodies. Or thought-forms. Or even electrical charges in the atmosphere.

1. The purpose of Passage 1 is to

   (A) give suggestions as to how to treat Cyclospora infection, based on findings by the SCDHEC investigation in 1996.

   (B) explain exactly what *Cyclospora cayetanensis* is and how it causes infection in humans, based on the 1996 SCDHEC investigation.

   (C) report the findings of the SCDHEC investigation into the digestive illness among attendees of a luncheon near Charleston on May 23, 1996.

   (D) justify funds spent by the SCDHEC on their investigation into the digestive illness among attendees of a luncheon near Charleston on May 23, 1996.

   (E) warn potential visitors to Charleston of the outbreak of *Cyclospora cayetanensis* that caused illness among the attendees of a luncheon near Charleston on May 23, 1996.

The correct answer is (C). A more specific reason behind the report is not given.

2. Which of the following statements about ghosts from Passage 2 is the most objective?

   (A) People often report sensing the presence of ghosts (line 1).
   (B) Contrary to common belief, they are not usually corporeal . . . (lines 5–6).
   (C) Ghosts can be either benevolent or malevolent (line 14).
   (D) You should not touch a ghost EVER (line 23).
   (E) No one knows for certain what they are (line 24).

The correct answer is (A). This is the most verifiable statement in the passage. For the other statements, the author does not offer proof and does not appeal to any authority. Even choice (E) cannot be verified absolutely—many people think they know, including the author of the passage, and it's possible someone may know.

3. Which of the following statements from Passage 1 is an opinion?

   (A) The first known cases of infection in humans were diagnosed in 1977 (lines 2–3).
   (B) Based on analysis by the SCDHEC, food items associated with illness included raspberries, strawberries, and potato salad (lines 12–14).
   (C) On May 23, a total of 95 persons attended a luncheon in an adjacent room and were served strawberries obtained from the same source . . . (lines 15–17).
   (D) One person who ate raspberries at the establishment that evening developed laboratory-confirmed infection; she had not attended either luncheon or eaten strawberries (lines 18–21).
   (E) There are no opinions in the passage, only facts.

The correct answer is (E). The passage is comprised entirely of verifiable statements.

4. Which of the following best describes the tone of Passage 1 as compared to that of Passage 2?

   (A) Passage 1 has a more assertive tone.
   (B) Passage 1 has a more objective tone.
   (C) Passage 1 has a more ironic tone.
   (D) Passage 1 has a more whimsical tone.
   (E) Passage 1 has a more somber tone.

The correct answer is (B). In Passage 2, the author seems to shout at times (note the capital letters and exclamation points), so Passage 1 seems more objective. The tone of Passage 2 is every bit as assertive, choice (A), as that of Passage 1—although offering no evidence, the author seems quite confident about the statements made. Neither passage seems ironic, whimsical, or somber.

5. Based on the passage, what was the most likely source of the *Cyclospora infection* described in Passage 1?

    (A) Strawberries
    (B) Potato salad
    (C) Raspberries
    (D) Other people
    (E) Laboratory contamination

The correct answer is (C). See the final sentence of the passage.

6. Based on Passage 2, ghosts usually present to human beings as

    (A) objects being moved about.
    (B) non-corporeal beings.
    (C) entities solid-seeming as a real person.
    (D) benevolent entities.
    (E) malevolent entities.

The correct answer is (B). See lines 5–8.

Consider all questions in the context of the passage. Whether you're looking for the main idea or the meaning of a particular word or phrase, pay attention to what's in the passage, rather than what you know about the real world. You may not agree with what the passage says; it's possible the author of the passage will be biased or even have the facts wrong. However, *unless the question asks you to do otherwise* (and it sometimes may), answer only on the basis of what the passage says. One cautionary note, however: At the same time you are reading the actual words, you must be alert to signs of the author's *attitude* toward the subject, which may be at variance with those words and which is usually revealed through diction, style, tone, and sometimes even punctuation. Consider the following two passages, which deal with the same topic.

Passage 1

Line   Astral projection is synonymous with OBE—that is, out-of-body experience. The person who experiences this phenom-enon leaves his or her physical body and enters what is called a *subtle body*, a kind of semi-transparent double that may be

(5)   either clothed or naked. In the astral form, OBE travelers can roam about the earth or even visit non-earthly realms, passing through objects and moving at the speed of thought.

Passage 2

Line   "Astral projection" is said to be synonymous with "OBE," or "out-of-body" experience. The so-called "traveler" leaves his or her body and enters what believers call a *subtle body*, which is a semi-transparent double that may be either clothed or
(5)   dressed in its birthday suit. In this "astral form," the person can move about the earth or even visit other worlds, passing through objects like Casper the Friendly Ghost, and moving at the speed of thought.

1. According to Passage 1, a *subtle body* is

   (A)   the guide that shows the astral traveler other realms, earthly and non-earthly.
   (B)   the illusion of a semi-transparent double that makes astral travel possible.
   (C)   an exit in the physical body through which the soul of the astral traveler can escape.
   (D)   the form in which the astral traveler makes his or her way to other places, earthly or non-earthly.
   (E)   the thought-projection that enables the astral traveler to move swiftly.

The correct answer is (D). You might pick choice (B) because you believe astral projection is an illusion, but remember that the question begins *According to Passage 1 . . .*

2. Which passage is more likely written by an author who accepts astral projection as fact? How can you tell?

   (A)   Passage 1, because that author seems more knowledgeable about the subject.
   (B)   Passage 1, because the tone is straightforward, with no sarcasm.
   (C)   Passage 2, because it has more detail and support from outside sources.
   (D)   Passage 2, because that author uses humor to make his piece more interesting.
   (E)   Both authors accept the idea as based on fact.

The correct answer is (B). The lack of sarcasm indicates a serious, accepting attitude toward the subject. There is no supporting evidence in either passage for what the authors say, which rules out choices (A) and (C). Just because a piece is interesting doesn't mean it is based on an accepting attitude, which rules out choice (D). The allusion to *birthday suit* and *Casper the Friendly Ghost* in Passage 2 lends a mocking attitude to Passage 2, ruling out choice (E).

3. What is the most likely reason the author of Passage 2 used quotation marks around words and phrases?

    (A) To make the passage seem more authoritative
    (B) To reinforce the impression of a sarcastic or tongue-in-cheek attitude toward the subject
    (C) To indicate that the words are from a secondary source
    (D) To make the technical information in the passage more clear
    (E) To differentiate technical words from the rest of the text

The correct answer is (B). Punctuation is more than just window dressing. In this case, it implies a tongue-in-cheek attitude toward the subject matter. Quotation marks can be used for the reasons mentioned in choice (A) and in choices (C) through (E), also. But remember, the question concerns the way they're used in *this passage* only—not all the ways in which they can be used in the real world.

Remember that there is a difference between fact and opinion. A fact is what actually happened or actually is; an opinion is the author's slant on it. You must become sensitive to the difference in order to do well on the Reading Skills portion of the PSAT.

> FACT: In her veterinary record, my cat is listed as a "domestic short-hair."

> OPINION: My short-haired cat is more pleasant to take care of than a long-haired cat, because I don't have to spend time brushing her.

The first statement can be *verified* in the real world by a trip to the veterinarian's office; the second *cannot be verified* and is therefore an opinion.

Look for what is implied as well as what is stated directly. The second of the two statements above *implies an attitude*—that it is unpleasant to spend time brushing a cat. You may agree; another person may disagree. In the final analysis, there is no truth or untruth.

Consider words only in their contexts. When asked the meaning of particular words or phrases in the passage, don't consider them in isolation—look closely at the surrounding words and phrases. For instance, the word *foot* means something very different in the following sentences:

- I hurt my *foot*.

- I can *foot* the bill.

Answer only the question that is asked. This may seem obvious, but in haste and under stress, it is easy to become sidetracked. When asked to *relate* parts of a passage to the whole passage or to other parts of it or when asked to *compare* two passages, be sure to choose answers that are pertinent to the question. For example, if asked to compare two authors in terms of their attitude toward romantic love, don't choose a "correct answer" that deals with their attitudes toward God, even if their attitudes toward God are extensively discussed in the passage.

Remember that the answers to the questions are in the passage itself. Do not be daunted by the subject matter of any passage you're asked to deal with. Remember: you need no outside knowledge except that which is gleaned from general experience and common sense.

Read the questions first only if that works best for you. There are differing opinions about whether you should read the questions before you read the passage. As you do the practice exercises, try both approaches and see which works for you.

Read the introductory lines and the footnotes. There will be two or three lines before the passage that tell you where it is from. These will orient you to what the passage is about, and they sometimes give a clue as to what the author's purpose and attitude might be. Occasionally, a passage will have footnotes to help you with context or meaning—these are important, too.

Practice Exercises

Now for more of that invaluable practice. Try your hand at reading the following passages and answering the questions that come after them. The answers appear on page 111.

The Single Passage

Here is an approximately 450-word passage that speculates on the nature of the universe.

Line   It is likely that, throughout all of history, human beings have
       wondered, Where did the universe come from? Did it spring
       out of nothing, for no reason? Did something or someone
       create it? Is it perhaps infinite, thus needing no creator?

(5)   An argument against the theory of an infinite universe—
       and the closest thing to scientific proof we have—is to be
       found in one of the basic laws of physics, the Second Law of
       Thermodynamics, which asserts that everything in the universe
       tends toward entropy—that is, toward disorder and decay.

(10)   Eventually, says this Second Law, all systems (whether they be
       stars, or the Brussels sprouts you had last night for dinner, or
       the houses you've lived in during your lifetime, or indeed you
       yourself and everyone you know) will eventually lose organiza-
       tion and energy, disintegrate, and die. Things may *seem* to gain

(15)   order—a baby grows into an adult, a house is built, a peach
       pit grows into a tree. However, the gain is illusory. For any
       entity to gain energy, it must steal energy from something else,
       and the overall stock of energy available in the universe is
       thereby diminished. (If a baby is to grow into an adult, it must

(20)   eat, and the food it eats loses energy and disintegrates in the
       process; to build a house one must kill part of a forest.)
       Scientists can prove this Second Law; entropy can be mea-
       sured.

           Now, if everything that exists eventually dissipates,

(25)   disintegrates, and dies, then someday the universe itself will do
       likewise, reaching a state of thermodynamic equilibrium, a
       cold, dead state in which nothing changes. If the universe is
       infinite, then it has already had infinite time to accomplish this
       state of equilibrium, and obviously it hasn't: In our universe,

(30)   the baby grows up and goes off to college, the Brussels sprouts
       spring up from our gardens, the stars still shine. Entropy is
       inexorable; it'll get us in the end. But it hasn't gotten us
       yet—therefore, the universe cannot be infinite.

(35) The science of physics has postulated a beginning, a point called a "singularity," from which the universe and all that is in it—including even space and time—emerged suddenly and violently. But what was here "before" the singularity? The answer is that there couldn't have been any "before," because time and space came into existence only *at* the singularity, so (40) the word "before" has no meaning. Paradoxically, it is at this juncture that the notion of infinity insinuates itself again. For the singularity is the ultimate unknowable, that point which physicist Paul Davies calls "the interface between the natural and the supernatural," the answer that still so far eludes us, (45) which some call nothingness, some call infinity, and some call God.

1. Which of the following choices best represents the main idea of the passage?

(A) Because we do not know what existed "before" the singularity from which the universe sprang, the possibility exists that the Second Law of Thermodynamics was formulated in error.

(B) The Second Law of Thermodynamics supports the idea of a finite universe, because, if the universe were infinite, it would have already succumbed to entropy, and obviously it has not.

(C) Although the Second Law of Thermodynamics supports the idea of a finite universe—such as the one physicists postulate sprang from a singularity—there is still no answer to the question of what came "before" the singularity.

(D) Physicists postulate that the universe sprang into existence at a singularity and point to the Second Law of Thermodynamics as proof.

(E) Throughout human history, people have wondered whether the universe sprang from nothing, for no reason; whether something or someone created it; or whether it's infinite.

2. In the context of the whole essay, the statement ". . . a peach pit grows into a tree" (lines 15–16) demonstrates that

(A) life cannot come from nothingness.
(B) it is possible that the universe has a creator.
(C) sometimes universal entropy decreases.
(D) at times, order seems to grow rather than diminish.
(E) there was probably life even before the singularity.

3. Which of the following details about the origin of the universe NOT mentioned in the passage would best support the argument that the universe is finite?

(A) Gravity is the weakest of nature's forces, but it is cumulative in power.

(B) Prior to 1930, scientists did not believe that matter could be created by natural means.

(C) Physicists do not generally believe time moves—like space, it just simply is.

(D) Using mathematics as a language, scientists can describe situations that are otherwise indescribable.

(E) The galaxies are rushing away from each other, as from a primal explosion science has named "the big bang."

4. What is the meaning of the word "inexorable," as used in line 32?

(A) Unexplainable

(B) Destructive

(C) Relentless

(D) Violent

(E) Regrettable

5. The author bolsters most of the arguments in the passage primarily by means of

(A) citing authoritative sources.

(B) appealing to our natural sense of wonder.

(C) using analogies that compare one theory of creation with another.

(D) using concrete details about various aspects of the subject.

(E) appealing to our religious convictions.

6. The final paragraph mainly represents

(A) definitions of terms used so far in the passage.

(B) a digression from the main subject of the passage.

(C) a summary of the main argument of the passage.

(D) a reversal of the main argument so far.

(E) an appeal to our religious convictions.

Paired passages may disagree about some subject or take differing perspectives on a single subject, or they may be about different subjects but have similar perspectives. Both passages below deal with the authors' perspectives on the natural world and its relation to good and evil.

Passage 1 is an excerpt from Ralph Waldo Emerson's Divinity School Address *delivered before the Senior Class in Divinity College, Cambridge, July 15, 1838.*

Passage 2 is taken from the journal of a fictional naturalist.

Passage 1

Line   In this refulgent summer, it has been a luxury to draw the breath of life. The grass grows, the buds burst, the meadow is spotted with fire and gold in the tint of flowers. The air is full of birds, and sweet with the breath of the pine, the balm-of-

(5)   Gilead, and the new hay. Night brings no gloom to the heart with its welcome shade. Through the transparent darkness the stars pour their almost spiritual rays. . . . The mystery of nature was never displayed more happily. The corn and the wine have been freely dealt to all creatures, and the never-

(10)   broken silence with which the old bounty goes forward, has not yielded yet one word of explanation. One is constrained to respect the perfection of this world, in which our senses converse . . . its fruitful soils; . . . its navigable sea; . . . its mountains of metal and stone; . . . its forests of all woods; in

(15)   its animals; . . . its chemical ingredients; . . . the powers and path of light, heat, attraction, and life. . . .

    What am I? and What is? asks the human spirit with a curiosity new-kindled, but never to be quenched. Behold these outrunning laws, which our imperfect apprehension can see

(20)   tend this way and that, but not come full circle. Behold these infinite relations, so like, so unlike; many, yet one. I would

study, I would know, I would admire forever. These works of thought have been the entertainments of the human spirit in all ages. . . .

(25)   These facts have always suggested . . . the sublime creed, that the world is not the product of manifold power, but of one will, of one mind; and that one mind is everywhere active, in each ray of the star, in each wavelet of the pool; and whatever opposes that will, is everywhere balked and baffled,

(30) because things are made so, and not otherwise. Good is positive. Evil is merely privative, not absolute: it is like cold, which is the privation of heat. All evil is so much death or nonentity. Benevolence is absolute and real.

Passage 2

Line   We are born in and of the natural world and so to us it is mundane, but, as Eisley writes, it's a queer place. Sometimes one would almost think that Nature, like the West African trickster god Edshu, were playing a joke on us.

(5)   Consider the variety of creatures that inhabit the world: the butterflies, lacewing flies, and fireflies that hover amongst the flowers in our gardens like fairies; the dragonflies that hang incandescent as small lanterns above our rivers. Consider the birds of the land—the swallow, robin, and bluebird that

(10) grace our summer landscape; and the birds of the open ocean—the storm petrel, shearwater, fulmar, and fabled albatross.

Yet consider, conversely, those other creatures that share our world: the carnivorous army ants of South America or the

(15) drivers of Africa, who swarm over their prey, butcher and devour it, deflected from their grisly task only by fire. Consider the reptile, that monarch of the desert, whose venom courses through its prey and kills in a heartbeat. Even among the birds, some species are parasitic. The glossy cowbird, for

(20) example (with its blue-black plumage that gives off greenish light), lays five or six eggs a season, each in a different nest, and then abandons them. The old world cuckoo deposits her clutch in the nest of the host that reared her, her young ejecting the host's offspring as soon as they are able. (The female is

(25) polyandrous and the male takes no care of the offspring at all.) Even the noble eagle emerges from its lofty aerie to descend upon the hapless rabbit, and the pure white seabird, the Fairy tern, is yet related to the gull, which is a scavenger and sometimes a cannibal.

(30)   Among the birds, the very covering of bright feathers that enchants us has developed from the scaly armor of reptiles. And the glorious gift of flight is yet shared with the abhorred bat.

Nature is adored by sentimentalists, and so she should
(35)   be—in part. Yet looking upon her whole, we can but weep.

7. Which of the following best expresses the main idea of Passage 1?

  (A) Nature is guided by a forgiving God.
  (B) Nature is mysterious and can never be understood.
  (C) The natural world is a place of trials, and human beings are the better for that.
  (D) The natural world is a place in which only goodness really exists.
  (E) Nature has well-defined rules and laws.

8. What is the meaning of the word "refulgent" as used in Passage 1, line 1?

  (A) Revered
  (B) Resplendent
  (C) Remorse
  (D) Redeemed
  (E) Relaxed

9. With which of the following statements would both of the authors likely NOT agree?

  (A) Nature regards us as her plaything.
  (B) Nature can be understood only through objective observation.
  (C) Nature is a conscious and purposive entity.
  (D) Nature is more powerful than humankind.
  (E) Nature yields up great bounty.

10. The main point of Passage 2 can be summed up best in which of the following statements?

  (A) Nature is sometimes beautiful and sometimes ugly.
  (B) Nature is unsentimental.
  (C) Nature is a trickster, sometimes cruel but more often kind.
  (D) Nature is a trickster, sometimes kind but more often cruel.
  (E) Nature, like God, can never be understood.

107

11. What is the meaning of the word "mundane" in line 2 of Passage 2?

    (A) Boring
    (B) Commonplace
    (C) Beloved
    (D) Sparkling
    (E) Esoteric

12. The author of Passage 2 would most likely call the author of Passage 1

    (A) evil.
    (B) delusional.
    (C) sentimental.
    (D) ignorant.
    (E) hypocritical.

Explanatory Answers

Sentence Completions

1. **The correct answer is (A).** The sentence is one of **cause-and-effect**. Note that the first half indicates that the season is winter. Although all of the choices denote fine qualities for a cat bed, only choice (A) connotes a snug, warm place. Remember, you should look for the *best* answer, not just an acceptable answer.

2. **The correct answer is (D).** This is a **cause-and-effect** sentence, although it is not explicitly marked as such by the word "because." It forces you to ask the questions "How would I stare at someone who rose straight into the air?" and "How would I describe someone's rise into the air?" The most attractive choices for the first blank would probably be choices (A), (B), and (D). Now look among these three choices for an appropriate second word. Taken in isolation, any one of them *might* work, but the *combination* in choice (D) is most plausible.

3. **The correct answer is (E).** This is a **comparison/contrast** sentence. The word *Although* indicates that you will be looking among the choices for a contrasting element. Ask yourself, "What kind of conclusion would I least expect a *flawlessly logical argument* to lead to?"

4. **The correct answer is (C).** This is a **cause-and-effect** sentence. Examining the first word of each choice, you will immediately throw out the silly one, choice (E), since it is hard to see how one could become *accustomed* to drinking a *deadly . . . potion*. After that, you can most logically discard the "soft" first words of choices (A) and (B), since they don't really seem to fit with being arrested and drinking poison. You are then left with choices (C) and (D). Common sense will tell you that it is improbable that there ever was an occasion when the general youth of Athens needed *eulogizing*.

5. **The correct answer is (B).** This is a **definition** sentence. You must know what the word *gullible* means. If you do not, you should look it up now.

6. **The correct answer is (C).** This is a **definition** sentence. Ask yourself, "What kind of medical information should not be transmitted over a public channel?"

7. **The correct answer is (D).** This is a **definition** sentence, so you must know what all the words mean in order to rule them in or out. If you do not know what they mean, look them up now.

109

8. **The correct answer is (B).** This is another **definition** sentence. Look up the words you do not recognize among these choices.

9. **The correct answer is (B).** This is a **comparison/contrast** sentence. Looking at the first blank, you will want to think what might offend non-Christians (in this case, pagans). Choices (C) and (E), reflecting positive attitudes toward the pagan cults, can be ruled out right away. Now turn to the second words. To *revert to*, choice (A), is to return to, and this doesn't fit, because Constantine was only baptized on his deathbed. So, you are left with choices (B) and (D), and, when speaking of a person's relationship to a religion, *converted* is clearly a better choice than *matriculated*, which is usually associated with admittance to college.

10. **The correct answer is (A).** You will want to rule out choices (B) and (E) right away, since an *optimistic* person and an *orderly* person can both bring joy. You can rule out choice (C) as well—we all know people who, although *unkempt*, are fun to be with. That leaves choices (A) and (D), and choice (A), being a near-synonym of *gloomy*, clearly has the edge.

11. **The correct answer is (E).** The *denotation* of a word is its dictionary definition. Each of the other choices means something entirely different. It would be a good idea to look these words up now.

12. **The correct answer is (A).** All the choices can be thrown out here, except for choices (A) and (C). Choice (A) is better because choice (C), *concede*, implies that there has been some sort of contest, which there hasn't.

Reading Skills

1. **The correct answer is (C).** It encompasses the main points in the passage—(1) that the Second Law of Thermodynamics supports the idea of a finite universe, (2) a brief explanation of the theory of the singularity, and (3) that the main question is still open. When confronted with a "main idea" question, the best first step is to eliminate the choices that simply are not in the passage or that distort its meaning seriously. Choice (A) fits these criteria—nowhere does the passage state or imply that the Second Law of Thermodynamics is erroneous. Likewise, choice (D) distorts the passage, because nowhere does the passage say that physics invokes the Second Law of Thermodynamics in support of a theory about the origin of the universe. Your next step is to eliminate the choices that are too broad and the ones that are too narrow. Choice (B) is too narrow: It leaves out the notion of the singularity and the question of what came before it, which are very prominent parts of the passage. Choice (E) is too broad, since it only restates the sweeping, general questions asked in the first paragraph and does not narrow down the content of the passage at all.

2. **The correct answer is (D).** Choices (A) and (E) are not in the passage. Choice (B) is in the passage, but not in the context of the *peach tree*. (Be sure not to choose an option just because it is somewhere in the passage. Read each question carefully.) Choice (C) is (tentatively) refuted in the passage.

3. **The correct answer is (E).** The discussion of the singularity should lead you to this answer. Consider lines 37–40. The other choices do not relate directly to the passage.

4. **The correct answer is (C).** Read all of lines 32–33, and note especially the statement "it'll get us in the end. . . ." Entropy can be described accurately using all the other choices, but only choice (C) defines it *as used in line 32*.

5. **The correct answer is (D).** The passage is full of concrete detail, though short on authoritative sources (there is only one named source).

6. **The correct answer is (D).** The main argument so far in the passage has been in support of the idea that the universe is finite. The final paragraph introduces a counterargument. Note especially the word *paradoxically* (line 40). The other choices are not reflected in the last paragraph. Regarding choice (E), the final paragraph does mention *God* as a possible source of the universe, but it also mentions *infinity* and *nothingness*.

7. **The correct answer is (D).** It builds to the final conclusion: *Good is positive. Evil is merely privative, not absolute.* Neither forgiveness, choice (A), nor trials, choice (C), is mentioned in the passage. The mystery of nature, choice (B), is mentioned but is too narrow to be the main idea.

8. **The correct answer is (B).** The sentences immediately following describe the bright splendor of summer, indicated especially by the words *fire* and *gold*.

9. **The correct answer is (B).** Based on the passages, both authors believe they at least partly understand Nature, and neither is objective in his observations. Support for choices (C) and (D) can be inferred from both passages. Support for choice (A) can be found in Passage 2 and for choice (E) in Passage 1.

10. **The correct answer is (D).** The other choices can perhaps be inferred from the passage, but only choice (D) encompasses the author's ambivalent, but on the whole rather dark, attitude toward Nature.

11. **The correct answer is (B).** Note that the line in question involves **comparison/contrast.**

12. **The correct answer is (C).** See the next-to-last sentence. The other choices are not reflected in the passage.

Chapter 3

Merriam-Webster's
Roots to Word Mastery

Introduction

If you're like many students today preparing for the PSAT, you probably have never taken a course in Latin, which means you may never have learned how most English words came to be based on words from older languages. And you may never have realized how the study of word roots can lead to a much larger vocabulary than you now have. Studying and mastering vocabulary words will certainly improve your PSAT critical reading score. So to maximize your chances of scoring high on your test, this chapter will set you on the path to learning a broad range of new vocabulary words.

You'll learn 50 of the Greek and Latin roots that form the foundation of most of the words in the English language as well as 150 English words based on those roots. Many of these 150 words will actually lead you to several more words each. By learning the word *credible*, you'll also understand *credibly* and *credibility* the next time you hear them; by learning *gratify*, you'll also learn *gratifying* and *gratification*; and by learning *theology*, you'll understand *theological*, *theologically*, and *theologian* when you run across them. So learning the roots and words in this chapter will help you to learn thousands of words!

Ancient Greek and Latin have been the sources of most words in the English language. (The third-biggest source is the family of Germanic languages.) And not just of the older words: Almost the entire English vocabulary was created long after the fall of the Roman empire, and it continues to expand to this day. Of the new words that are constantly being invented, the majority—especially those in the sciences, where most new words are introduced—are still based on Greek and Latin roots. Even new buzzwords that you

For more vocabulary-building exercises, visit Merriam-Webster's Web site at www.m-w.com.

113

think appear out of nowhere may be Greek or Latin in origin. For instance, *morph* is a short form of *metamorphose*, which comes almost straight from Latin; *def* is short for *definitely*, which is also based on Latin; *hype* is probably short for *hyperbole,* which comes straight from Greek; and *rad* is short for *radical*, which comes from the Latin *radix*—which actually means "root"!

Besides improved test scores, what can you expect to gain from expanding your vocabulary?

A large vocabulary will allow you to read a wider range of writing than you had previously, and in the process, it will broaden your range of interests. If you've always limited your leisure reading to magazines about rock musicians and film stars, or cars and sports, or clothing and style, or fantasy and electronic games, you'll soon discover that newsweeklies, biographies, literary fiction, nature writing, or history can give you more pleasure and expand your mind at the same time.

Just as important, you'll find that a larger vocabulary will help you express your ideas more clearly. It will encourage you to describe, say, a film or a musician with more informative words than "really good" or "cool" or "awesome," and it will give you more precise ways to talk about, say, a news story, a mental state, a new building, or a person's face—in fact, almost any aspect of everyday life.

But it will also help make you more competent in your chosen career. According to research studies, people with large vocabularies are far more likely to be found in the most important and interesting and desirable jobs.

Let's suppose you want to become a doctor, nurse, or pharmacist. Doctors today prescribe thousands of drugs and treat thousands of identified medical conditions. Many of these drugs and conditions have long and complex names, almost all of which are derived from Greek and Latin. In your chosen career, you'd naturally want to have memorized as many of these names as possible. But since most of us don't have perfect memories, having a good grasp of Greek and Latin roots is the best way to be sure your memory is jogged whenever you come across a long medical or pharmaceutical term. Knowing a single Latin suffix or prefix (many short word endings are called suffixes, and many short word beginnings are called prefixes) or a root can prepare you to understand hundreds

114

of words in which it appears. For instance, since the suffix *-itis* means "disease" or "inflammation," seeing a word with that ending (*gastroenteritis, nephritis, phlebitis,* etc.) will let you identify at once the class of words to which it belongs. *Hemo-* means "blood," so *hemophilia, hemoglobinopathy, hemorrhagic fever,* and *hemolytic anemia* are all conditions involving the blood. And let's not forget the middles of words. In *gastroenteritis,* the root *-enter-* refers to the intestines.

As you can see, many words contain more than one root. A single word may be a mix of Greek and Latin and even Germanic roots or elements, and a long scientific term may contain four or more elements. Such complex words are much less common in ordinary vocabulary, but even a conversation between elementary-school children will contain many words based on classical roots.

In a technical field, mastering a technical vocabulary may be a requirement for your job. But a broad nontechnical vocabulary can be highly valuable as well. Even in a narrowly focused field such as accounting or computer programming, a large vocabulary can prove to be of real practical value. And in a field such as law, which tends to get involved in many aspects of life, a large general vocabulary can turn out to be very advantageous.

While root study is very valuable, be cautious when you begin exploring it. A portion of a word may resemble a root only by coincidence. For example, the word *center* doesn't have anything to do with the root *cent* (meaning "hundred"), and the words *interest* and *interminable* don't have anything to do with the root *inter* (meaning "between"). It may take time to recognize which words actually contain the roots you think you see in them. Another problem is that not every root you think you've identified will necessarily be the right one. For example, *ped* may mean either "foot" or "child," and *liber* may mean either "book" or "free." A third problem is that many common roots are too short to recognize or change their spelling in a confusing way from word to word. So even though *perception, deceive, recipe, capture,* and *receipt* can all be traced to the same Latin root, the root changes form so much—*cip, cept, cap,* etc.—that root study probably won't help the student looking for a memory aid. Similarly, when the Latin word *ad* (meaning "to" or "toward") becomes a prefix, it usually changes to *ac-, ad-, af-, ag-, am-, an-,* or some other form, so the student can rarely recognize it. In addition, the meanings of some roots can change from word to word. So even though the *cip-cept-cap* root means "grasp," "seize," or "take," it may seem to change its meaning completely when combined with a prefix (*per-, de-*, etc.).

As long as you are aware of such difficulties, root study is an excellent way to learn English vocabulary (not to mention the vocabularies of Spanish, French, Italian, and Portuguese, all of which are based on Latin). In fact, it's the *only* method of vocabulary acquisition that relies on broadly useful memory aids. Without it, vocabulary study consists of nothing but trying to memorize unrelated words one by one by one.

So from here on, it's up to you. The more fun you can have learning your new vocabulary, the better you'll do. And it *can* be fun. For one thing, the results are instantaneous—you can show off your new knowledge any time you want. And you'll almost feel your mind expanding as your vocabulary expands. This is why people talk about the "power" of a large vocabulary; you'll soon realize your mental capacities are actually becoming more powerful with every new word.

Take every opportunity to use the words you're learning; the most effective way to keep a new word alive in your vocabulary is to use it regularly. Look and listen for the new words you've learned—you'll be surprised to find yourself running into them often, especially if you've also begun reading more demanding books and magazines in your leisure time. Challenge your friends with them, even if just in a joking way. Make up games to test yourself, maybe using homemade flash cards.

And don't stop acquiring new vocabulary words after you've mastered this chapter. Whenever you're reading, look for roots in the new words you keep encountering and try to guess each word's meaning before looking it up in a dictionary (which you should try to keep close at hand). Once you've acquired the habit, you'll be astonished at how quickly your vocabulary will grow.

Instructions

On the following pages, we introduce you to 50 of the most useful Greek and Latin roots (omitting the prefixes and suffixes that almost everyone knows—*anti-, co-, de-, -ism, mis-, non-, un-, vice-*, etc.). We call these roots useful because they are common and also because they nearly always keep their meaning in an obvious way when they appear in an English word. So if you encounter an unfamiliar word on your test, these roots may be the key to making an educated guess as to its meaning.

Each root is discussed in a short paragraph. Each paragraph is followed by three vocabulary words derived from the root. For each word, we provide the pronunciation, the definition, and a sentence showing how the word might actually be used in writing or conversation.

You'll be quizzed after every 15 words, and finally you'll be tested on every one of the 150 words. (All answers are given at the end of the chapter.) These tests will ensure that the words and roots become permanently fixed in your memory, just as if you'd been drilled on them in class.

For further study on your own, near the end of the chapter we list an additional 50 useful roots, along with three English words based on each one.

50 Roots to Success

Pronunciation Guide: \ə\ abut   \ər\ further   \a\ ash   \ā\ ace   \ä\ mop, mar   \aů\ out   \ch\ chin   \e\ bet   \ē\ easy   \g\ go   \i\ hit   \ī\ ice   \j\ job \ŋ\ sing   \ō\ go   \ȯ\ law   \ȯi\ boy   \th\ thin   \th\ the   \ü\ loot   \u\ foot \y\ yet   \zh\ vision

agr Beginning Latin students traditionally learn the word *agricola*, meaning "farmer," in their very first class. Though most of us tend to think of the Romans as soldiers, senators, and citizens of the city of Rome, most inhabitants of the empire were actually farmers. We see the root today in words such as **agriculture.**

agronomy \ə-'grä-nə-mē\ A branch of agriculture dealing with field-crop production and soil management.
- The poor country was in dire need of an agronomy team to introduce its farmers to new crops and techniques.

agrochemical \ˌa-grō-'ke-mi-kəl\ An agricultural chemical (such as an herbicide or an insecticide).
- The river's pollution was easily traced to the runoff of agrochemicals from the cornfields.

agrarian \ə-'grer-ē-ən\ Of or relating to fields, lands, or farmers, or characteristic of farming life.
- The team of sharply dressed lawyers seemed nervous and awkward in this agrarian landscape of silos and feed stores.

ante *Ante* means "before"; its opposite, *post*, means "after." Both almost always appear as prefixes (that is, at the beginnings of words). *Ante* is easy to confuse with *anti*, meaning "against." **Antebellum** means "before the war," and we often speak of the antebellum South—that is, the South before the Civil War, not the "antiwar" South.

antedate \'an-ti-ˌdāt\ 1: To date as of a date prior to that of execution. 2: To precede in time.
- It appeared that Crowley had antedated his check to the contractors, helping them evade taxes for work done in the new year.

antecedent \ˌan-tə-'sē-dənt\ Prior, preceding.
- As Mrs. Perkins told it, the scuffle had started spontaneously, and any antecedent events involving her rowdy son had been forgotten.

anterior \an-'tir-ē-ər\ Situated before or toward the front.
- Dr. Singh was going on about anterior and posterior knee pain, but in her agony Karen could hardly remember a word.

anthro The Latin *anthro* means "man" or "mankind." Thus, in English we call the study of mankind **anthropology**. *Anthro* is very close to the Greek and Latin *andro*, which shows up in such words as **android**.

anthropoid \\'an-thrə-ˌpoid\\ Any of several large, tailless apes.
- The anthropoids—chimpanzees, bonobos, gorillas, orangutans, and gibbons—had diverged from the human evolutionary line by 5 million years ago.

misanthrope \\'mi-sən-ˌthrōp\\ A person who hates or distrusts mankind.
- Over the years she had retreated into an increasingly bitter solitude, and her former friends now dismissed her as a misanthrope.

philanthropy \\fə-'lan-thrə-pē\\ Active effort to promote human welfare.
- His philanthropy was so welcome that no one cared to inquire how he'd come by his fortune.

aqu The Greek and Latin root *aqu-* refers to water. The ancient world regarded all matter as made up of four elements—earth, air, fire, and water. Today, the root is found in such familiar words as **aquarium**, **aquatic**, and **aquamarine**.

aquaculture \\'ä-kwə-ˌkəl-chər\\ The cultivation of the natural produce of water, such as fish or shellfish.
- Having grown hugely, the aquaculture industry now produces 30 percent of the world's seafood.

aquifer \\'a-kwə-fər\\ A water-bearing stratum of rock, sand, or gravel.
- The vast Ogallala aquifer, which irrigates most of the Great Plains, is monitored constantly to ensure that it isn't dangerously depleted.

Aquarius \\ə-'kwar-ē-əs\\ 1: A constellation south of Pegasus pictured as a man pouring water. 2: The 11th sign of the zodiac in astrology.
- Many believe that the great Age of Aquarius began in 1962; others believe it commenced in 2000 or hasn't yet begun.

arti This root comes from the Latin word for "skill." *Art* could also mean simply "cleverness," and we still describe a clever solution as **artful**. Until recent centuries, almost no one made a real distinction between skilled craftsmanship and what we would now call **art**. So the words **artistic** and **artificial** turn out to be very closely related.

artifice \\'är-tə-fəs\\ 1: Clever skill. 2: A clever trick.
- She was stunned to find she'd been deceived by a masterpiece of artifice—the lifelike figure of a seated man talking on the phone, a lit cigarette in his right hand.

artifact \\'är-ti-ˌfakt\\ A usually simple object, such as a tool or ornament, made by human workmanship.
- Among the artifacts carried by the 5,000-year-old Iceman was a fur quiver with fourteen arrow shafts.

artisan \\'är-tə-zən\\ A skilled worker or craftsperson.
- Ducking down an alley, he weaved quickly through the artisans hawking their wares of handworked brass and leather.

Quiz 1

Answers appear at the end of this chapter.

1. Carnegie spread his _____ more widely than any previous American, building almost 1,700 libraries.

2. A long list of _____s—mainly herbicides and pesticides—were identified as health threats.

3. News of the cave's discovery soon leaked out, and local youths were soon plundering it of its Indian _____s.

4. Stalin moved swiftly to uproot Russia's _____ traditions and substitute his new vision of collectivized agriculture.

5. They had drilled down 85 feet before they struck the _____ and water bubbled to the surface.

6. The first X-ray image, labeled "_____," showed a frontal view of her heart.

7. George Washington Carver, a hero of American _____, transformed Southern agriculture through his research into the peanut.

8. The throne itself, its surface glittering with ornaments, was the most extravagant example of the sculptor's _____.

9. In his lecture on "The _____ Causes of the Irish Famine," he expressed wonder at rural Ireland's absolute dependency on the potato by 1840.

10. Before the development of _____, the Atlantic salmon was threatened by overfishing.

11. Her brother, always suspicious and unfriendly, was by now a genuine _____, who left his phone unplugged and refused all invitations.

12. Any contracts that _____ the new law by five years or more will remain in effect.

13. The man resembled an _____, with powerful sloping shoulders and arms that seemed to brush the ground.

14. A young boy pouring water into the basin below reminded her of the astrological symbol of _____.

15. All the handcrafts turned out to be the work of a large family of _____s.

bene In Latin, *bene* means "well"; its near-opposite, *mal*, means "bad" or "poorly." Both usually appear at the beginnings of words. We may hope to use this root often to list **benefits** and describe **beneficial** activities.

benediction \ˌbe-nə-'dik-shən\ The pronouncement of a blessing, especially at the close of a worship service.
- The restless children raced out to the church picnic immediately after the benediction.

beneficent \bə-'ne-fə-sənt\ Doing or producing good; especially performing acts of kindness or charity.
- Even the busy and poor willingly contribute to organizations recognized as beneficent.

benefactor \'be-nə-ˌfak-tər\ A person or group that confers aid, such as a charitable donation.
- Construction of the new playground had been funded by a generous benefactor.

bio *Bio* comes from the Greek word for "life." Thus, **biology** means the study of all living forms and life processes, and **biotechnology** uses the knowledge gained through biology. **Antibiotics** fight off bacteria, which are life forms, but not viruses, which may not be.

bionic \bī-'ä-nik\ Having normal biological ability enhanced by electronic or mechanical devices.
- A 1970s TV series featuring "the Bionic Woman" sparked interest in robotics.

biopsy \'bī-ˌäp-sē\ The removal and examination of tissue, cells, or fluids from the living body.
- Until the biopsy results came back, there was no way to tell if the lump was cancerous.

symbiosis \ˌsim-bē-'ō-səs\ The intimate living together of two dissimilar organisms, especially when mutually beneficial.
- In a display of symbiosis, the bird stands on the crocodile's teeth and pecks leeches off its gums.

chron This root comes from the Greek word for "time." A **chronicle** records the events of a particular time. **Chronometry** is the measuring of time, which can be done with a **chronometer**, a timepiece more accurate than an ordinary watch or clock.

chronic \\'krä-nik\\ Marked by long duration or frequent recurrence; habitual.
- Her roommate was a chronic complainer, who started off every day grumbling about something new.

anachronism \\ə-'na-krə-ˌni-zəm\\ 1: The error of placing a person or thing in the wrong period. 2: One that is out of its own time.
- After the collapse of the Soviet Union, some analysts felt that NATO was an anachronism.

chronology \\krə-'nä-lə-jē\\ An arrangement of events in the order of their occurrence.
- Keeping a journal throughout her trip gave Joan an accurate record of its chronology afterward.

circum *Circum* means "around" in Latin. So to **circumnavigate** is "to navigate around," often around the world, and **circumference** means the "distance around" a circle or other object. A **circumstance** is a fact or event accompanying ("standing around") another.

circumvent \\ˌsər-kəm-'vent\\ To evade or defeat, especially by trickery or deception.
- During Prohibition, many citizens found ways to circumvent the laws against alcohol.

circumspect \\ˌsər-kəm-'spekt\\ Careful to consider all circumstances and consequences; cautious; prudent.
- Unlike his impulsive twin brother, Claude was sober, circumspect, and thoughtful.

circumstantial \\ˌsər-kəm-'stan-shəl\\ 1: Describing evidence based on inference, not directly observed facts. 2: Incidental.
- The fact that he was gone all night was only circumstantial evidence, but still extremely important.

cosm *Cosm* comes from the Greek word meaning "order." Ultimate order, for the Greeks, related to the universe and the worlds within it, so **cosmos** for us means the universe. A **cosmonaut** was a space traveler from the former Soviet Union.

cosmopolitan \ˌkäz-mə-ˈpä-lə-tən\ International in outlook; sophisticated; worldly.
- The cosmopolitan actress Audrey Hepburn was born in Belgium and educated in England but won fame in America.

cosmology \käz-ˈmä-lə-jē\ 1: A branch of astronomy dealing with the origin and structure of the universe. 2: A theory that describes the nature of the universe.
- New Age philosophies and science fiction suggest a variety of possible cosmologies.

microcosm \ˈmī-krə-ˌkä-zəm\ An individual or community thought of as a miniature world or universe.
- Early thinkers saw the whole human world as a microcosm of the universe, which was considered the macrocosm.

Quiz 2

Answers appear at the end of this chapter.

1. In ant–aphid _____, the aphids are protected by the ants, who "milk" them for their honeydew.

2. A _____ witch could end a drought by casting a spell to bring rain.

3. The diner's hours depended on such _____ factors as whether the cook's car had gotten repossessed.

4. Phenomena such as time warps and black holes made theoretical _____ the strangest subject in the curriculum.

5. Church members were surprised by the closing _____, "May God *deny* you peace, but grant you love."

6. Neuroscientists believe they will soon have developed a complete _____ ear.

7. Identifying a suspicious tumor almost always calls for a _____ procedure.

8. The children's clinic was built soon after a significant gift by a single _____.

9. Both candidates had managed to _____ campaign finance laws through fraud.

10. Measles and flu are acute illnesses, while asthma and diabetes are _____ conditions.

11. Shakespeare's *Macbeth*, set in the eleventh century, contains such _____s as a reference to clocks.

12. A detailed _____ of the actions of company executives from April to July revealed some suspicious patterns.

13. Office life, with all its dramas and secrets, seemed to her a
_____ of the world outside.

14. When we have only flimsy evidence, we should be _____
in our opinions.

15. With its international nightlife and a multitude of languages spoken
on its beaches, Martinique is a _____ island.

cred This root comes from *credere*, the Latin verb meaning "to believe." Thus something **incredible** is almost unbelievable. We have a good **credit** rating when institutions believe in our ability to repay a loan, and we carry **credentials** so that others will believe we are who we say we are.

credence \'krē-dəns\ Mental acceptance as true or real; belief.
  • Giving credence to gossip—or even to corporate financial reports these days—is risky.

credible \'kre-də-bəl\ Trustworthy; believable.
  • The defense team doubted that the ex-convict would make a credible witness.

creed \'krēd\ A statement of the essential beliefs of a religious faith.
  • The Nicene Creed of A.D. 381 excluded Christian beliefs considered incorrect.

dis In Latin, *dis* means "apart." In English, its meanings have increased to include "do the opposite of" (as in **disobey**), "deprive of" (as in **disillusion**), "exclude or expel from" (**disbar**), "the opposite or absence of" (**disaffection**), and "not" (**disagreeable**).

disarming \di-'sär-miŋ\ Reducing hostility or criticism; ingratiating.
  • Their ambassador to the United Nations has a disarming manner but a cunning mind.

disburse \dis-'bərs\ To pay out; distribute.
  • The World Bank agreed to disburse $20 million to Bolivia in recognition of its economic reforms.

discredit \dis-'kre-dət\ 1: To cause disbelief in the accuracy or authority of. 2: To disgrace.
  • Lawyers with the states suing the tobacco company sought to discredit testimony of its chief witness.

dyna The Greek root *dyna* means "to be able" or "to have power." **Dynamite** has enough power to blow up the hardest granite bedrock. A **dynamic** person or group is powerful and energetic. A **dynamometer** measures mechanical force, which is measured in **dynes**.

dynamo \'dī-nə-ˌmō\ 1: A power generator. 2: A forceful, energetic person.
  • The early dynamo was a mysterious mechanism for many, who saw no relation between steam and electric current.

dynasty \'dī-nə-stē\ 1: A line of rulers from the same family. 2: A powerful group or family that maintains its position for a long time.
  • After the Mongols and before the Manchus, the Ming dynasty provided China a very stable era.

hydrodynamic \ˌhī-drō-dī-'na-mik\ Of or relating to the motion of fluids and the forces acting on moving bodies immersed in fluids.
  • Water temperature, resistance, and depth are among the hydrodynamic aspects of rowing.

127

dys In Greek, *dys* means "bad" or "difficult." As a prefix in English, it has the additional meanings "abnormal" and "impaired." **Dyspnea** is difficult or labored breathing. **Dyspepsia** is indigestion (or ill humor). A **dysfunctional** family is one that functions badly.

dyslexia \dis-ˈlek-sē-ə\ A disturbance of the ability to read or use language.
  • Dyslexia is regarded as the most widespread of the learning disabilities.

dysentery \ˈdi-sən-ˌter-ē\ An infectious intestinal disease with abdominal pain and severe diarrhea.
  • Considering the poor sanitation, travelers were not surprised to find dysentery widespread.

dystrophy \ˈdis-trə-fē\ A disorder involving wasting away of muscular tissue.
  • The telethon raises over $50 million a year to battle muscular dystrophy and related diseases.

epi Coming from the Greek, this root means various things, particularly "on" and "over." An **epicenter** is the part of the earth's surface directly over the focus of an earthquake. The **epidermis** is the outer layer of the skin, overlying the inner "dermis." An **epitaph** is an inscription upon a tomb in memory of the person buried there.

epithet \ˈe-pə-ˌthet\ A characterizing and often abusive word or phrase.
  • Classic epithets used by Homer include "*rosy-fingered* dawn" and "Zeus, *the cloud-gatherer.*"

epigraph \ˈe-pə-ˌgraf\ 1: An engraved inscription. 2: A quotation set at the beginning of a literary work to suggest its theme.
  • Chapter 5, describing the great battle, bears the Shakespearean epigraph "Let slip the dogs of war."

epilogue \ˈe-pə-ˌlôg\ A concluding section, especially to a literary or musical work.
  • Not until the novel's epilogue do we realize that all the characters were based on the author's family.

Quiz 3

Answers appear at the end of this chapter.

1. Most early Christian _____s developed around the act of baptism, where adult candidates proclaimed their faith.

2. With his _____ smile and quiet humor, he charms even the wariest clients.

3. Amoebic _____ is not just traveler's diarrhea—it is contracted by people who live in unclean conditions, too.

4. The dictator scornfully attempted to _____ the proceedings at his war crimes trial.

5. New reports lent _____ to the captive's story that the enemy had fled.

6. When students with undiagnosed _____ go on to higher education, their coping mechanisms often fall apart.

7. Henry Ford founded a _____; his great-grandson is now the company's chairman.

8. The listing of _____s included 40,000 reports of inscriptions found on Roman ruins.

9. Katie's research focused on the _____ drag of small sea kayaks.

10. Relief agencies explored how best to _____ funds and food to the disaster victims.

11. At the close of Shakespeare's *The Tempest*, Prospero speaks the wise _____.

12. Lou Gehrig's disease is one of about forty diseases in the area of muscular _____.

13. The shoplifter hurled obscene _____s at the guard conducting her to the office.

14. Her story is hardly _____, since she's already changed the facts twice.

15. Mayor Fiorello La Guardia of New York was considered a _____ in an already dynamic city.

extra This root, from Latin, places words "outside" or "beyond" their usual or routine territory. **Extraterrestrial** events take place "beyond" the Earth. Something **extravagant**, such as an **extravaganza**, goes beyond the limits of moderation. And **extra** is itself a word, a shortening of **extraordinary**, "beyond the ordinary."

extrapolate \ik-'stra-pə-ˌlāt\ To project (known data) into an unknown area to arrive at knowledge of the unknown area.
- Her department pored over export-import data endlessly in order to extrapolate present trade trends and predict the future.

extrovert \'ek-strə-ˌvərt\ An outgoing, sociable, unreserved person.
- Linda's boss is an extrovert, always happiest in a roomful of people.

extraneous \ek-'strā-nē-əs\ Not forming a vital part; irrelevant.
- Coaching in diving and dance often seeks to reduce extraneous movements.

fid *Fid* comes from *fides*, the Latin word for "faith." An **infidel** is someone who lacks a particular kind of religious faith. An **affidavit** is a sworn statement, a statement you can have faith in. Something that's **bona fide** is in "good faith"—absolutely genuine, the real deal.

fiduciary \fə-'dü-shē-ˌer-ē\ 1: Involving a confidence or trust. 2: Held or holding in trust for another.
- Corporate directors have often forgotten their fiduciary responsibility to their companies' stockholders.

confidante \'kän-fə-ˌdänt\ A person to whom secrets are entrusted, especially a woman.
- The famed advice columnist Ann Landers was in many ways America's confidante.

fidelity \fə-'de-lə-tē\ 1: The quality or state of being faithful. 2: Accuracy, as in sound reproduction.
- Harriet's comment left Lisa wondering about her husband's fidelity.

geo From the Greek word for "earth," *geo* almost always appears as a prefix. **Geography** describes the Earth's surface; **geology** deals with its history. We measure the Earth—and relationships of its points, lines, angles, surfaces, and solids—using **geometry**.

geopolitical \ˌjē-ō-pə-'li-ti-kəl\ Combining geographic and political factors such as economics and population spread, usually with reference to a state.
- Any invasion might trigger a series of geopolitical consequences, including the fall of other governments.

geosynchronous \ˌjē-ō-'siŋ-krə-nəs\ Having an orbit such that its position is fixed with respect to the Earth.
- Satellites in geosynchronous orbits are usually positioned over the equator.

geothermal \ˌjē-ō-'thər-məl\ Of, relating to, or using the heat of the Earth's interior.
- Geothermal energy technology is most developed in areas of volcanic activity.

131

graph This root is taken from the Greek word meaning "to write." Something **graphic** is "vividly described." **Graphology** is the study of handwriting. A **graph** is a diagram representing changes in something that varies. But *graph*, or *graphy*, actually most often appears at the end of a word.

spectrography \spek-'trä-grə-fē\ The dispersing of radiation (such as electromagnetic radiation or sound waves) into a spectrum to be photographed or mapped.
- Spectrography can determine what elements stars are made of and how fast they are moving.

seismograph \'sīz-mə-ˌgraf\ An apparatus for measuring and recording earthquake-related vibrations.
- Only recently have seismographs been enabling earthquake predictions that actually save lives.

topography \tə-'pä-grə-fē\ 1: The detailed mapping of geographical areas showing their elevations and natural and manmade features. 2: The contours of a geographical surface.
- Watching for the next El Niño, NASA monitors ocean surface topography from space for clues.

grat This root comes from *gratus*, the Latin word meaning "pleasing, welcome, or agreeable," or from *gratia*, meaning "grace, agreeableness, or pleasantness." A meal that is served **graciously** will be received with **gratitude** by **grateful** diners, unless they want to risk being called **ingrates**.

gratify \'gra-tə-ˌfī\ 1: To be a source of pleasure or satisfaction. 2: To give in to; indulge or satisfy.
- The victim's family was gratified by the guilty verdict in the murder trial.

ingratiate \in-'grā-shē-ˌāt\ To gain favor by deliberate effort.
- Backers of the proposed new mall sought to ingratiate themselves with community leaders.

gratuitous \grə-'tü-ə-təs\ Uncalled for; unwarranted.
- Luckily for Linda and all concerned, her gratuitous and offensive remark was not recorded.

Quiz 4

Answers appear at the end of this chapter.

1. An _____ may assume that introverts are odd and antisocial.

2. To be named a child's guardian is to enter an important _____ relationship.

3. Broadcast journalists' microphones now reduce surrounding _____ noise to a whisper.

4. He kept the embarrassing details a secret from everyone but Kendra, his longtime _____.

5. The growth of telecommunications is causing a rapid increase in the number of _____ satellites.

6. Her scheme to _____ herself with the president began with freshly baked cookies.

7. _____ energy usually derives from the heat associated with young volcanic systems.

8. CAT scans and _____ are being used to analyze old bones from the Southwest.

9. After polling 840 well-chosen Americans, the firm _____s its results to the entire country.

10. The stock-market chart looked as if it had been produced by a _____ set on the San Andreas fault.

11. Chief Justice John Marshall called for an oath of _____ to the Constitution.

12. Haters of junk e-mail formed NAGS—Netizens Against _____ Spamming.

13. The map detailed the region's _____, indicating the approximate altitude of every square foot of land.

14. He hoped the award would _____ her without swelling her head.

15. Foster was devoted to national politics, but had no interest in wider _____ issues.

hydr *Hydr* flows from the Greek word for "water." **Hydrotherapy** uses water for healing physical infirmities. Water may spout from a **hydrant**. "Water" can also be found in the lovely flower called **hydrangea**: its seed capsules resemble ancient Greek water vessels.

hydraulic \hī-'drȯ-lik\ 1: Operated or moved by water. 2: Operated by the resistance offered or the pressure transmitted when a quantity of liquid is forced through a small opening or tube.
- The hydraulic brake system used in automobiles is a multiple piston system.

dehydrate \dē-'hī-ˌdrāt\ 1: To remove water from. 2: To lose liquid.
- To minimize weight on the challenging trail, the hikers packed dehydrated fruits and vegetables.

hydroelectric \ˌhī-drō-i-'lek-trik\ Of or relating to production of electricity by waterpower.
- Hydroelectric power sounded clean and renewable, but some asked about its social and environmental impact.

hyper This Greek prefix means "above and beyond it all." To be **hypercritical** or **hypersensitive** is to be critical or sensitive beyond what is normal. To **hyperextend** means to extend a joint (such as a knee or elbow) beyond its usual limits. Clicking on a **hyperlink** may take you beyond the Web site where you found it.

hyperbole \hī-'pər-bə-lē\ Extravagant exaggeration.
- The article called him the college's most popular professor, which even he thought was hyperbole.

hypertension \ˌhī-pər-'ten-shən\ The condition accompanying high blood pressure.
- Hypertension ran in Rachel's family and seemed to be linked to her relatives' heart attacks.

hyperventilate \ˌhī-pər-'ven-təl-ˌāt\ To breathe rapidly and deeply.
- Competitive short-distance runners hyperventilate briefly before running.

hypo Coming from Greek, *hypo* as a prefix can mean "under" or "below normal." A **hypocrite** says or does one thing while thinking or feeling something entirely different underneath. Many *hypo-* words are medical. A **hypodermic** needle injects medication under the skin. **Hypotension**, or low blood pressure, can be just as unhealthy as hypertension.

hypochondriac \ˌhī-pə-'kän-drē-'ak\ A person depressed in mind or spirits because of imaginary physical ailments.
- My grandmother is a hypochondriac; every time she hears about a new disease on the news, she thinks she has caught it.

hypothetical \ˌhī-pə-'the-ti-kəl\ Involving an assumption made for the sake of argument.
- The dating service provides hypothetical questions designed to predict success or failure.

hypothermia \ˌhī-pō-'thər-mē-ə\ Subnormal body temperature.
- Confusion and slurred speech are signs of hypothermia, a silent killer in all seasons.

inter This prefix is the Latin word meaning "between or among." Someone who **interferes** comes between two people; a player who **intercepts** a pass comes between the ball and its intended receiver. An **intermission** is a break between acts of a play. An **international** event takes place between or among nations.

intercede \ˌin-tər-'sēd\ 1: To act between parties as a mediator. 2: To plead on another's behalf.
- The bishop prayed, asking Mother Mary to intercede for us.

interdict \'in-tər-ˌdikt\ To destroy, cut off, or damage.
- U.S. Kosovo Force soldiers sought to interdict weapons at the Serbian and Albanian borders.

interface \'in-tər-ˌfās\ 1: A surface forming a common boundary between two bodies, spaces, or phases. 2: The place where independent systems meet and act on each other.
- Long before the computer age, the auto dashboard was designed as a man−machine interface.

jur *Jur* comes from the Latin verb *jurare*, "to swear or take an oath," and the noun *juris*, "right" or "law." A **jury**, made up of **jurors**, makes judgments based on the law. A personal **injury** caused by another person is "not right."

perjury \\'pər-jə-rē\\ Violation of an oath to tell the truth; lying under oath.
- Lying to a TV reporter is one thing; perjury before a Senate committee is another.

jurisprudence \\ˌj ̇ur-əs-'prü-dəns\\ 1: A system of laws. 2: The science or philosophy of law.
- Juliana's heroes were the crusaders of 20th-century jurisprudence, especially Thurgood Marshall.

abjure \\ab-'j ̇ur\\ 1: To give up, renounce, recant. 2: To abstain from.
- To the prison counselor, the three conspirators always solemnly abjured a future life of crime.

Quiz 5

Answers appear at the end of this chapter.

1. The novelist Lord Archer was found guilty of _____ for lying during his libel suit.

2. "As a _____ example," she said, "let's suppose it were the other way around."

3. Jared led the team up the river to visit the principal _____ power plant in the region.

4. In the thinner air near the mountain top, the climbers began to _____.

5. _____ technology uses fluid to give bulldozers and cranes their great power.

6. There are often no warning signs before _____ triggers a stroke, heart attack, or heart failure.

7. By 19 he was a _____, calling his mother daily about some new ache or sniffle.

8. They urged the UN Secretary-General to _____ in the bloody Middle East conflict.

9. By then her face was caked with ice and _____ had caused her heart to stop.

10. In Web site design, a user-friendly _____ is essential.

11. Accepting the peace prize, Hume again stressed the need to _____ violence.

12. To preserve fruits, we learned how to can and freeze and even _____ them.

13. Feminist _____ is a philosophy of law based on the political, economic, and social equality of the sexes.

138

14. Jason's mom said he read thick books and took quantities of notes, but this was surely _____.

15. Once the enriched uranium left the lab, there would be no chance to _____ it.

mal *Mal*, from the Latin, means "bad." **Malodorous** things smell bad. A **malefactor** is someone guilty of bad deeds. A **malady** is a disease or disorder. **Malnutrition** is faulty or inadequate nutrition. **Dismal** means particularly bad.

malevolent \mə-'le-və-lənt\ Having, showing, or arising from intense ill will, spite, or hatred.
  • Bookstores report that children still like stories with hairy beasts and malevolent aliens.

malign \mə-'līn\ To speak evil of; defame.
  • Amanda didn't wish to malign her neighbors, but the late-night partying had to stop.

malpractice \ˌmal-'prak-təs\ An abandonment of professional duty or a failure of professional skill that results in injury, loss, or damage.
  • The soaring cost of malpractice insurance forced many doctors into early retirement.

mar From the Latin word *mare*, meaning "sea," *mar* brings its salty tang to English in words like **marine**, "having to do with the sea," and **submarine**, "under the sea." It also forms part of such place names as Del Mar ("of the sea"), California. **Aquamarine** is the color of clear seawater in sunlight.

maritime \'mar-ə-ˌtīm\ Of or relating to the sea, navigation, or commerce of the sea.
  • She achieved a national practice in maritime law, specializing in ship insurance.

marina \mə-'rē-nə\ A dock or basin providing secure moorings for pleasure boats.
  • Florida has marinas all along its coast to meet the needs of watercraft from enormous yachts to flimsy sailboats.

mariner \'mar-ə-nər\ A sailor.
  • Ann was haunted by some lines about the old mariner in Coleridge's famous poem.

morph This form comes from the Greek word for "shape." It appears in **anthropomorphic**, meaning "having human form." And **morph** is itself a new English word; by morphing, filmmakers can alter photographic images or shapes digitally, transforming them in astonishing ways.

amorphous \ə-'mȯr-fəs\ Shapeless; formless.
- The sculptor swiftly molded an amorphous lump of clay into a rough human shape.

metamorphosis \ˌme-tə-'mȯr-fə-səs\ 1: A change in physical form or substance. 2: A fundamental change in form and often habits of an animal as part of the transformation of a larva into an adult.
- Day by day we watched the gradual metamorphosis of the tadpoles into frogs.

morphology \mȯr-'fä-lə-jē\ A branch of biology dealing with the form and structure of organisms.
- As an example, she mentioned the morphology of whales, whose fins evolved from legs.

mort / mori These roots come from the Latin noun *mors* (and its related form *mortis*), meaning "death." A **mortuary** is a place where dead bodies are kept until burial, and a **mortician** prepares corpses for burial or cremation. **Memento mori**, a Latin phrase used in English, means "a reminder of death," such as a skull.

moribund \'mȯr-ə-bənd\ 1: Dying or approaching death. 2: Inactive or becoming outmoded.
- Evidence of the sagging industrial economy could be seen in the moribund factories and towns.

mortify \'mȯr-tə-ˌfī\ 1: To subdue or deaden (the body) with self-discipline or self-inflicted pain. 2: To embarrass greatly; humiliate.
- The parents' attempts to act youthful mortified their kids, who almost died of embarrassment when their friends were around.

mortality \mȯr-'ta-lə-tē\ 1: The state of being subject to death. 2: The proportion of deaths to population.
- The preacher takes every occasion to remind us of our mortality, as does the insurance agent.

mut *Mut* comes from the Latin *mutare*, "to change." Science-fiction movies often focus on weird mutations, changes in normal people or animals that lead to death, destruction, or comedy. A governor may **commute** or change a prison sentence; a person **commuting** between cities "exchanges" one location for another.

permutation \ˌpər-myù-'tā-shən\ 1: The changing of the order of a set of objects. 2: An ordering of a set of objects.
- The letters A, B, and C have six possible permutations: ABC, ACB, BAC, BCA, CAB, and CBA.

immutable \i-'myü-tə-bəl\ Unchangeable or unchanging.
- The physical world is governed by the immutable laws of nature.

transmute \trans-'myüt\ To change in shape, appearance, or nature, especially for the better; transform.
- A meek person may dream of being transmuted into a tyrant, or a poor person into a rich one.

Quiz 6

Answers appear at the end of this chapter.

1. The _____ at Hyannis has over 180 slips for deep-draft sailboats, motorboats, and yachts.

2. _____ suits are being filed today against even fine doctors who have made no errors.

3. The monarch's transformation from caterpillar to butterfly represents a dramatic _____.

4. Computer users were warned about a _____ virus hiding in e-Christmas cards.

5. The fabled dream of the alchemist was to _____ lead into gold.

6. The store's nautical antiques and pond yachts should interest the armchair _____.

7. It would _____ her if she ever heard herself described as "middle-aged."

8. Al Capp's Shmoo was an _____ blob-like creature who sometimes helped his friends solve mysteries.

9. The moment he left the party, she started to _____ him mercilessly.

10. In terms of _____, bats' wings are skeletal hands with very long fingers, webbed with membranes.

11. The day the first CD appeared in the stores, the vinyl LP was _____.

12. The number of different ways eight people can line up in a row provides a nice illustration of _____s.

13. Detailed _____ records are kept by the National Center for Health Statistics.

14. The National _____ Museum was displaying personal possessions of the *Bounty* mutineers.

15. In an ever-changing world, people hunger for standards and qualities that are _____.

neo Old as its Greek source, *neo* means "new." **Neon** was a new gas when found in 1898. A **neoconservative** is a liberal who has become a conservative. A **neophyte** is a new convert, or a beginner. And a **neologism** is a new word.

neoclassical \ˌnē-ō-'kla-si-kəl\ Of or relating to a revival or adaptation of the style of classical antiquity.
- Neoclassical paintings are dignified and restrained, and they often radiate a noble spirit.

Neolithic \ˌnē-ə-'li-thik\ Of or relating to the latest period of the Stone Age, characterized by polished stone implements.
- Doctors have asked how the life spans of the Neolithic farmers compared with those of earlier hunter-gatherers.

neoplasm \'nē-ə-ˌpla-zəm\ A new growth of tissue serving no useful purpose in the body; tumor.
- Using digital X-rays, the dentist examined Tom's gums for neoplasms and cysts.

omni This comes from the Latin prefix meaning "all." Thus an **omnidirectional** antenna will draw in stations from all directions. Something **omnipresent** is thought to be present at all places and at all times. An **omnivorous** animal might eat almost everything. Some companies apparently meaning to be everything to their customers name themselves simply "Omni."

omnibus \'äm-ni-bəs\ Of, relating to, or providing for many things at once.
- The Senate's omnibus bill includes money for everything from snail research to new bombers.

omnipotent \äm-'ni-pə-tənt\ Having unlimited authority or influence; almighty.
- The question arises, If God is good and omnipotent, why do bad things happen?

omniscient \äm-'ni-shənt\ Having infinite awareness, understanding, insight, or knowledge.
- His stories usually have an omniscient narrator, who reveals the thoughts of all the characters.

ortho *Ortho* comes from *orthos*, the Greek word for "straight," "right," or "true." **Orthotics** is a therapy that straightens out the stance or posture of the body by providing artificial support for weak joints or muscles. **Orthograde** animals, such as humans, walk with their bodies in an upright position. **Orthography** is correct spelling.

orthodox \\'or-thə-ˌdäks\\ 1: Holding established beliefs, especially in religion. 2: Conforming to established rules or traditions; conventional.
- Gerald preferred orthodox, mainstream cancer treatments to untested alternative therapies.

orthopedist \\ˌor-thə-'pē-dist\\ A medical specialist concerned with correcting or preventing skeletal deformities.
- A local orthopedist eventually managed to correct the child's spinal curvature.

orthodontic \\ˌor-thə-'dän-tik\\ Pertaining to irregularities of the teeth and their correction.
- As much as she dreaded braces, Jennifer knew the time had come for orthodontic work.

pan Directly from Greek, *pan* means "all"; as a prefix in English it can also mean "completely," "whole," or "general." A **panoramic** view is a complete view in every direction. **Pantheism** is the worship of all gods. A **pandemic** outbreak of a disease will affect an exceptionally high proportion of the population, though probably not literally "all" people.

panacea \\ˌpa-nə-'sē-ə\\ A remedy for all ills or difficulties; a cure-all.
- Educational reform is sometimes seen as the panacea for society's problems.

panoply \\'pa-nə-plē\\ 1: A magnificent or impressive array. 2: A display of all appropriate accessory items.
- The full panoply of a royal wedding was a thrilling sight for millions.

pantheon \\'pan-thē-ˌän\\ 1: The gods of a people. 2: A group of illustrious people.
- Even during Dickens's lifetime, the critics had admitted him into the literary pantheon.

phon This Greek root means "sound" or "voice." It shows up in such words as **telephone** ("far sound"), **microphone** ("small sound"), and **xylophone** ("wood sound"). **Phonics** teaches reading by focusing on the sounds of letter groups. A **phonograph** is an instrument for reproducing sounds.

cacophony \ka-ˈkä-fə-nē\ Harsh or discordant sound.
  • According to his grandfather, popular music since Bing Crosby had been nothing but cacophony.

phonetic \fə-ˈne-tik\ Relating to or representing the sounds of the spoken language.
  • Some schools teach reading by the phonetic method, linking sounds with letters.

polyphonic \ˈpä-lē-ˈfä-nik\ Of or relating to music in which two or more independent melodies are sung or played against each other in harmony.
  • Children singing "Three Blind Mice" are performing the simplest kind of polyphonic music.

Quiz 7
Answers appear at the end of this chapter.

1. Some saw the antidepressant drug Prozac as a psychological
   _____.

2. Prehistory, the period of no written records, included the
   _____ and Bronze Ages.

3. Suzanne, age 16, said if she were _____ for a day, she
   would bring about world peace and save the rainforest.

4. Adventurous young people often challenge _____ religious belief systems.

5. The _____ Trade and Competitiveness Act touched on
   many aspects of labor, global commerce, and regulation.

6. The conductor chose a balanced program by composers from the
   musical _____.

7. A _____ alphabet was developed by NATO to be
   understandable by all allies in the heat of battle.

8. The checkup produced one cause for concern: a small
   _____ on the bile duct.

9. My _____ traces all our lower back problems to the time
   when the first humans stood erect.

10. Sandra's new sequencer could take complex _____
    music and convert it into written notation.

11. Even several university degrees and eyes in the back of your head do
    not make you _____.

12. Looking down the long row of _____ buildings, we
    almost thought we were in ancient Rome.

13. His mouth was a disaster area, and his crooked rows of teeth had never had a minute of _____ attention.

14. Out over the ocean, the winter sky spread a brilliant _____ of stars.

15. The kids who liked producing the most outrageous music soon were styling themselves the "_____ Club."

photo Coming from the Greek word for "light," *photo* enlightens us in words like **photography**, which is the use of light to create an image on film or paper. A **photocopy** is a printed copy made by light on an electrically charged surface. A **photogenic** person is one highly suitable for being photographed.

photon \'fō-ˌtän\ A tiny particle or bundle of radiant energy.
- *Star Trek*'s photon torpedoes destroy their targets with intense radiation in the X-ray range.

photosynthesis \ˌfō-tō-'sin-thə-səs\ The process by which green plants use light to produce organic matter from carbon dioxide and water.
- Sagebrush is a hardy plant that can carry on photosynthesis at very low temperatures.

photoelectric \ˌfō-tō-i-'lek-trik\ Relating to an electrical effect from the interaction of light with matter.
- Photoelectric cells would trigger the yard lights when they sensed motion.

post *Post* comes from a Latin word meaning "after" or "behind." A **postscript** is a note that comes after an otherwise completed letter, usually as an afterthought. **Postpartum** refers to the period just after childbirth and all of its related concerns. To **postdate** a check is to give it a date after the date when it was written.

posterior \pä-'stir-ē-ər\ Situated behind or on the back; rear.
- A posterior view of the animal revealed unusual coloring and an extremely long tail.

posthumous \'päs-chə-məs\ Following or happening after one's death.
- The late singer achieved posthumous success when her film became a huge hit.

postmortem \ˌpōst-'mȯr-təm\ 1: Occurring after death. 2: Following the event.
- In 1999 the institute had issued a postmortem report on the Bosnian war, "NATO's Empty Victory."

pre One of the most common of all English **prefixes**, *pre* comes from *prae*, the Latin word meaning "before" or "in front of." A TV program **precedes** another by coming on before it. You **predict** an event by saying it will happen before it does. A person who **presumes** to know assumes something before having all the facts.

precocious \pri-'kō-shəs\ Showing mature qualities at an unusually early age.
  • Some thought the sitcom's precocious child star was cute; others thought she was a show-off.

prerequisite \prē-'re-kwə-zət\ An action, event, or object required in advance to achieve a goal.
  • Certain courses were prerequisites for majoring in engineering at the university.

predisposed \ˌprē-di-'spōzd\ Influenced in advance or made persuadable.
  • The commissioner was predisposed to vote for the project since its developer had given his campaign a large contribution.

prim *Prim* comes from *primus*, the Latin word for "first." A **prime minister** is the chief minister of a ruler or state. Something **primary** is first in time, rank, or importance. Something **primitive** seems to be in an early stage of development.

primal \'prī-məl\ 1: Original or primitive. 2: First in importance.
  • Much of civilization seems designed to disguise or soften the rawness of our primal urges.

primordial \prī-'mȯr-dē-əl\ Existing in or from the very beginning.
  • He assumed his ancestors emerged from the primordial ooze, and not as gods.

primate \'prī-māt\ A member of an order of mammals that includes humans, apes, and monkeys.
  • Do we have anything important to learn about human behavior from our cousins the primates?

rect This root comes **directly** from the Latin word *rectus*, meaning "straight" or "right." A **rectangle** is a four-sided figure whose straight sides meet at right angles. To **correct** something is to make it right. To stand **erect** is to stand straight.

rectitude \'rek-tə-ˌtüd\ Correctness in judgment; moral integrity.
  • The school superintendent wasn't popular, but no one could question his fairness and rectitude.

rectify \'rek-tə-ˌfī\ To make or set right; correct.
  • Problems with the Bowl Championship Series were rectified by a simple four-team playoff.

rectilinear \ˌrek-tə-'li-nē-ər\ Characterized by straight lines.
  • In its rectilinear structure, the sculpture reflects the surrounding office buildings.

151

Quiz 8

Answers appear at the end of this chapter.

1. Hamstrings, deltoids, and gluteus maximus are human muscles on the _____ side.

2. The lighting engineering firm offered _____ sensors for many uses.

3. The West Point students' reputation for _____ was badly damaged by the cheating scandal.

4. Average parents of specially gifted or _____ children face unusual challenges.

5. With the dead man now proven innocent, his relatives sought a _____ pardon.

6. The power of lasers results from a focused concentration of _____s.

7. For many, retreating to a rough-hewn home in the woods seems to satisfy a _____ urge.

8. Some children may be _____ to asthma by their genes.

9. Green plants don't graze, hunt, or shop; they make food by using sunlight through _____.

10. The association called on Congress to _____ the unfairness of health care funding.

11. During the _____ exam, the medical examiner discovered a mysterious blackening of the liver tissue.

12. Her study of baboons earned Gloria a fellowship to the _____ research center.

13. Over ten billion years ago, the Milky Way was just a giant _____ gas cloud.

14. Simple _____ designs with bold vertical and horizontal lines dominated the hotel's decor.

15. Detailed knowledge of psychology is not a _____ for interviewing of job applicants.

retro *Retro* means "back," "behind," or "backward" in Latin. **Retro** itself is a fairly new word in English, meaning "nostalgically old-fashioned," usually when describing styles or fashions. To **retrogress** is to go back to an earlier and usually worse state. A **retrograde** action is a backward or reverse action.

retroactive \ˌre-trō-'ak-tiv\ Intended to apply or take effect at a date in the past.
  • The fact that the tax hike was retroactive was what annoyed the public the most.

retrofit \'re-trō-ˌfit\ To furnish something with new or modified parts or equipment.
  • Owners were offered "fast-track" permits to retrofit their homes against earthquakes.

retrospective \ˌre-trə-'spek-tiv\ Of or relating to surveying the past.
  • Excitement grew in anticipation of the rare retrospective exhibition of Avedon's photographs.

scrib / scrip This root comes from the Latin verb *scribere*, "to write." A **script** is written matter, such as lines for a play. **Scriptures** are sacred writings. **Scribble** means to write or draw carelessly. A written work that hasn't been published is a **manuscript**.

circumscribe \'sər-kəm-ˌskrīb\ To limit the range or activity of.
  • Various laws have circumscribed the freedom of labor unions to strike and organize.

inscribe \in-'skrīb\ 1: To write, engrave, or print. 2: To dedicate (a book) to someone.
  • As Mike turned to leave, the store clerk offered to inscribe the diamond ring free.

proscribe \prō-'skrīb\ 1: To prohibit. 2: To condemn or forbid as harmful.
  • If the doctor proscribes certain foods, you'd better not eat them.

sub *Sub* means "under," as in **subway**, **submarine**, and **substandard**. A **subject** is a person who is under the authority of another. **Subconscious** activity exists in the mind just under the level of awareness. To **subdue** is to bring under control.

subjugate \'səb-ji-ˌgāt\ To bring under control; conquer; subdue.
- Bringing criminal charges against reporters seemed a government attempt to subjugate the media.

subliminal \sə-'bli-mə-nəl\ Not quite strong enough to be sensed or perceived consciously.
- Worried parents claimed that some songs contained disturbing subliminal messages.

subversive \səb-'vər-siv\ 1: Tending to overthrow or undermine by working secretly from within. 2: Tending to corrupt someone or something by weakening loyalty, morals, or faith.
- In the 1950s the nation became alarmed that subversive communists were lurking everywhere.

syn From the Greek word meaning "with" or "together with," *syn* as a prefix in English can also mean "at the same time." Thus **synesthesia** is the remarkable awareness of another sense (such as color) at the same time as the one being stimulated (such as sound). **Synergy** is the useful "working together" of distinct elements. **Syntax** is about how words are put together.

synthesis \'sin-thə-səs\ The combination of parts or elements into a whole.
- Chemical analysis separates a substance into its elements; chemical synthesis combines elements to produce something new.

synopsis \sə-'näp-səs\ A condensed statement or outline.
- Having read the synopsis, Bill did not feel a need to read the full report.

syndrome \'sin-ˌdrōm\ A group of signs and symptoms that occur together and characterize a particular abnormality.
- Sufferers from chronic fatigue syndrome fought for a decade to have their symptoms recognized as a specific illness.

tele *Tele* comes from the Greek word for "far off"; in English its basic meaning is "distant" or "at a distance." A **telescope** looks at faraway objects. A **telephoto** lens on a camera magnifies distant objects for a photograph. A **television** allows us to watch things taking place far away (or sometimes not far enough away).

teleological \ˌte-lē-ə-ˈlä-ji-kəl\ Relating to design, purpose, or cause, especially in nature.
- The traditional teleological argument claims that humans are so remarkable that only God could have designed them.

telepathic \ˌte-lə-ˈpa-thik\ Communicating from one mind to another without known sensory means.
- Suzanne never considered herself telepathic, but she awoke with a start when her brother died at 2:00 a.m. 3,000 miles away.

telemetry \tə-ˈle-mə-trē\ The transmission, especially by radio, of measurements made by automatic instruments to a distant station.
- Satellite telemetry allowed the tracking of this year's great caribou migration.

156

Quiz 9

Answers appear at the end of this chapter.

1. Highly responsive to each other's actions, the twins at times seemed almost _____.

2. The catalog featuring vintage dinnerware of the 1940s through the 1970s was really a _____ display of modern design.

3. As a semi-invalid, she led a _____d life, rarely venturing beyond her garden.

4. Approval of the pay increase was confirmed, _____ to January 1st.

5. Did an early experiment in _____ advertising at a movie theater result in increased popcorn sales?

6. A cherub helped an angel _____ words so beautiful they fell like roses from her feather pen.

7. Her new album seemed to be a _____ of country and world music.

8. The scary part was when the _____ failed and the astronauts vanished from the screens.

9. Once in power, the mullahs proceeded to _____ the Westernized women of Tehran.

10. Smoking is now _____d in many U.S. medical and restaurant settings.

11. A Hollywood-based Web site offers a helpful _____ of the plots of hundreds of films.

12. The mayor hoped to _____ the vehicles to increase the mobility of the disabled.

13. The new special police unit was entrusted with intelligence gathering and monitoring _____ activities.

14. Schizophrenia is a _____ related to a variety of causative factors.

15. The claim that a gopher's cheek pouches are *intended* for carrying food is, to zoologists, a _____ statement.

terr This root was dug up from the Latin *terra*, "earth." **Terra firma** is a Latin phrase that means "firm ground," as opposed to the swaying seas. A **terrace** is a leveled area along a sloping hill; **territory** is a specific piece of land. A **terrier**, literally an "earth dog," was originally used by hunters to dig for small game.

subterranean \ˌsəb-tə-'rā-nē-ən\ Underground.
- The region, it was believed, was home to subterranean beings that emerged from their burrows only at night.

terrestrial \tə-'res-trē-əl\ 1: Having to do with the earth or its inhabitants. 2: Having to do with land as distinct from air or water.
- Unlike frogs, most toads are terrestrial, entering the water only to lay their eggs.

terrain \tə-'rān\ The surface features of an area of land.
- Mountain unicycling proved especially challenging over such rough terrain.

therm Still warm from centuries of use, *therm* comes from the Greek word meaning "heat." A **thermometer** measures heat; a **thermostat** makes sure it stays at the same level. A rising body of warm air, used by hawks and sailplanes, is called a **thermal**.

thermal \'thər-məl\ 1: Of, relating to, or caused by heat. 2: Designed to prevent loss of body heat.
- Thermal vents on the ocean floor release steam as hot as 600°.

thermodynamic \ˌthər-mō-dī-'na-mik\ Of or relating to the physics of heat.
- A chemical's thermodynamic properties indicate how it will behave at various temperatures.

thermonuclear \ˌthər-mō-'nü-klē-ər\ Of or relating to changes in the nucleus of atoms of low atomic weight brought about by very high temperatures.
- In those days thermonuclear devices were being proposed for such uses as excavating canals.

trans This root comes across from Latin to indicate movement "through, across, or beyond" something. A **translation** carries the meaning across languages. A TV signal is **transmitted** or "sent through" the air (or a cable) to your set. Public **transportation** carries you across a distance, though you may need to **transfer** from one bus or subway across to another.

transient \'tran-shənt\ 1: Passing through a place and staying only briefly. 2: Of brief duration.
- Tristan's inn in Vermont attracted transient tourists come to gaze at the autumn foliage.

transcendent \tran-'sen-dənt\ 1: Exceeding usual limits; surpassing. 2: Beyond comprehension.
- The symphony's hushed ending, with the solo violin melody trailing off into silence, is almost transcendent.

transfusion \trans-'fyü-zhən\ 1: The process of diffusing into or through. 2: The process of moving (as of blood) into a vein.
- Travelers needing blood transfusions have usually suffered severe accidents.

uni *Uni* comes from the Latin word for "one." A **uniform** is clothing of one design. A **united** group has one opinion or forms one **unit**. A **unitard** is a one-piece combination leotard and tights, very good for skating, skiing, dancing—or riding a one-wheeled **unicycle**.

unicameral \ˌyü-ni-'kam-rəl\ Having a single legislative house or chamber.
- Passing new laws was comparatively quick and easy in the unicameral government.

unilateral \ˌyü-ni-'la-tə-rəl\ Having, affecting, or done by one side only.
- Russia's unilateral withdrawal from Afghanistan, in return for nothing, astonished the world.

unison \'yü-nə-sən\ 1: Sameness of musical pitch. 2: A state of harmonious agreement; accord.
- Unable to read music well enough to harmonize, the village choir sang only in unison.

viv *Viv* comes from *vivere*, the Latin verb meaning "to live or be alive." A **vivid** memory is a lively one. A **survivor** has lived through something terrible. A **revival** brings something back to life—whether an old film, interest in a long-dead novelist, or the religious faith of a group.

vivacious \və-'vā-shəs\ Lively, sprightly.
- For the cheerleading squad, Sheri chose the most outgoing, energetic, and vivacious candidates.

vivisection \ˌvi-və-'sek-shən\ Experimental operation on a living animal.
- The firm reluctantly agreed to avoid research involving vivisection in favor of alternative methods.

convivial \kən-'viv-yəl\ 1: Enjoying companionship in feasting and drinking. 2: Festive.
- Alberta was known for hosting relaxed and convivial gatherings, where the wine flowed freely.

Quiz 10

Answers appear at the end of this chapter.

1. At the height of the Cold War, some Americans began digging _____ fallout shelters.

2. The _____ properties of metals affect technologies we don't think of as heat-related.

3. Forty-nine states have bicameral legislatures; only Nebraska's is _____.

4. Any chemical reaction that produces heat is a _____ reaction.

5. Over such rugged _____, mules were the only hope for transporting needed supplies.

6. It's a noisy, _____ crowd that gathers at McSorley's Restaurant after 5:00.

7. His bright idea turned out to be a _____ one, and he had soon moved on to something new.

8. He returned from the backpacking trip energized as if he'd been given a _____ of new blood.

9. Detonating a _____ bomb requires temperatures exceeding a million degrees Fahrenheit.

10. While singing in parts is difficult, singing modern compositions for _____ voices has challenges of its own.

11. Jessie was so _____ that she livened up every party she ever attended.

12. She emerged from the concert hall in a daze, feeling she had undergone a _____ experience.

13. Alabama has over 500 species of marine mollusks, and many _____ mollusks as well.

14. Animal lovers of every stripe wrote in, claiming that _____ had little scientific merit.

15. After failed negotiations with its neighbors, Iran announced a _____ decision to develop its own oil wells in the Caspian Sea.

REVIEW TEST

Fill in each blank in the sentences on the following pages with one of the following words. Answers appear at the end of this chapter.

abjure	discredit	marina	primate
agrarian	dynamo	mariner	primordial
agrochemical	dynasty	maritime	proscribe
agronomy	dysentery	metamorphosis	rectify
amorphous	dyslexia	microcosm	rectilinear
anachronism	dystrophy	misanthrope	rectitude
antecedent	epigraph	moribund	retroactive
antedate	epilogue	morphology	retrofit
anterior	epithet	mortality	retrospective
anthropoid	extraneous	mortify	seismograph
aquaculture	extrapolate	neoclassical	spectrography
Aquarius	extrovert	Neolithic	subjugate
aquifer	fidelity	neoplasm	subliminal
artifact	fiduciary	omnibus	subterranean
artifice	geopolitical	omnipotent	subversive
artisan	geosynchronous	omniscient	symbiosis
benediction	geothermal	orthodontic	syndrome
benefactor	gratify	orthodox	synopsis
beneficent	gratuitous	orthopedist	synthesis
bionic	hydraulic	panacea	telemetry
biopsy	hydrodynamic	panoply	teleological
cacophony	hydroelectric	pantheon	telepathic
chronic	hyperbole	perjury	terrain
chronology	hypertension	permutation	terrestrial
circumscribe	hyperventilate	philanthropy	thermal
circumspect	hypochondriac	phonetic	thermodynamic
circumstantial	hypothermia	photoelectric	thermonuclear
circumvent	hypothetical	photon	topography
confidante	immutable	photosynthesis	transcendent
convivial	ingratiate	polyphonic	transfusion
cosmology	inscribe	posterior	transient
cosmopolitan	intercede	posthumous	transmute
credence	interdict	postmortem	unicameral
credible	interface	precocious	unilateral
creed	jurisprudence	predisposed	unison
dehydrate	malevolent	prerequisite	vivacious
disarming	malign	primal	vivisection
disburse	malpractice		

1. Keith _____d the novel "To Melissa, my only muse and inspiration."

2. After the first trial, Collins was called to answer charges of _____ and evidence tampering.

3. Is it _____ to say that an eagle's wings were "designed" for soaring?

4. Rafael's clumsy attempt to _____ the contract led to his arrest for fraud.

5. Some interactive games let players achieve virtual destruction worse than that of a _____ bomb.

6. After his divorce, his legal practice shrank and a _____ suit almost bankrupted him.

7. _____ apes resemble humans in that they lack tails and walk semi-erect.

8. The "facts" on the "Astounding Facts" Web site turned out not to be very _____.

9. _____ runoff is blamed for creating a huge "dead zone" in the Gulf of Mexico.

10. Most people picture _____s as underground lakes rather than as expanses of soaked gravel.

11. The Water-Carrier, _____, is an old constellation carved in stones of the Babylonian Empire.

12. The formal gardens were showplaces of _____, with every tree and shrub shaped by human hands.

13. Aaron's fossil hunting in Alaska led to his unearthing of unusual ancient _____s.

14. The prison's star inmate, he had undergone a _____ from hardened criminal to contributing citizen.

15. The blonde Evita was seen by Argentina's poor as a _____ angel dispensing charity.

16. Paleolithic hunters, with their tools of chipped stone, gave way to _____ farmers, with their polished stone tools.

17. What anonymous _____ had contributed $500,000 to the medical fund?

18. Her aunt, previously blind, could now recognize faces with her new _____ eye.

19. For years Carol had managed her _____ heart condition through careful diet and exercise.

20. Using a telephone in a play set in 1765 is an obvious _____.

21. Veterinarians have often relied on _____ examinations in diagnosing disease.

22. A newly hired 22-year-old had easily managed to _____ the computer security system.

23. The sunny and _____ Doris Day started out as a jazz singer in the 1940s.

24. When asked about Russia's own success fighting corruption, the official quickly became _____.

25. The club was chic and _____, and everyone seemed to have a French or German accent.

26. Rural Maine is home to many _____s: woodworkers, potters, weavers, and the like.

27. The findings of Copernicus and Galileo proposed nothing less than a new _____.

28. Some building codes require _____ sensors, which are quick to detect smoky fires.

29. The _____ provided needed services after an exhausting day on choppy seas.

30. The game of Monopoly seems to present a _____ of the world of real-estate dealing.

166

31. Scientists often refer to the ocean's surface as the ocean-atmosphere
_____.

32. A new find lends _____ to the claim that the first
Americans came from Europe.

33. She was skeptical about what lay behind his smooth and
_____ manner.

34. Society often depends on _____ to fill the gaps left by
government spending.

35. The new president turned out to be a ferociously energetic human
_____.

36. Each winter, outdoor adventure groups often publicize the best
ways to avoid frostbite and _____.

37. She was always reading about alternative therapies, but her doctor
was as _____ as they come.

38. Muscular _____ is actually a family of disorders that
causes muscle degeneration.

39. A passage from *Othello* appeared as the _____ of the
long-awaited report.

40. The author's _____ listed the adventurers' whereabouts
five years after their rescue.

41. She told him his concerns were _____ and he should
stick to the subject at hand.

42. A data recorder and transmitters and receivers formed part of the
satellite's _____ system.

43. A prominent political _____, the Kennedy family has
seen many of its members elected to office.

44. He was a drifter, hardly the kind of person for a _____
responsibility such as executor of a will.

45. "Attack ads" attempt to _____ political candidates,
often with half-truths and lies.

46. Whether the coup succeeded or failed depended on the
_____ of the general's soldiers.

47. The clinic, in Canada's far north, serves a _____ Inuit
population not likely to return for regular checkups.

48. Could _____ tensions in faraway Asia actually affect
the national elections?

49. Study of the sun's magnetic fields requires _____ to
reveal the solar spectrum.

50. For the America's Cup yachts, the keel by itself presents complex
_____ problems.

51. Severe stomach distress ruined their trip, and it turned out they
both had _____.

52. The Princeton Earth Physics Project tracks earthquakes using a
network of _____s.

53. There were arguments about how best to _____
financial aid following the disaster.

54. Sandra knew it would _____ her husband if she wore
the necklace he'd given her.

55. The fetus had gotten turned around into the _____
position, which can make the birthing process difficult.

56. Much modern _____ still is practiced in small mom-
and-pop fishpond operations.

57. Those lurching virtual-reality thrill rides are powered by _____,
pressurized-fluid technology.

58. Nick, the family _____, played touch football, organized reunions, and was his company's top salesman.

59. Astonishing examples of cooperative living between species appear
as _____.

60. Having quit smoking, he was told he must now adopt a strict diet
for his _____.

61. The meteorite, billions of years old, offered clues about the _____ solar system.

62. Best-selling novelists can sell a book idea to their publishers with nothing but a short _____.

63. The Garden of Eden is the biblical vision of a _____ paradise.

64. Melanie's problems with spelling and math were finally traced to _____.

65. Having entered the virtual body, the doctor may test a range of _____ drug interactions.

66. The response from the opposition was full of _____ insults and slurs.

67. A United Nations force was asked to _____ on behalf of both combatants and restore peace.

68. With public-relations help, the Nigerians hoped to _____ reports of genocide during the Biafran war.

69. As a context for discussion, Abu handed out a detailed _____ of Muslim history.

70. At halftime, the _____ mass of band musicians abruptly snapped into a tight formation.

71. The greatest Supreme Court justices could often be called philosophers of _____.

72. The awesome _____ of the procession made the hometown parade seem like a coronation.

73. Fascinated by plant breeding, Heather began to enroll in _____ courses.

74. After a terrible two-month binge, he solemnly _____d alcohol forever.

75. That nasty remark was her first hint that her beloved Alex had a _____ streak.

76. Two _____ power plants were being built near the volcano's base.

77. Following the hijackings, the airline was forced to _____ its jets with new cockpit doors.

78. To celebrate its seagoing history, the port city established a _____ museum.

79. A specialist in vertebrate _____, he usually explained skeleton structures in terms of evolution.

80. Looser laws in Canada may make it harder for the U.S. to _____ drug trafficking.

81. Devout medieval Christians sought to "_____ the flesh"—to reduce their sensitivity to hunger, cold, and discomfort.

82. Shuffling the deck ensures that the cards will be dealt in almost infinite _____s.

83. The foes of freedom have tried to suppress books, films, and songs, calling them _____.

84. The congregation then recites the _____, a concise statement of Christian beliefs.

85. Many _____ sculptures from the 1780s could be mistaken for works from ancient Rome.

86. It would take a heartfelt apology to _____ the situation.

87. Before taking Tree Physiology, you must have completed such _____s as Forest Botany.

88. The Senate finally threw everything together into a single _____ bill.

89. Though there had been no eyewitnesses, the _____ evidence was enough to convict him.

90. After a time, the supposed illnesses of a _____ no longer attract the sympathy of friends.

91. The investigation was focusing on a 48-year-old man—a single, unemployed loner and _____.

92. One need not be _____ to write an encyclopedia, but it would help.

93. The company produces a sports guard, dentures, braces, and other _____ appliances.

94. Lawyers argued that the state constitution _____d the legislature's power in cases like this one.

95. Having failed to form a coalition, the president began to consider taking _____ action.

96. Apollo and Dionysus were two of the most widely worshiped gods in the Greek _____.

97. New to New York, Carol couldn't fall asleep with the _____ of street sounds.

98. With her fortune declining, even Lady Armstrong could see that the great estate was _____.

99. To prevent moisture-related spoilage, Gretchen said we could _____ some foods.

100. The lawyers had argued that her injuries were actually _____ to the accident.

101. With a liver _____, a small piece of tissue can be examined for signs of disease.

102. Several simultaneous melodies combined to form a rich texture of _____ sound.

103. The river's _____ dams block downstream movement of large wood, disturbing aquatic habitats.

104. The verdict awarded her complete survivor's benefits, _____ to the date of her husband's death.

105. She would later claim that she had _____d her grief into the songs that made her famous.

106. The university awarded _____ degrees to seniors killed in the crash.

107. Sandra tried using _____ motivational tapes while sleeping to improve her attitude.

108. _____ reading ability in children may not be matched by advanced writing skills.

109. Lottman's film was an odd _____ of ancient myth, film noir, and alternative comics.

110. Gazing into a campfire at night, we feel a _____ connection with our prehistoric ancestors.

111. Any system that turns heat into mechanical energy represents a _____ process.

112. A salty _____ may throw a tub of sea jargon at you to expose your ignorance.

113. It required all his charm to _____ himself with the power brokers.

114. Several Roman emperors, convinced that they were _____, declared themselves gods.

115. Sitting up straight at the table isn't necessarily an outward sign of moral _____.

116. The U.S. Geographic Survey has modeled and mapped the entire American _____.

117. The center compiled data on illness and _____ from blood diseases.

118. The region's _____ is dramatic, with sheer cliffs descending to parched plains.

119. Hilda's sleek, _____ designs featured sharp clean lines and squared corners.

120. His CAT scan revealed a large _____, but it turned out to be harmless.

121. With remarkable skill and patience, the _____ had restored Tyler's spine by surgical means.

122. The _____ exhibit on Project Apollo began with its birth in 1961.

123. Brett's doctors called on his close relatives to donate blood for the _____.

124. Even in war there are rules and norms of behavior that _____ the worst offenses.

125. The Founding Fathers rejected the idea of a _____ legislature, favoring a House and Senate to balance each other.

126. Wherever the great khan's army marched, it would conquer and _____ the local tribes.

127. From these incomplete statistics we can easily _____ the complete data.

128. People with this rare _____ are smart and mentally retarded at the same time.

129. Some groups argue that _____ is a barbaric and unjustified form of animal cruelty.

130. Audrey claims to have _____ communication with her pet ferrets while she's at the office.

131. Many have wondered if some murderers were biologically _____ to kill.

132. In 1880 a traveling salesman might have tried to sell you a single _____ for everything from mumps to arthritis.

133. Prehistoric peoples in harsh climates often lived in caves or even _____ dwellings.

134. He delivered his praise as solemnly as a priest's _____.

135. _____ orbits are ideal for maintaining contact with a specific location on Earth.

136. We distinguish between outright lies on the one hand and mere
_____ on the other.

137. These get-togethers start out quietly but always become
_____, and sometimes even rowdy.

138. She emitted the kind of radiant energy that isn't measured in
_____s.

139. Giant tubeworms live on the ocean floor near _____
vents spouting scalding water.

140. The broken jawbone was clearly visible in the X-ray image that
showed an _____ view of his skull.

141. The mob outside the _____ research center called for
an end to tests on monkeys.

142. After awakening from her coma, she recounted a _____
experience of light and bliss.

143. Phyllis used the _____ approach with her first-graders,
sounding out syllables one by one.

144. The student complaint involved the alleged yelling of racial
_____s.

145. The new Web site, called "_____.com," is "for those
who like to tell and those who like to listen."

146. It's common, but also dangerous, for freedivers to
_____ in order to stay underwater longer.

147. The rebellious workers began chanting in _____, "No
Contract, No Work!"

148. Economic growth in poor countries often depends on
_____ reform and rural development.

149. In green plants, light energy is converted into chemical energy
during _____.

150. Alicia kept a fixed and _____ order to her household,
especially in the sock drawers.

174

50 More Roots

The roots and derived words in the table below are intended for further study. Learn the meanings of any of the words you are unfamiliar with (perhaps by drilling yourself with homemade flash cards), and try using each of them in sentences. Try to think of other terms that use each of the roots in the left-hand column.

aud ("hear")	auditor	audition	auditory
aut/auto ("same, self")	automaton	autonomy	autocratic
bell ("war")	bellicose	belligerent	antebellum
bi ("two")	bipartisan	binary	bipolar
carn ("flesh")	carnage	incarnation	carnal
cata ("down")	catalyst	catacomb	catatonic
cent ("hundred")	centenary	centigrade	centimeter
cid ("kill")	genocide	infanticide	fungicide
corp ("body")	corporal	corpulent	corporeal
crac/crat ("power")	bureaucrat	aristocracy	autocrat
crypt/cryph ("hidden")	cryptic	apocryphal	crypt
culp ("guilt")	culpable	exculpate	mea culpa
cur ("care")	curator	sinecure	curative
dec ("ten")	decathlon	decimate	decibel
demo ("people")	demotic	endemic	demographic
dict ("speak")	diction	edict	indict
domin ("lord")	domineer	predominant	dominion
duct ("lead")	abduct	duct	induct
ego ("I")	alter ego	egocentric	egoist
equi ("equal")	equivocal	equity	equilibrium
eu ("good")	euphemism	euphoria	euthanasia
flu ("flow")	influx	confluence	fluent
grad ("step")	degradation	gradient	gradation
grav ("heavy")	grave	gravitate	gravitas
hemi/demi/semi ("half")	hemiplegic	semiconductor	demigod
homo ("same")	homogeneous	homogenize	homologous
later ("side")	bilateral	collateral	unilateral
medi ("middle")	mediate	intermediary	median
mono ("single")	monotone	monologue	monotheism
neuro ("nerve")	neurology	neuron	neurotransmitter

175

PETERSON'S getting you there

50 More Roots (continued)

nom ("name")	misnomer	nomenclature	nominal
patr/pater ("father")	patriarch	patrimony	patrician
pun/pen ("punish")	punitive	impunity	penal
peri ("around")	peripheral	peripatetic	perimeter
phob ("fear")	agoraphobia	xenophobia	acrophobia
plac ("please")	placate	implacable	placebo
popul ("people")	populist	populace	depopulate
proto ("first")	protocol	protagonist	prototype
quadr ("four")	quadrennial	quadriplegic	quadruped
sacr/sanct ("holy")	sanctify	sacrosanct	sanctuary
simil/simul ("like")	simile	simulate	assimilate
son ("sound")	sonority	sonata	sonic
super/supra ("above")	superannuated	superimpose	superfluous
the/theo ("god")	theocracy	monotheism	theology
topo ("place")	topical	topographical	utopia
tri ("three")	trilogy	trinity	trimester
turb ("confused")	perturb	turbid	turbine
ver/veri ("true")	aver	veracity	veritable
verb ("word")	verbiage	verbose	proverb
vert ("turn")	subvert	revert	avert

Answer Key

Quiz 1
1. philanthropy
2. agrochemical
3. artifact
4. agrarian
5. aquifer
6. anterior
7. agronomy
8. artifice
9. antecedent
10. aquaculture
11. misanthrope
12. antedate
13. anthropoid
14. Aquarius
15. artisan

Quiz 2
1. symbiosis
2. beneficent
3. circumstantial
4. cosmology
5. benediction
6. bionic
7. biopsy
8. benefactor
9. circumvent
10. chronic
11. anachronism
12. chronology
13. microcosm
14. circumspect
15. cosmopolitan

Quiz 3
1. creed
2. disarming
3. dysentery
4. discredit
5. credence
6. dyslexia
7. dynasty
8. epigraph
9. hydrodynamic
10. disburse
11. epilogue
12. dystrophy
13. epithet
14. credible
15. dynamo

Quiz 4
1. extrovert
2. fiduciary
3. extraneous
4. confidante
5. geosynchronous
6. ingratiate
7. geothermal
8. spectrography
9. extrapolate
10. seismograph
11. fidelity
12. gratuitous
13. topography
14. gratify
15. geopolitical

Quiz 5
1. perjury
2. hypothetical
3. hydroelectric
4. hyperventilate
5. hydraulic
6. hypertension
7. hypochondriac
8. intercede
9. hypothermia
10. interface
11. abjure
12. dehydrate
13. jurisprudence
14. hyperbole
15. interdict

Quiz 6
1. marina
2. malpractice
3. metamorphosis
4. malevolent
5. transmute
6. mariner
7. mortify
8. amorphous
9. malign
10. morphology
11. moribund
12. permutation
13. mortality
14. maritime
15. immutable

Quiz 7
1. panacea
2. Neolithic
3. omnipotent
4. orthodox
5. omnibus
6. pantheon
7. phonetic
8. neoplasm
9. orthopedist
10. polyphonic
11. omniscient
12. neoclassical
13. orthodontic
14. panoply
15. cacophony

Quiz 8
1. posterior
2. photoelectric
3. rectitude
4. precocious
5. posthumous
6. photon
7. primal
8. predisposed
9. photosynthesis
10. rectify
11. postmortem
12. primate
13. amorphous
14. rectilinear
15. prerequisite

Quiz 9
1. telepathic
2. retrospective
3. circumscribe
4. retroactive
5. subliminal
6. inscribe
7. synthesis
8. telemetry
9. subjugate
10. proscribe
11. synopsis
12. retrofit
13. subversive
14. syndrome
15. teleological

Quiz 10
1. subterranean
2. thermal
3. unicameral
4. thermodynamic
5. terrain
6. convivial
7. transient
8. transfusion
9. thermonuclear
10. unison
11. vivacious
12. transcendent
13. terrestrial
14. vivisection
15. unilateral

Review Test
1. inscribe
2. perjury
3. teleological
4. antedate
5. thermonuclear
6. malpractice
7. anthropoid
8. credible
9. agrochemical
10. aquifer
11. Aquarius
12. artifice
13. artifact
14. metamorphosis
15. beneficent
16. Neolithic
17. benefactor
18. bionic
19. chronic
20. anachronism
21. postmortem
22. circumvent
23. vivacious
24. circumspect
25. cosmopolitan
26. artisan
27. cosmology
28. photoelectric
29. marina
30. microcosm
31. interface
32. credence
33. disarming
34. philanthropy
35. dynamo
36. hypothermia
37. orthodox
38. dystrophy
39. epigraph
40. epilogue
41. extraneous
42. telemetry

43. dynasty
44. fiduciary
45. malign
46. fidelity
47. transient
48. geopolitical
49. spectrography
50. hydrodynamic
51. dysentery
52. seismograph
53. disburse
54. gratify
55. posterior
56. aquaculture
57. hydraulic
58. extrovert
59. symbiosis
60. hypertension
61. primordial
62. synopsis
63. terrestrial
64. dyslexia
65. hypothetical
66. gratuitous
67. intercede
68. discredit
69. chronology
70. amorphous
71. jurisprudence
72. panoply
73. agronomy
74. abjure
75. malevolent
76. geothermal
77. retrofit
78. maritime
79. morphology
80. interdict
81. mortify
82. permutation
83. subversive
84. creed
85. neoclassical
86. rectify
87. prerequisite
88. omnibus
89. circumstantial
90. hypochondriac
91. misanthrope
92. omniscient
93. orthodontic
94. circumscribe
95. unilateral
96. pantheon
97. cacophony
98. moribund
99. dehydrate
100. antecedent
101. biopsy
102. polyphonic
103. hydroelectric
104. retroactive
105. transmute
106. posthumous
107. subliminal
108. precocious
109. synthesis
110. primal
111. thermodynamic
112. mariner
113. ingratiate
114. omnipotent
115. rectitude
116. terrain
117. mortality
118. topography
119. rectilinear
120. neoplasm
121. orthopedist
122. retrospective
123. transfusion
124. proscribe
125. unicameral
126. subjugate
127. extrapolate
128. syndrome
129. vivisection
130. telepathic
131. predisposed
132. panacea
133. subterranean
134. benediction
135. geosynchronous
136. hyperbole
137. convivial
138. photon
139. thermal
140. anterior
141. primate
142. transcendent
143. phonetic
144. epithet
145. confidante
146. hyperventilate
147. unison
148. agrarian
149. photosynthesis
150. immutable

Mathematical Reasoning Review

Standard Multiple Choice

What to Expect

The format for multiple-choice problems is fairly intuitive—you've most likely seen questions like this on many standardized tests. The problem is presented to you with five options, labeled (A) through (E). The answer key has five columns of ovals, one for each possible solution. Your job is to fill in the oval that corresponds to the correct solution.

For standard multiple-choice questions, you will be instructed as follows:

Time—25 Minutes • 20 Questions

Solve problems 1–20, then select the best of the choices given for each one and fill in the corresponding oval on the answer sheet. You may use available space on the page for scratch work.

Notes:

1. You may use a calculator. All of the numbers used are real numbers.

2. You may use the figures that accompany the problems to help you find the solution. Unless the instructions say that a figure is not drawn to scale, assume that it has been drawn accurately. Each figure lies in a plane unless the instructions say otherwise.

Reference Information

$A = \pi r^2$
$C = 2\pi r$ $A = \ell w$ $A = \frac{1}{2}bh$ $V = \ell wh$ $V = \pi r^2 h$ $c^2 = a^2 + b^2$ Special Right Triangles
The number of degrees of arc in a circle is 360.
The measure in degrees of a straight angle is 180.
The sum of the measures in degrees of the angles of a triangle is 180.

How to Approach Standard Multiple-Choice Questions

Look at the answer choices before beginning each question so you'll know what you're looking for in the problem.

If the problem looks impossible and you're tempted to skip it, don't—at least at first. There's a lot of overlap in math—you may know enough arithmetic to help you figure out algebra problems or enough algebra to help you with geometry.

If you don't see your answer listed as one of the choices, it may be the same as one of the choices but written in a different mathematical form. Try changing the form of the answer.

Try working the problem backward, testing the choices to find the right one.

Simplify your task by using numbers in place of variables when you can do so quickly—they're easier to work with.

When checking your choices, use your calculator.

Student-Produced Response

Student-Produced Response (SPR) Questions (Grid-ins)

Another name for student-produced response questions is "grid-ins." These questions test the same skills as the multiple-choice questions; the difference is that you're not given possible solutions from which to choose. Instead, you have to come up with your own answer and enter it onto the answer sheet using a grid.

For grid-in questions, you will be instructed as follows:

Directions for Student-Produced Response Questions

Each of the remaining 10 questions requires you to solve the problem and enter your answer by marking the ovals in the special grid, as shown in the examples below.

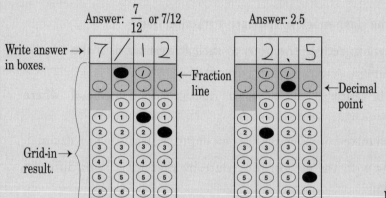

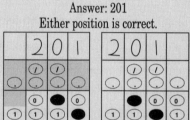

Note: You may start your answers in any column, space permitting. Columns not needed should be left blank.

- Mark no more than one oval in any column.
- Because the answer sheet will be machine-scored, **you will receive credit only if the ovals are filled in correctly.**
- Although not required, it is suggested that you write your answer in the boxes at the top of the columns to help you fill in the ovals accurately.
- Some problems may have more than one correct answer. In such cases, grid only one answer.
- No question has a negative answer.
- **Mixed numbers** such as $2\frac{1}{2}$ must be gridded as 2.5 or 5/2. (If $\boxed{2\ 1\ /\ 2}$ is gridded, it will be interpreted as $\frac{21}{2}$, not $2\frac{1}{2}$.)

- **Decimal Accuracy:** If you obtain a decimal answer, **enter the most accurate value the grid will accommodate.** For example, if you obtain an answer such as 0.6666 . . . , you should record the result as .666 or .667. **Less accurate values such as .66 or .67 are not acceptable.**

Acceptable ways to grid $\frac{2}{3}$ = .6666 . . .

How to Approach Student-Produced Response Questions

The most important point to keep in mind when working with grid-ins is to fill in the ovals! The handwritten answer at the top of the grid is not scored by the machine. If the ovals are left blank, the machine will treat the answer as if it were left blank and all your hard work will have been for naught.

Be sure to use the slash mark to indicate a fraction bar.

It is not necessary to reduce fractions to their lowest terms if the answer will fit in the grid.

Answers can be entered as either a fraction or a decimal where appropriate.

Be sure to enter a mixed number as either an improper fraction or a decimal.

Become familiar with the grid-in procedure by practicing with different types of answers.

If a grid-in question has more than one correct answer, you will get credit for any correct answer.

Arithmetic

Skill in arithmetic has been important ever since our Paleolithic ancestors first learned how to count cave bears. Today, skill in arithmetic will help you survive in a different, but no less important, way. It will help you to do well on the PSAT and the SAT, which will improve your chances of getting into the college of your choice. You will use arithmetic throughout your life, so study this section carefully to make sure you understand it and can apply its methods quickly.

These are the important elements of arithmetic that you need to know:

- Numbers and the properties of integers
- The number line
- Fundamental operations used in arithmetic
- Working with fractions
- Decimals
- Percentage
- Ratio and proportion
- Averages
- Word problems

Numbers

Numbers, like words, are symbols that represent something. Like language, numbers are a code that you can learn. Arithmetic is the branch of mathematics that deals with basic computations using real numbers.

Here is what you need to know about numbers for the PSAT.

Real Numbers

There are two categories of real numbers, rational and irrational.

Rational Numbers

These can all be written as fractions like

$$\frac{4}{9}, -3, 6\frac{1}{2}, \text{ or } \frac{-3}{8}.$$

Irrational Numbers

This kind of number cannot be written as a fraction. Numbers such as pi, the square root of 2, or the cube root of 9 are irrational.

Whole Numbers

These are natural numbers such as 1, which are obtained by repeatedly adding 1 to it. For example: 3, 99, and 271 are whole numbers.

Prime Numbers

A prime number is a whole number with exactly two whole number factors; namely itself and the number 1. (So the number 1 is not prime since it has exactly one factor.) Some examples of prime numbers are: 3, 5, 7, 11, 13, and 17.

Integers

These are whole numbers and may be positive, negative, or zero. These are the kind of numbers you will work with most on the PSAT.

Properties of Integers

- They do not include fractions or decimals.

- An integer that is divisible by 2 is an **even** number, like −4, −2, 0, 2, and 4.

- **Zero** is an even number.

- All other integers are **odd** numbers, like −3, −1, 1, and 3.

- Integers in sequence with a difference of 1 between them are **consecutive** integers.

The Number Line

The number line is a horizontal line that graphically represents the real number system. To construct a number line, choose a point to represent zero, called the **origin**, then make marks at equal intervals to the left, or negative direction, and the right, or positive direction. These marks represent whole numbers, the integers. Plot all the other real numbers between these integers. The number line extends indefinitely in both the positive and negative directions.

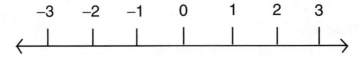

Signed Numbers

All numbers except zero have an algebraic sign. The sign is positive if the number is to the right of the origin on the number line and negative if the number is to the left of the origin. A number without a sign in front of it is assumed to be positive.

Absolute Value

The absolute value of a number is just the number itself with the sign removed. Absolute value is designated by two vertical bars, one before and one after the number. For instance, the absolute value of a number y is represented by: $|y|$. Another way to think of absolute value is as the magnitude or distance away from the origin irrespective of the direction. For example, the absolute value of -7 is:

$$|-7| = 7$$

Basic Operations in Arithmetic

There are four fundamental operations in arithmetic: addition, subtraction, multiplication, and division. There are also two important, and related, operations: exponentiation and finding roots of a number. The order in which these operations are performed is important, and you must work in the right order to get the correct answer.

Addition

Combines two numbers together to get one **total** or **sum.** The operation of addition is indicated by the "**+**" sign. For example:

$$\begin{array}{r} 2 \\ +3 \\ \hline 5 \end{array} \quad \text{or} \quad 2 + 3 = 5$$

186

Subtraction

Removes one number from another number. The result is the **difference**. The operation of subtraction is indicated by the "−" sign. For example:

$$\begin{array}{r} 3 \\ -1 \\ \hline 2 \end{array} \quad \text{or} \quad 3 - 1 = 2$$

Subtracting one number from another is the same thing as adding its opposite sign, as in: $x - y = x + (-y)$

Multiplication

Adds a number to itself the specified number of times. The result is the **product**. The operation of multiplication is indicated by the "×" or "•" sign. For example:

$$\begin{array}{r} 7 \\ \times 3 \\ \hline 21 \end{array} \quad \text{or} \quad 7 \bullet 3 = 21$$

Since multiplying 7×3 is the same as adding $7 + 7 + 7$, you can think of multiplication as abbreviated addition.

Division

Separates one number into another number of equal parts. The result is the **quotient**, which tells how many times one number can be multiplied by another. The operation of division is indicated by the "÷" or "/" sign. For example:

$$\frac{6}{2} = 3 \quad \text{or} \quad 6 \div 2 = 3$$

You can think of division as the reverse of multiplication. And remember, you cannot divide by zero.

Exponentiation

This is a special case of multiplication. In exponentiation, a number is multiplied by itself the number of times specified by the power of the exponent. For example, squaring a number $(x)^2$ is the same as multiplying the number by itself 2 times. Cubing a number $(x)^3$ is accomplished in the same way. For example:

$$5 \text{ cubed} = 5 \times 5 \times 5 = 5^3 = 125$$

Finding Roots

This is the reverse process of exponentiation. The root of a number is a number that, when multiplied by itself the root number of times, will yield the number under the radical sign. For example:

The cube root of $125 = \sqrt[3]{125} = 5$

Order of Operations (PEMDAS)

To solve an arithmetic problem on the PSAT, you may be asked to perform several different operations in sequence. To get the right answer, you need to perform the operations in the correct order, so memorize this acronym:

PEMDAS   It stands for <u>P</u>lease <u>E</u>xcuse <u>M</u>y <u>D</u>ear <u>A</u>unt <u>S</u>ally.

PEMDAS is an easy way to remember to perform arithmetic operations in this order: those inside <u>P</u>arentheses first, then <u>E</u>xponents, followed by <u>M</u>ultiplication and <u>D</u>ivision in order from left to right, then <u>A</u>ddition and <u>S</u>ubtraction in order from left to right.

Using Parentheses

One easy way to reduce careless mistakes and confusion in your thinking is to put parentheses around numbers that form groups of similar operations. For example:

$$\frac{(3 + (9 \times 4))}{12}$$

The parentheses in this example make it clear which operations to do in what order. First, the numbers in the inner set of parentheses, (9×4), followed by the $+3$ in the second set of parentheses, and finally, division by 12. The answer is: 3.25.

Fractions

Think of fractions as a different way to indicate division. For example, the fraction $\frac{4}{5}$ is another way of saying $4 \div 5$.

Adding and Subtracting Fractions

If the fractions have a common denominator, simply add the numerators together to get your answer. For example, what does the sum of $\frac{3}{7} + \frac{2}{7}$ equal?

$$\frac{3 + 2}{7} = \frac{5}{7}$$

If the denominators are not the same, you will need to find a common denominator before you can add or subtract. An easy way to do this is to multiply each fraction by 1, but in a different form. Remember, 1 can be expressed not only as 1 or $\frac{1}{1}$, but also as $\frac{5}{5}$, or $\frac{271}{271}$, and so forth. Any whole number divided by itself will always equal 1. For example:

$$\frac{1}{4} + \frac{1}{3} = ?$$

First, find the common denominator by multiplying by 1:

$$\frac{1}{4} \times \frac{3}{3} \quad \text{and} \quad \frac{1}{3} \times \frac{4}{4}$$

This gives you: $\frac{3}{12} + \frac{4}{12}$

Now, add the numerators together to get the answer: $\frac{7}{12}$

Multiplying Fractions

To perform this operation on fractions, multiply all the numerators together, then multiply all the denominators together. Put these products together in the same way, numerator over denominator, and you have the answer.

For example, find the product of $\frac{8}{5} \times \frac{3}{6} \times \frac{1}{2}$.

Multiply all the numerators together: $8 \times 3 \times 1 = 24$

Multiply all the denominators together: $5 \times 6 \times 2 = 60$

The answer is $\frac{24}{60}$, which can be simplified to $\frac{2}{5}$.

Simplifying Fractions

Simplifying a fraction to its simplest form will make your calculations easier, especially when you have a problem involving several steps. For instance, $\frac{2}{5}$ is much easier to work with than $\frac{24}{60}$.

189

Dividing Fractions

Divide one fraction into another by multiplying the reciprocal. To find the reciprocal fraction, put the numerator in the denominator and the denominator in the numerator. For example:

$$\frac{\frac{1}{4}}{\frac{3}{8}} = \left(\frac{1}{4}\right)\left(\frac{8}{3}\right) = \frac{8}{12} = \frac{2}{3}$$

Decimals

Decimals are a special case of fractions. You can represent any fraction as a decimal by dividing the numerator by the denominator. Working with decimals is easy when you use a calculator; but remember, always keep the decimal point lined up when you need to write them out.

Example

$$\frac{3}{4} = .75 \quad \text{or} \quad 4\overline{)3.00}$$

$$\begin{array}{r} .75 \\ 4\overline{)3.00} \\ 2.80 \\ \hline .20 \\ .20 \\ \hline .00 \end{array}$$

Decimal Equivalents

These decimal equivalents of fractions are so common that they should be memorized:

$$\frac{1}{4} = .25$$

$$\frac{1}{3} = .333...$$

$$\frac{1}{2} = .50$$

$$\frac{2}{3} = .666...$$

$$\frac{3}{4} = .75$$

$$\frac{1}{1} = 1.00$$

190

Percentages

Percentages, like decimals, are a special case of fractions. In a percentage, the denominator is always 100. The root, *cent*, actually means *100* (*cent*ury, *cent*ennial). The numerator is the number of parts per 100. For example:

$$5\% = \frac{5}{100} = 0.05$$

$$50\% = \frac{50}{100} = 0.50$$

In order to make sure you understand percentages, you may want to review fractions and decimals.

How to Represent Percents as Fractions

1. Remove the percent sign and write the number over 100.

2. Simplify.

Example: $40\% = \frac{40}{100} = \frac{4}{10} = \frac{2}{5}$

How to Represent Fractions as Percents

1. Divide the numerator by the denominator.

2. Move the decimal point two digits to the right, then add the percent sign.

Example: $\frac{40}{100} = 40 \div 100 = 0.40 = 40\%$

How to Represent Percents as Decimals

1. Remove the percent sign.

2. Move the decimal point two digits to the left.

Example: $40\% = .40$

How to Represent Decimals as Percents

1. Move the decimal point two digits to the right. (If there aren't enough digits to do this, add more zeros on the right.)

2. Remove the decimal point.

3. Attach the percent sign.

Example: $0.4 = 0.40 = 40. = 40\%$

Ratio and Proportion

These two concepts are closely related; here's how.

Ratio

A ratio is the quotient of one quantity divided by another, or one number compared to another. Let two quantities to be compared be called x and y. The ratio of x to y is:

$$\frac{x}{y} \quad \text{or} \quad x : y$$

For example: A city lot is 75 feet wide by 150 feet long. What is the ratio of its width to length?

The ratio is: $\quad \frac{75}{150} \quad$ or $\quad 75 : 150$

This simplifies to: $\frac{1}{2} \quad$ or $\quad 1 : 2$

Proportion

A proportion is just two ratios set equal to each other. For example:

$$\frac{4}{5} = \frac{80}{100}$$

The right-hand term is equal to the left-hand term in a proportion.

Proportions can often be used to solve for an unknown part of a ratio. You can use it to solve for an unknown length of a triangle, using the method of similar triangles. For example, the ratio of two sides of one triangle is known to be 2 : 1. The first side of a second triangle is known to be 10. What is the length of the second side of the second triangle? Sounds ugly, but if you create a proportion, it all falls into place:

$$\frac{2}{1} = \frac{10}{x}$$

You can solve this by cross-multiplying:

$$2x = 10$$

or

$$x = 5$$

Averages

Three numbers that are favorites of scientific investigators around the world are:

- Mean
- Median
- Mode

A favorite word of advertisers is *average*:

"People who use *Never Die* vitamins live an average of 27 years longer."

Now the mean, median, and mode are technically all **averages**. However, what is usually meant by the word "average" is the *arithmetic mean*, or just the *mean*.

Mean

This is the sum of a group of numbers divided by the number of numbers. It has the general form:

$$\frac{a + b + c}{n}$$

Where a, b, and c represent measured quantities and n is the number of measurements.

Example

In a zoo there are 4 cages, each holding several tigers, as follows:

Cage A holds 5 tigers

Cage B holds 3 tigers

Cage C holds 6 tigers

Cage D holds 5 tigers

Cage E holds 6 tigers

What is the average number of tigers per cage?

Let x = the average number of tigers per cage

Number of tigers is 25 (5 + 3 + 6 + 5 + 6)

Number of cages is 5

$$x = \frac{25}{5} = 5$$

This means there is an **average** of 5 tigers per cage.

Median

The median is the middle number of a group of numbers when the data is arranged in order from least to greatest:

   3, 5, <u>5</u>, 6, 6   (The median is 5.)

If there are an even number of numbers, the median is the average of the two middle numbers:

   3, <u>5</u>, <u>5</u>, 6   (The median is 5, because the average of 5 + 5 = 10, and 10 divided by 2 = 5.)

   3, <u>5</u>, <u>6</u>, 6   (The median is 5.5, because the average of 5 + 6 = 11, and 11 divided by 2 = 5.5.)

Mode

The mode is the number that appears most often in the group:

   <u>5</u>, 3, <u>5</u>, 6   (The mode is 5.)

If more than one number appears an equal number of times, the result is **bimodal**:

   <u>5</u>, 3, <u>6</u>, <u>5</u>, <u>6</u>   (The modes are 5 and 6.)

Word Problems

A word problem can be looked at as a little story told with numbers or variables (that is, a letter that represents an unknown number). At the end of the story, you are asked a question.

Example

Jochim spent $17 at the food court in the mall on Saturday, whereas Milton (who had four extra orders of fries) spent $23. How much more did Milton spend at the food court than Jochim?

Word problems are found in all types of math, from arithmetic to algebra to geometry.

To approach word problems, take the following steps:

1. Read in small segments, rather than trying to make sense of the whole problem at once. <u>Underline</u> each important segment—this will help you separate the math problem from the story.

    <u>Jochim spent $17</u> at the Food Court in the Mall on Saturday, whereas <u>Milton</u> (who had four extra orders of fries) <u>spent $23</u>. How much more did Milton spend at the Food Court than Jochim?

    (A) $6
    (B) $15
    (C) $23
    (D) $30
    (E) $40

The correct answer is (A). $23 − $17 = $6.

2. If the problem is a complex one, you might want to **circle the question**, just to help you keep in mind what you're looking for.

3. For multiple-choice questions, **look over the answers** before you begin working the problem. Work in fractions if the answer is in fractions, and in decimals if the answer choices are in decimals.

4. DON'T fall for the most obvious answer choice—**work the problem**, even if you're sure what the outcome will be. In the above example, you're not likely to get confused, but if the problem were larger and more complex, you MIGHT, in haste, choose the *sum* of the numbers, choice (E), rather than the *difference* between them. Test-writers love to include answers that seem right but aren't.

5. **Check your answer.** Again, it could match one of the choices but still be wrong.

Practice Exercises

1. 2% =

   (A) 2.0
   (B) 0.2
   (C) 0.02
   (D) 0.002

2. 2.0 =

   (A) 0.20%
   (B) 2.0%
   (C) 20.0%
   (D) 200%

3. $\dfrac{1}{4}$ =

   (A) 25%
   (B) 0.25%
   (C) 0.025%
   (D) 0.0025%

4. $0.65 \times 0.42 =$

5. What is four and five hundredths written as a decimal?

6. $4\dfrac{1}{3} + 3\dfrac{1}{3} =$

7. $\dfrac{5}{12} - \dfrac{3}{8} =$

8. $30 \div 2\dfrac{1}{2} =$

9. $\dfrac{3}{7} \times \dfrac{7}{3} =$

10. $4 \times \dfrac{1}{3} =$

Explanatory Answers

1. **The correct answer is (C).** Move the decimal two places to the left and take away the % sign—0.02.

2. **The correct answer is (D).** Move the decimal two places to the right and add the percent sign—200%

3. **The correct answer is (A).** $\frac{1}{4} = 0.25 = 25\%$. It helps to have memorized the fractional equivalents to decimals here.

4. 0.273

5. $4 + \frac{5}{100} = 4.05$

6. $4 + 3 + \left(\frac{1}{3} + \frac{1}{3}\right) = 7\frac{2}{3}$

7. $\frac{5}{12} - \frac{3}{8} = \frac{10}{24} - \frac{9}{24} = \frac{1}{24}$

8. $30 \div 2\frac{1}{2} = \frac{30}{2.5} = 12$

9. $\frac{3}{7} \times \frac{7}{3} = [(3)(7)] \div [(7)(3)] = \frac{21}{21} = 1$

10. $4 \times \frac{1}{3} = (4)(1) \div 3 = \frac{4}{3}$

Algebra

Algebra is the second leg of the tripod of basic math knowledge you will need to do well on the PSAT. Remember, algebra is really just a generalization of the principles of arithmetic, except, in algebra, you must manipulate both numbers and letters, called variables, to get the answer. If you have reviewed the arithmetic section carefully, you are ready to begin working with algebraic concepts now.

To be well prepared for the PSAT, you should have a solid grasp of these fundamental elements of algebra:

- Basic operations with signed numbers
- Factoring
- Simplifying algebraic expressions
- Solving algebraic equations and inequalities
- Substitution
- Simple quadratic equations
- Exponents and roots
- Word problems

Do you know these important algebraic terms?

Variable	A letter used to represent numbers or groups of numbers, x or y, for example.
Factor	Numbers or letters that form a product when multiplied together. For instance, 3 and 2 are factors of 6.
Coefficient	Often refers to the number in an algebraic expression, but can be any factor of the term. In the expression $7x^2$, 7 is the coefficient.
Equation	Is used to indicate that two expressions are equal. $9y = 27$, for example, is an equation that is true only when $y = 3$.
Root	A number that makes an equation true. The number 1 is the root of the equation $17x - 12x = 5$, because $5x = 5$, which means $x = 1$.
Exponent	Tells how many times a number, or variable, is multiplied by itself (used as a factor). Exponents are indicated by a small superscript to the right of the number, or variable.
Polynomial	An expression that contains several algebraic terms. For example, a monomial has one term, a binomial has two terms, and a trinomial has three terms.

Basic Operations with Signed Numbers

In algebra, we work with variables, which are letters that represent numbers, or groups of numbers. Signed numbers, you will recall, are numbers with a positive sign or a negative sign. If the number is positive, the (+) sign is usually omitted. When working with signed numbers, we can use the same basic operations in algebra that we use in arithmetic.

Addition

The distributive law is useful when adding and subtracting algebraic expressions. The distributive law says:

> For addition: $ab + ac = a(b + c)$

When you see a term such as $3x + 3y$, you can use the distributive law to change the form of the expression to $3(x + y)$.

> For subtraction: $ab - ac = a(b - c)$

Thus, a term like $4x - 4z$, becomes $4(x - z)$ using the distributive law.

Adding polynomials

If you want to add two polynomials, arrange the terms in vertical columns with like terms over one another. For instance, to add $x^2 + 9x - 2$ and $4x^2 - 4x + 5$, proceed as follows:

$$\begin{array}{r} x^2 + 9x - 2 \\ + \ 4x^2 - 4x + 5 \\ \hline 5x^2 + 5x + 3 \end{array}$$

Subtracting polynomials

If you want to subtract two polynomials, arrange the terms in vertical columns with like terms over one another. Now, change the sign of all terms in the lower polynomial and add. For example, to subtract $5x^2 + 7x - 3$ from $8x^2 - 15x + 10$, proceed as follows:

$$\begin{array}{r} 8x^2 - 15x + 10 \\ + \ -5x^2 - \ 7x + 3 \\ \hline 3x^2 - 22x + 13 \end{array}$$

Multiplication

How you multiply algebraic expressions depends on whether they are monomials, binomials, or polynomials.

Multiplication of Monomials

If you want to multiply a monomial by a monomial, first multiply the coefficients together, then add the exponents of variables with the same base. For instance:

$$(2x^3)(7x^4) = 14x^7$$

To multiply a monomial by a polynomial, multiply each term in the polynomial by the monomial. Do you recognize the distributive law at work here? Here's an example:

$$3x(5x - 2x + 1) = (3x)(5x) - (3x)(2x) + (3x)(1)$$
$$= 15x^2 - 6x^2 + 3x$$
$$= 9x^2 + 3x$$

Multiplication of Binomials

Binomials have an important use in factoring. To multiply two binomials together, apply the distributive law as follows:

$$(a + b)(c + d) = a(c + d) + b(c + d)$$
$$= ac + ad + bc + bd$$

For example, what is the result of multiplying $(x + 3)$ and $(x - 4)$?

$$(x + 3)(x - 4) = (x)(x) + (x)(-4) + (3)(x) + (3)(-4)$$
$$= x^2 + (-4x + 3x) + (-12)$$
$$= x^2 - x - 12$$

Multiplication of Polynomials

To multiply one polynomial by another, multiply each term of one polynomial by each term of the other. As in the example above, you want to extend the method used for binomials to polynomials, using the distributive law:

$$(a + b + c)(d + e + f) = a(d + e + f) + b(d + e + f) + c(d + e + f)$$

Division

How you divide algebraic expressions depends, again, on whether they are monomials, binomials, or polynomials.

Division of Monomials

In order to divide one monomial by another, divide the coefficients, then subtract the exponents of variables with the same base. For example:

$$6x^3 \div 3x^2 = \left(\frac{6}{3}\right)(x^{3-2}) = 2x$$

Division of Polynomials

Division of one polynomial by another polynomial is done by dividing each term of one by each term of the other, according to the distributive law as follows:

$$\frac{a + b + c}{(d + e + f)} = \frac{a}{(d + e + f)} + \frac{b}{(d + e + f)} + \frac{c}{(d + e + f)}$$

Remember, you won't be expected to make long, tedious calculations on the PSAT. When you encounter a problem that appears to require you to do this, look for an obvious shortcut. Is the calculation really necessary to get the answer? Can you divide common terms?

Factoring

To factor an expression means to find other expressions that, when multiplied together, will yield the original expression. You are likely to see these kinds of factors on the PSAT.

Prime Factors

The prime factors of an expression are itself and 1.

Common Factors

An expression has common factors if it has a monomial that can be divided into it to get a second factor. For example, 3 and 4 are factors of 12, or $(x + 3)$ and x are factors of $x^2 + 3x$.

Difference of Two Squares

Factor polynomials that are the difference of two perfect squares by finding the square root of each term. One factor is the sum of each square root. The other factor is the difference of each square root. For example, the factors of $x^2 - 9$ are:

$$x^2 - 9 = (x + 3)(x - 3)$$

Simple Quadratics

These are trinomials in the form of $ax^2 + bx + c$, and their factors are two binomials. For instance, the factors of $x^2 + x - 6$ are:

$$(x + 3)(x - 2)$$

If a trinomial can be factored, it will meet this test:

$$b^2 - 4ac = \text{perfect square}$$

Simplyfing Algebraic Expressions

Often, math questions on the PSAT will have expressions that look complicated and difficult to solve. But, if you look closely, you will usually find that these expressions can be simplified to something much easier. These are some important ways to simplify algebraic expressions:

Combine Terms

If an algebraic expression has several terms of the same degree, you can combine them into one term. For instance, if you see $x^2 + 3x - 4x^2$, combine both of the second-degree terms. This simplifies the expression to $3x - 3x^2$.

Divide Terms

An expression like $\left(\dfrac{(28x^2)(48y)}{(48y)(14x)} \right)$ may look difficult at first glance, but notice that $48y$ appears in both the numerator and the denominator. These terms divide out because $\dfrac{48y}{48y} = 1$. This simplifies the expression to $\dfrac{28x^2}{14x}$, which can be further simplified to $2x$. The expression wasn't so difficult after all.

Reduce to Simplest Form

Often, algebraic expressions will be in a form that can be further simplified. You will want to reduce expressions to their simplest form in many cases, because it will simplify and speed up your work.

As an example, take the expression:

$$\left(\frac{108x^{13}}{12x^{12}}\right) - \left(\frac{72x^8}{18x^7}\right).$$

It can be simplified to:

$$\left(\frac{(9)(12)x^{13}}{12x^{12}}\right) - \left(\frac{(4)(18)x^8}{18x^7}\right) = \left(\frac{9x^{13}}{x^{12}}\right) - \left(\frac{4x^8}{x^7}\right)$$

Which can be further simplified to: $9x - 4x = 5x$

Change the Form of the Expression

Sometimes you may want to change the form of an expression to work with it or recognize it as a correct answer. For instance, $32t + 3y$ is the same as $3y + 32t$, and $\frac{3x}{6x}$ is the same as $\frac{1}{2}$. Be alert to the possibility that you may need to change the form of the expression if you don't see your answer listed as a choice.

Factor the Expression

Our old friend the factor is one of the most important ways to simplify some algebraic expressions. PSAT questions will often have factors in both the numerator and denominator that divide out and make the resulting simplified expression the correct answer. Consider this expression:

$$\frac{x^2 - x - 2}{x^2 - 3x + 2} = \frac{(x + 1)(x - 2)}{(x - 1)(x - 2)} = \frac{(x + 1)}{(x - 1)}$$

Solving Algebraic Equations and Inequalities

An algebraic equation is created by setting two expressions equal to each other. An equation has three parts: a left-hand side, an equal sign, and a right-hand side.

Similarly, an inequality is created by setting one expression greater than the other. An inequality also has three parts: a left-hand side, an inequality sign, and a right-hand side.

These are some important definitions and properties of equations:

Root	An equation's root is the number that makes the equation equal. The root of the equation $3x = 24$ is 8, because when $x = 8$, $3x = (3)(8) = 24$. Some equations (i.e., quadratic equations) have more than one root. If so, these multiple roots are sometimes called the *solution set.*
Identity	An equation that is true for all values of the unknown is called an identity. This equation is an identity: $x^2 + x - 6 = (x - 2)(x + 3)$.
Number of unknowns	Equations are categorized by the number of unknowns (variables) they have. $D = RT$ is an equation with three unknowns, whereas $4x + 5y - 12 = 0$ has only two unknowns.
Conditional equations	If an equation is true only for certain values of an unknown, it is called a conditional equation. For instance, $x^2 - 6 = 10$ is true only when $x^2 = 16$, or when $x = +4$, and $x = -4$.
Degree	An equation's degree is the same as its greatest degree term. For instance, $y = mx + b$ is a first-degree equation (mx^1), and $y = ax^2 + bx + c$ is a second-degree equation (ax^2).

Solving Equations

The process of finding an equation's root, or roots, is called solving. Solving equations usually involves manipulating one, or both, of its sides until it is in a form that can be solved. On the PSAT, most of the equations will be linear (first-degree) equations. Here are some useful ways to solve an equation:

Mathematical Operations

This is one of the most useful ways to manipulate the equation into the form you want. There are two important points to keep in mind, however:

First, you must perform the mathematical operation on **both sides** or the equality will not be served. For example, consider:

$$2x = 10$$

In order to solve the equation (find its root), we divide **both sides** by 2:

$$\frac{2x}{2} = \frac{10}{2}$$

This gives us the solution: $x = 5$

Second, you must perform the operation on each side **as a whole**, not term by term. For example:

$$\frac{1}{y} = \frac{1}{5} + \frac{1}{3}$$

To solve this one, take the reciprocal of the equation **as a whole**:

$$y = \frac{1}{\frac{1}{5} + \frac{1}{3}} = \frac{1}{\frac{8}{15}} = \frac{15}{8}$$

If you were to incorrectly solve this by taking the reciprocal of each individual term, you would get $y = 8$ for your answer. Wrong. But, if this were a question on the PSAT, 8 would probably be one of the answer choices.

Transposing

Another very useful method for solving equations is called transposing. Transposing is moving a term from one side of the equation to the other. This is done by **subtracting** it from **both sides** (to preserve the equality). This removes the term from its original location and places it on the opposite side with an opposite sign. For example:

$$x + 3 = 15$$
$$x + 3 - 3 = 15 - 3$$
$$x = 12$$

Do you know what these symbols mean?

Less than:	$<$	The left-hand side is less than the right-hand side.
Less than or equal to:	$\leq$	The left-hand side is less than or equal to the right-hand side.
Greater than:	$>$	The left-hand side is greater than the right-hand side.
Greater than or equal to:	$\geq$	The left-hand side is greater than or equal to the right-hand side.

Solving Inequalities

In general, you can solve inequalities using the same methods as those used to solve equalities. However, there is an important point you need to remember when working with inequalities:

Direction of the Inequality

The direction of the inequality is reversed when you multiply or divide both sides by a negative number. For example:

$$3 < 7 \quad \text{but} \quad (-1)(3) > (-1)(7)$$
$$-3 > -7$$

Similarly, if:

$$x > 0 \quad \text{then} \quad -x < 0$$

or

$$x < 0 \quad \text{then} \quad -x > 0$$

Substitution

When working with more than one equation, you may want to use a handy technique called substitution to solve the problem. Substitution, or plugging-in, is often useful when you have two equations with two unknowns. First, solve one equation for one of the two unknowns. Second, plug this solved equation into the first by replacing the unknown with the solved equation. Let's try an example.

What is the value of x, given:

$$7x - 5y + 11 = 0 \text{ and } 3y - 13 = 23$$

First, solve for y in the second equation.

$$3y = 23 + 13 = 36$$
$$y = \frac{36}{3}$$
$$y = 12$$

Second, substitute 12 for y in the first equation and solve for x.

$$7x - 5y + 11 = 0$$
$$7x - (5)(12) + 11 = 0$$
$$7x - 60 + 11 = 0$$
$$7x - 49 = 0$$
$$7x = 49$$
$$x = \frac{49}{7}$$
$$x = 7$$

Simple Quadratic Equations

A quadratic equation is a second-degree polynomial equation whose general form is:

$$ax^2 + bx + c = 0$$

You won't need to use the quadratic formula to solve problems on the PSAT. In a simple quadratic equation, you should get two answers. Most of the time, working with quadratic equations will involve factoring. For example:

$$x^2 - 4x - 21 = 0$$

We want to find factors with the general form:

$$ac + ad + bc + bd = (a + b)(c + d)$$

In this case, we are looking for factors of 21 whose sum is -4.

The factors of 21 are: 1, 3, 7, 21

Of these factors, the only possible combinations are 7 and 3.

Now, plug them into the general form:

$$(a + b)(c + d)$$

And find the combination that works:

$$(x + 3)(x - 7)$$

The two answers are:

$$x = -3 \text{ and } x = 7$$

Exponents and Roots

Complex calculations or manipulations of exponents or roots are not found in PSAT problems. Neither are exponents that are not whole numbers. These are the important things you should know about exponents and roots.

Exponents

How you manipulate exponents depends upon whether you are multiplying, dividing, or raising one power by another power.

Multiplying Expressions

When you are multiplying algebraic expressions with the same base, **add** the exponents:

$$(x^2)(x^5) = x^{2 + 5} = x^7$$

Dividing Expressions

When you are dividing algebraic expressions with the same base, **subtract** the exponents:

$$\frac{x^6}{x^2} = x^{6 - 2} = x^4$$

Raising One Power by Another Power

When an algebraic expression of one power is raised to another power, **multiply** the exponents:

$$(x^4)^3 = x^{4 \times 3} = x^{12}$$

Roots

The root of a number is another number, a factor, that when multiplied by itself the root number of times, becomes the original number. For instance, a square root of 4 is 2 because when 2 is multiplied by itself the root number of times (twice for a square root), the product is 4, the original number. Stated algebraically, this is: $\sqrt{4} = 2$ because $2^2 = 2 \times 2 = 4$. Another square root of 4 is -2 because $(-2)(-2) = 4$ also.

Do you know these important parts of a root?

Radical

A radical specifies a root of an expression or number, $\sqrt[y]{x}$.

Index

The index of a root is written as a small number over the radical sign. It specifies how many equal factors the radical represents. The most common indexes are 2, the square root, and 3, the cube root. By convention, a radical sign without an index is taken to mean a square root, $\sqrt{}$.

Here are some examples:

$$\sqrt[2]{x}$$

The index 2 means take the square root of x, but the 2 is usually omitted.

$$\sqrt[3]{x}$$

An index of 3 means take the cube root of x.

$$\sqrt[4]{x}$$

An index of 4 means take the fourth root of x.

Working with Radicals

Just like exponents, how you handle radicals depends on whether you are adding, subtracting, multiplying, or dividing.

Addition and Subtraction of Radicals

Combine all like radicals. For example:

$$3\sqrt{3} + 7\sqrt{3} = 10\sqrt{3}$$

or

$$7\sqrt{7} - 4\sqrt{7} = 3\sqrt{7}$$

Unlike radicals must be rewritten, then combined. For example:

$$\sqrt{45} + \sqrt{20} = \sqrt{(9)(5)} + \sqrt{(4)(5)}$$
$$= 3\sqrt{5} + 2\sqrt{5}$$
$$= 5\sqrt{5}$$

Multiplication of Radicals

The product of the roots of two algebraic expressions equals the root of the product of the two expressions. For example:

$$(\sqrt{18})(\sqrt{2}) = \sqrt{(18)(2)} = \sqrt{36} = 6 \text{ and } -6$$

or

$$(3\sqrt{24})(5\sqrt{6}) = (3)(5)\sqrt{(24)(6)}$$
$$= 15\sqrt{144}$$
$$= (15)(12)$$
$$= 180$$

Division of Radicals

The quotient of the roots of two algebraic expressions equals the root of the quotient of the two expressions. For example:

$$\frac{\sqrt{48}}{\sqrt{3}} = \sqrt{\frac{48}{3}} = \sqrt{16} = 4 \text{ and } -4$$

or

$$\frac{100\sqrt{200}}{4\sqrt{50}} = \frac{100}{4}\sqrt{\frac{200}{50}} = 25\sqrt{4} = 50 \text{ and } -50$$

Word Problems

As is the case with arithmetic, word problems in algebra tell a little story, this time requiring you to translate the words into algebraic expressions. Word problems test not only your math skills, but also your ability to reason. When working with word problems, proceed systematically as follows:

- Read carefully to be sure you understand the problem.

- Understand what you are being asked to solve for.

- Figure out what information you are given.

- Figure out what information you need.

- Decide how to solve the problem.

- Solve the problem.

- Check your answer to make sure it answers the question.

If you become familiar with the key words and phrases used in word problems, they will be much easier to solve. It's a good idea to memorize these words along with their algebraic translations because they are used often on the PSAT:

The Words	The Translation	Example
Is, has, was	=	Jill **is** three years older.
Sum of, greater than, more than, further than	+	A town is 5 miles **further than**
Difference, less than, fewer, younger than	−	The cost is $1.75 **less than**
Of what number?	%	20 is $\frac{1}{5}$ **of** what number?
$\frac{2}{3}$ of a tank of gas	×	The car used $\frac{2}{3}$ **of** a tank of gas.
Per, for hour	÷	Hiking at 3 miles **per** hour
shoes sold **for** every hat	ratio	3 pair of shoes **for**

Sample Word Problem

48 is 80 percent of what number?

- Read the problem carefully.

- You are being asked to find a number; let's call it x. We want to solve for x.

- We are given two pieces of information: 48 and what it represents, 80% of x.

- We have enough information to solve the problem once we translate it into algebra.

  The translation is: $48 = 80\%$ of x

  $$48 = .80x$$

- Solve the problem: $x = \dfrac{48}{.80}$ or $x = 60$

- Check your answer: 60 makes sense, answers the question, and checks $(.80)(60) = 48$.

Practice Exercises

1. $5n + 25 = 65$

   Solve for n.

2. The sum of a number and its double is 51. What is the number?

3. Which value of x will make this number sentence true? $x + 30 \leq 14$

   (A) 13
   (B) 11
   (C) -15
   (D) -22

4. Which of the following are three consecutive even integers whose sum is 36?

   (A) 7, 9, 11
   (B) 8, 10, 12
   (C) 9, 11, 13
   (D) 10, 12, 14

5. What values of x will make the following inequality true?
   $3x - 12 \leq 3$

6. Simplify: $\dfrac{(x^2 - 4)}{(x + 2)}$

7. Which of the following is equivalent to $x^2 + 4x$?

   (A) $x(x + 4)$
   (B) $2(x + 4)$
   (C) $(x + 4)^2$
   (D) $(x + 1)(x + 4)$

8. What is the equivalent of $4x(3xy + y)$?

9. What is equivalent to $(2y^2 + 2)$?

10. An equation of the form $\dfrac{a}{b} = \dfrac{c}{d}$ is a(n)

    (A) inequality.
    (B) constant.
    (C) proportion.
    (D) monomial.

Explanatory Answers

1. $5n = 65 - 25 = 40$

   $n = \dfrac{40}{5}$

   $n = 8$

2. $n + 2n = 51$

   $\quad 3n = 51$

   $\quad\ \ n = 17$

3. The correct answer is **(D)**.

   $x + 30 \leq 14$

   $\quad x \leq 14 - 30$

   $\quad x \leq -16$

4. The correct answer is **(D)**. This is the only choice that is true.

5. $3x - 12 \leq 3$

   $\quad 3x \leq 3 + 12$

   $\quad 3x \leq 15$

   $\quad\ \ x \leq 5$

6. $(x^2 - 4) = (x + 2)(x - 2)$

   So, $\dfrac{(x + 2)(x - 2)}{(x + 2)} = (x - 2)$

7. The correct answer is **(A)**. An x can be factored out and the expression restated as $x\,(x + 4)$.

8. $12x^2y + 4xy$

9. $2(y^2 + 1)$

10. The correct answer is **(C)**. This is an example of a proportion, which is two ratios set equal to each other.

Geometry

Study this geometry review carefully and it will improve your ability to recognize the properties of geometric figures and to use this knowledge to solve many of the PSAT math problems. Although much of this material will be review, take the time to be sure you understand it well. The time you invest now will pay off later.

These are the basic concepts in geometry you will need to know:

- Points, lines, planes, and angles
- Special angles, special lines, and their properties
- Triangles, such as right, equilateral, and isosceles
- Special triangles and their properties
- Circles and their properties
- Other polygons and their properties
- Volume and surface area of solids
- Basic coordinate geometry

Points, Lines, Planes, and Angles

Points, lines, planes, and angles are the basic elements in geometry. Most geometric figures are constructed out of these building materials. Understanding these basic elements and how they fit together to form more complicated geometric figures is the key to correctly solving the geometry problems on the PSAT.

Point

A point specifies location and nothing else. It has no size. A point is most often represented as a dot and labeled with an upper case letter.

• B

On a graph, the location of a point is given by a set of coordinates; (3,8), for example.

Line

A line is a set of consecutive points that extend infinitely in two directions. A line can be represented as a lowercase letter at one end of the line or by naming two points on the line.

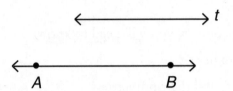

Plane

A plane exists in two dimensions. It has infinite length and infinite width but no thickness. A plane is typically represented graphically as a four-sided figure and labeled with an uppercase letter in one corner.

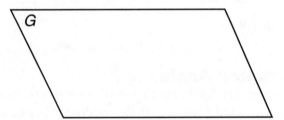

Angle

Two lines that meet at a point form an angle. Each line is called a side of the angle, and the point at which they meet is called the vertex of the angle. The ∠ symbol is used to designate an angle.

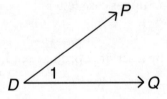

The angle shown above can be labeled in several ways:

- By a number, as in ∠1

- By a letter indicating the vertex, as in ∠D

- By the use of three letters, such as ∠PDQ (The second letter has to list the vertex.)

Important Terms

These important terms are often used when describing points, lines, planes, and angles:

Ray

A line extending from a point to infinity, in one direction only, is called a ray.

Line segment

A line segment is that part of a line that lies between two endpoints. In the example below, $\overline{AB}$ designates this line segment:

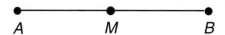

Collinear

Points that are on the same line are called collinear. In the preceding diagram, points A, M, and B are collinear.

Midpoint

The midpoint is the point that is equidistant from each endpoint and thus divides a line segment into two smaller line segments, each having the same length.

In the preceding diagram, point M is the midpoint.

Congruent

Line segments that have the same length are congruent. Congruent line segments are marked alike. In the example under "Bisect" below, PQ and QR are congruent.

Bisect

If a line intersects another line in such a way as to divide it into two equal, or congruent, line segments, the line is said to bisect it. In the example below, $\overline{AB}$ bisects $\overline{PR}$.

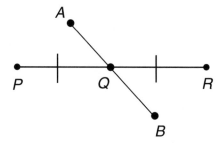

Coplanar

Points that are on the same plane are coplanar. In the example below, points *C* and *D* are coplanar because they are both on plane *G*.

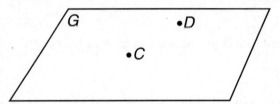

Degree

An angle's size is determined by measuring how far apart its two sides are. The unit of measurement for an angle is the degree (°).

If an angle is small, it has only a few degrees. If an angle is large, it has many degrees.

Congruence

Angles that have the same degree measure are called congruent and are marked alike. The ≅ symbol indicates that two angles are congruent.

Special Angles

There are several types of special angles you need to be familiar with:

Straight angle

This angle is a straight line. Its angle measure is 180°.

Right angle

This angle forms a square corner and is the result of the intersection of two perpendicular lines. The little square in the corner of the angle designates a right angle, which is 90°.

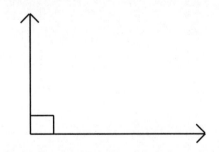

Acute angle

An acute angle is one with an angle measure of less than 90°.

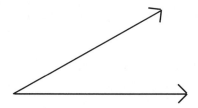

Obtuse angle

An obtuse angle is one with an angle measure of more than 90° and less than 180°.

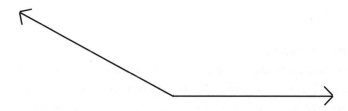

Special Angle Pairs

Also, there are three types of special angle pairs you should know:

Vertical angles

When two lines cross, they form two pairs of vertical angles. Vertical angles are congruent to each other. In the example below, $\angle A$ and $\angle C$ is one vertical angle pair and $\angle B$ and $\angle D$ is the second vertical angle pair. This means $\angle A \cong \angle C$ and $\angle B \cong \angle D$.

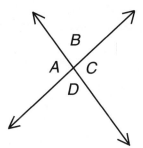

Complementary angles

Two angles are complementary if the sum of their measure is 90°. In the example below, m∠*BAC* + m∠*CAD* = 90°, which makes them complementary angles. The two angles need not be adjacent to each other to be complementary.

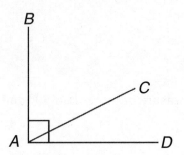

Supplementary angles

Two angles are supplementary if the sum of their measure is 180°. In the example below, m∠*QPR* + m∠*RPS* = 180°, making them supplementary angles. The two angles need not be adjacent to each other to be supplementary.

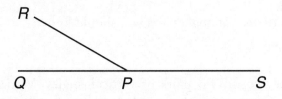

220

Special Lines

There are two very important types of special lines: perpendicular lines and parallel lines. Learn how to recognize them quickly and work with them easily.

Perpendicular lines

Two lines that cross at right angles are perpendicular. They form four right angles. Perpendicular lines are indicated with this symbol: $\perp$. In the diagram below, $\overline{CD} \perp \overline{AB}$. Only one right angle symbol is needed to mark the lines as perpendicular.

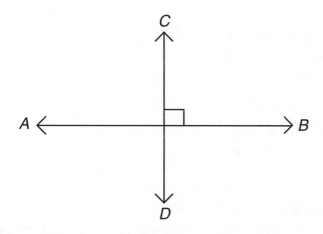

Parallel lines

Two lines in the same plane that never intersect are parallel. Parallel lines are indicated with this symbol: $\parallel$. In the following diagram, two parallel lines, m and n are intersected by transversal, t. A transversal is a line that intersects two lines.

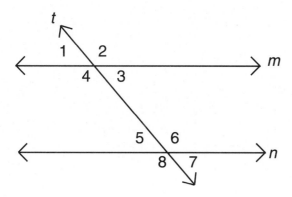

Parallel line-angle Relationships

The intersection of two parallel lines with a transversal creates a group of angles with relationships that are important for you to know. These relationships are as follows:

Alternate interior angles

Alternate interior angles are congruent. In the diagram below, the alternate interior angles are: $\angle 3 \cong \angle 5$ and $\angle 4 \cong \angle 6$.

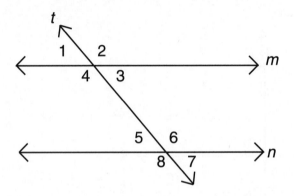

Corresponding angles

Corresponding angles are congruent. In the diagram, the corresponding angles are: $\angle 1 \cong \angle 5$, $\angle 2 \cong \angle 6$, $\angle 3 \cong \angle 7$, $\angle 4 \cong \angle 8$.

Interior angles

Interior angles that lie on the same side of a transversal are supplementary. In the diagram, the supplementary interior angles, which add up to 180°, are: $\angle 3$ and $\angle 6$, as well as $\angle 4$ and $\angle 5$.

Triangles

A triangle is a three-sided polygon. When three points that don't lie on the same line are connected by line segments, a triangle is formed. The Δ symbol is used to indicate a triangle. In the figure below, ΔABC lies in plane G.

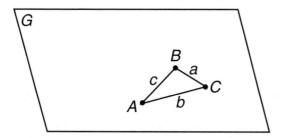

The usual way to designate the side of a triangle is to:

- Name the line segment that forms it, such as $\overline{AB}$.

- Label it as a lowercase letter that matches the angle opposite the side; for example, side *a* would be opposite ∠A.

The usual way to designate an angle of a triangle is to:

- Name the three letters of the angle that form it, such as ∠BAC. (The vertex is always listed second. Here, the vertex is A: ∠BAC.)

- Name the letter of the angle at the vertex, such as ∠A.

An essential property of triangles is: the sum of their angle measure equals 180°, or m∠1 + m∠2 + m∠3 = 180°. If you know or can figure out the measure of two of the angles, all you need to do to find the measure of the third angle is subtract their measure from 180°. Consider the following example:

If m∠2 = 30° and m∠3 = 85°, what is the measure of ∠1?

$$m\angle 1 = 180° - m\angle 2 - m\angle 3$$
$$= 180° - 30° - 85°$$
$$= 180° - 115°$$
$$m\angle 1 = 65°$$

223

Area of a Triangle

To find the area (A) of a triangle, multiply $\frac{1}{2}$ the base (b) times the height (h) of the triangle.

$$\text{Area} = \frac{1}{2}(\text{base} \times \text{height}) \qquad \text{or} \qquad A = \frac{1}{2}bh$$

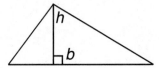

For example, what is the area of a triangle with base 10 and height 5?

$$A = bh = \frac{1}{2}(10)(5) = 25$$

Types of Triangles

The following are four main types of triangles.

Scalene Triangle

Has no congruent sides or angles.

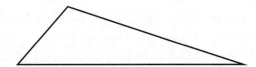

Isosceles Triangle

Has at least two congruent angles, called base angles, and a vertex angle. Has two congruent sides that are opposite the congruent angles.

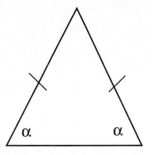

224

Equilateral Triangle

Has three congruent sides and three congruent angles, each 60°. This type of triangle is also isosceles.

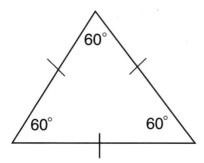

Right Triangle

Has one right angle measuring 90°. The side opposite this angle is the hypotenuse, which is the longest side of the triangle. A right triangle can also be scalene or isosceles.

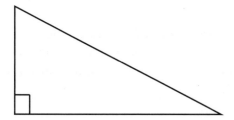

Special Triangles—The Right Triangle

The right triangle is a special case. It has so many useful properties that it deserves a section of its own. Much of the branch of mathematics called trigonometry is based on the properties of the right triangle and the circle. For the PSAT, you won't need to know trigonometry, but you will need to know about the Pythagorean Theorem and three important special types of right triangles. If you memorize the information in this section, you will be able to work faster and more accurately on the PSAT math questions.

Pythagorean Theorem

This theorem says: *the square of the hypotenuse of a right triangle is equal to the sum of the squares of the legs.* Stated algebraically, the Pythagorean Theorem is: $c^2 = a^2 + b^2$. If you haven't memorized the Pythagorean Theorem already, now would be a good time to do so because you will use it all the time.

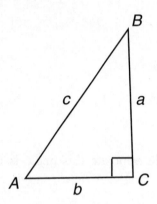

3-4-5 Right Triangle

True to its name, the lengths of the sides of a 3-4-5 right triangle are 3, 4, and 5, or some multiple (x) of these numbers. The 5 side will always be opposite the 90° angle. The diagram below shows the relationships of the sides.

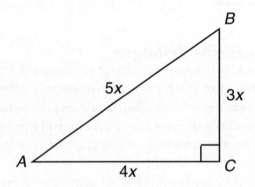

45°-45°-90° Right Triangle

This type of right triangle is also called an isosceles right triangle. Both of the base angles are 45°, and the vertex angle is 90°. The following diagram of a 45°-45°-90° right triangle shows the relationships of the sides to the angles. If you know or can figure out one side of this triangle, it is easy to find the other two sides because each side is a multiple of *x*.

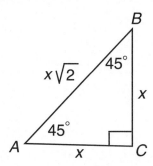

30°-60°-90° Right Triangle

This is a very common triangle. As its name implies, the angles of this triangle are 30°, 60°, and 90°. The diagram below illustrates the relationships between the sides and the angles of this triangle.

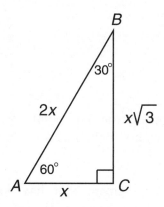

Circles

A circle is a closed plane curve whose every point is equidistant from a fixed point called the center. A circle is round. The following diagram shows a typical circle. Point *C* is the center of the circle, line segment *BD* is the diameter of the circle, and line segments *BC* and *CD* are each a radius of the circle. Circles are important geometric shapes. You will see many questions that relate to them on the PSAT, so be sure you understand them.

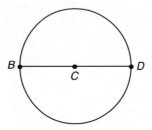

Important Facts about Circles

These are the facts you need to know to work effectively with circles:

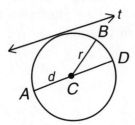

Radius

The radius is the length of a line segment from any point on the circle to the center of the circle. The symbol for radius is *r*.

Diameter

The diameter is the length of a line segment that has both endpoints on the circle and passes through the center of the circle. The symbol for diameter is *d*.

Tangent of a Circle

A line that passes through only one point on the circle is called the tangent or tangent line. The tangent just nicks the circle. In the figure above, line *t* is a tangent.

Pi

The ratio of the circumference of a circle to its diameter is called pi. A letter of the Greek alphabet, π is used as the symbol for this ratio. The value of π to four decimal places is 3.1416.

Circumference

The circumference is the distance around the perimeter of the circle. The formula for circumference is:

$$C = 2\pi r$$

Since the diameter is twice the radius, or $d = 2r$, the formula can also be written as:

$$C = \pi d$$

Arc

An arc is some portion of a circle. An arc is created by connecting radii from the endpoints of the arc to the center of the circle. This forms an angle.

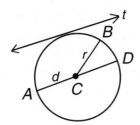

In the figure above, $\angle BCD$ forms arc BD. The degrees of arc BD are equal to the degrees of $\angle BCD$.

$$\text{Length of an arc} = \left(\frac{n}{360}\right)(2\pi r) \text{ where } n = \text{degrees of arc}$$

Area

To find the area (A) of a circle, multiply π times the square of the radius (r^2):

$$A = \pi r^2$$

Sector

A sector is that portion of the area of a circle that is bounded by the two radii and the included arc of the circle. It is like a slice of pie.

Area of a Sector: There are three steps to finding the area of a sector. First, find what percent of the total area the sector represents. Do this by dividing the number of degrees of arc (n) by 360°. Second, find the area of the whole circle. Finally, multiply the two together to get the area of the sector.

What is the area of a 90° sector of a circle with radius 4?

$$\textbf{First, } \text{sector \% of total area} = \frac{n}{360°} = \frac{90°}{360°} = 25\%$$

$$\textbf{Second, } \text{area of circle} = \pi r^2 = \pi(4^2) = 16\pi$$

$$\textbf{Third, } \text{area of sector} = (25\%)(16\pi) = 4\pi$$

Quadrilaterals and Other Polygons

A quadrilateral is a plane figure formed by connecting line segments to four points, no three of which lie on the same line. A quadrilateral is a four-sided polygon. It and the triangle are the most common types of polygons. Every so often, though, a test question will ask you about other polygons, such as pentagons, hexagons, or octagons; so it's a good idea to know how to work with other polygons, too.

Types of Quadrilaterals and Their Measurement

The quadrilaterals that you are most likely to find on the PSAT are the parallelogram, the rectangle, and the square.

Parallelogram

This quadrilateral has opposite sides that are parallel. The opposite sides are equal in length and the opposite angles are equal in measure, as shown in the diagram below, where $QR = PS$ and $QP = RS$.

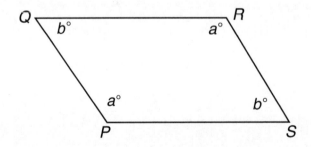

Rectangle

A rectangle is a special type of parallelogram, in which all the angles are right angles (90°).

Square

A square is a special type of rectangle. The sides of a square are all equal and the angles are all right angles (90°).

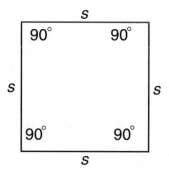

Measurement of Quadrilaterals

You may be asked to find the perimeter or area of a quadrilateral or you may be asked to find the angle measure of some part of a quadrilateral. Here's how to do it:

Perimeter

The perimeter (P) of a quadrilateral is just the sum of its four sides (s).

$$P = s_1 + s_2 + s_3 + s_4$$

Area

The area (*A*) of a quadrilateral is its length (*L*) multiplied by its width (*W*).

Area of a rectangle is: $A = L \times W$

Area of a square (where $L = W$) is: $A = s^2$

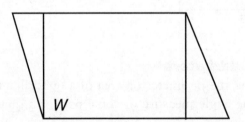

Area of a Parallelogram

To find the area of a parallelogram, treat it as if it were a rectangle, but use the perpendicular distance, not the slant distance, as the width (*W*). You can do this because the slanted ends can be squared up by dropping a perpendicular line at each end. The part cut off from one side fits exactly into the empty space on the other end to form a rectangle with the same area as the parallelogram.

Other Polygons

These types of polygons don't occur on the PSAT so frequently as triangles and quadrilaterals, but it pays to know about them. Here is an easy way to find their total number of degrees of interior angle.

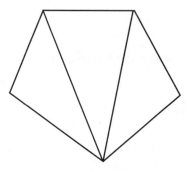

Interior Angles of a Polygon

Find the total number of degrees in a polygon's interior angles by dividing the interior into as many non-overlapping triangles as you can. Count the number of triangles. Since each triangle has 180° of interior angle, the total number of degrees of interior angle of the polygon is 180° times the number of triangles. For example, in the pentagon above, there are three triangles, $180° \times 3 = 540°$. This means there are 540° of interior angle in a pentagon.

Volume and Surface Area of Solids

Solids are three-dimensional figures. For the purposes of the PSAT, they are usually quadrilaterals with the added dimension of depth, or thickness. A rectangular solid is a favorite example of a solid.

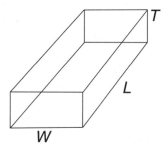

Volume

In order to find the volume (V) of a solid, multiply the length (L) by the width (W), and the thickness (T). For instance, a rectangular solid of length 4 inches, width 3 inches, and thickness 2 inches has a volume of:

$$V = L \times W \times T$$

$$V = 4 \times 3 \times 2 = 24 \text{ cubic inches}$$

In the case of a cube, all side dimensions are the same so the volume is:

$$V = s^3$$

For example, a cube with side 3 inches has a volume of:

$$V = 3^3 = 27 \text{ cubic inches}$$

Surface Area

You can find the surface area (S) of a solid by adding together the areas of each surface. To find the surface area of the rectangular solid in the example above, proceed as follows:

The total surface area is made up of three pairs of surfaces: 2 ends, 2 sides, and 2 plates. Stated algebraically, this becomes

$$
\begin{aligned}
S &= 2(T \times W) + 2(T \times L) + 2(W \times L) \\
&= 2(2 \times 3) + 2(2 \times 4) + 2(3 \times 4) \\
&= 2(6) + 2(8) + 2(12) \\
&= 12 + 16 + 24 \\
&= 52 \text{ square inches}
\end{aligned}
$$

Coordinate Geometry

Coordinate geometry applies principles of algebra to the solution of geometric problems. You establish a coordinate system by drawing two number lines perpendicular to each other. These lines are the axes. One line, the X-axis, runs horizontally. The second line, the Y-axis, runs vertically. This divides the plane into four quadrants. The point at which these lines meet is called the origin.

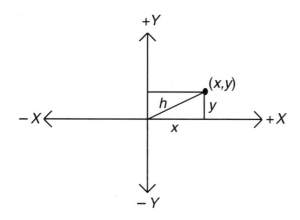

Specifying a Point

You can specify a position on this coordinate system by using an ordered pair, composed of two numbers: the abcissa, and the ordinate, or (x,y). These two numbers locate a point on the plane. The first number, the abcissa, is the distance away from the origin on the X-axis. The second number, the ordinate, is the distance away from the origin on the Y-axis. From each of these points on the axes, extend a line parallel to the other axis. The point at which these lines meet is the point (x,y).

Distance between Two Points

Find the distance between two points on the coordinate system by making use of the Pythagorean Theorem. Have you memorized this theorem yet? The Pythagorean Theorem is useful here because you can treat the distance between two points as the length of the hypotenuse of a right triangle. In the simple case above, seeking the distance from the origin $(0,0)$ to the point (x,y) is the same as finding the length (h) of the hypotenuse of a right triangle with sides x and y. Solving for h, we have:

$$h^2 = x^2 + y^2$$

or

$$h = \sqrt{x^2 + y^2}$$

The general formula for finding the distance (d) between two points is:

$$d = \sqrt{(x_1 - x_2)^2 + (y_1 - y_2)^2}$$

Slope of a Line

The slope of a line (m) can be found by using the following formula:

$$m = \frac{y_2 - y_1}{x_2 - x_1}$$

Midpoint of a Line Segment

The midpoint (M) of a line segment can be found by using the following formula:

$$M = \left(\frac{1}{2}(x_1 - x_2), \frac{1}{2}(y_1 - y_2)\right)$$

Practice Exercises

1. How many faces does a cube have?

2. What is an acute angle?

3. What is a right angle?

4. Which of the following statements is true?

   (A) Parallel lines intersect at obtuse angles.
   (B) Parallel lines never intersect.
   (C) Intersecting lines always have two points in common.
   (D) Perpendicular lines never intersect.

5. In a triangle, the measure of angle A is 65 degrees and the measure of angle B is 25 degrees. What does angle C measure?

   (A) 80 degrees
   (B) 85 degrees
   (C) 90 degrees
   (D) 100 degrees

6. A polygon is a closed plane figure made up of connecting lines. What is the least number of lines that can make a polygon?

   (A) 3
   (B) 4
   (C) 5
   (D) 6

7. The top side of a rectangle is 4 times that of its adjoining side. If the adjoining side is x inches long, what is the area of the rectangle?

8. What is the complementary angle to 36 degrees?

9. What is the supplementary angle to 140 degrees?

10. What is the circumference of a circle with a diameter of 5 inches?

Explanatory Answers

1. A cube has 6 faces: four sides plus the top and bottom.

2. The definition of an acute angle is that it has a measure of less than 90° and greater than 0.

3. A right angle measures exactly 90°.

4. **The correct answer is (B).** All the other statements are false.

5. **The correct answer is (C).** The sum of the interior angles of a triangle is 180°, so the measure of angle C must be 90°.

6. **The correct answer is (A).** There must be at least 3 lines to form a closed plane figure, a triangle.

7. The area of a rectangle is length multiplied by width. In this case, the length is $4x$ and the width is x, making the area $= (4x)(x) = 4x^2$.

8. The complementary angle is one that, when added to 36°, makes 90°. This means the complementary angle is $90° - 36° = 54°$.

9. The supplementary angle to 140° is one that, when added to 140°, makes 180°. This means the supplementary angle is $180° - 140° = 40°$.

10. The formula for the circumference of a circle is $C = 2\pi r = \pi d$. Since the diameter of the circle is 5, we have $C = 5\pi$.

Chapter

5

Writing Skills Review

Identifying Sentence Errors

What to Expect

Identifying Sentence Error questions are designed to measure your ability to identify:

- Grammatical errors

- Incorrect usage

- Poor diction (word choice)

- Faulty use of idiom (an expression peculiar to the English language that is considered correct, even though it is illogical if taken literally—for example, "many a day has passed" or "adverse to" as opposed to the incorrect "adverse against")

(See Directions on the following page.)

How to Approach Identifying Sentence Errors Questions

Following are pointers on how to prepare for and deal with Identifying Sentence Errors questions.

Read Widely

Here we go again. There's no way around this one: reading is the best way to develop an ear for correct, standard written English—and an ear for mistakes. In the Identifying Sentence Errors section, you will be asked only to spot errors; you will not be asked to say what those errors are. Many times, an error will be a segment of the sentence that just sounds wrong. If you're used to reading and speaking correct English, you can usually trust your instincts to choose the correct answer.

239

For Identifying Sentence Error questions, you will be instructed as follows:

Directions: The following questions will test your knowledge of grammar, usage, diction, and idiom.

Some sentences are correct.

No sentence contains multiple errors.

In each sentence below, five elements, labeled (A) through (E), are underlined and lettered. One (and ONLY one) of the underlined elements may contain an error. In choosing your answer, be sure to follow the rules of standard written English. You can assume that the parts of the sentences not underlined are correct.

If the sentence has no error, choose Ⓔ, "No error."

Example:

My dog Sally and my cat Buster

<u>gets along well</u> with each <u>other, eating and</u>
      A   B
sleeping <u>together, playing</u> quietly,
                   C
and <u>sharing</u> their food and treats. <u>No error.</u>
     D   E

Sample Answer:

●

Write Whenever You Get the Chance

Write postcards and letters. Write for your own amusement—stories and anecdotes. Keep a diary. Do ALL your written homework between now and test time so you can get feedback. Although the writing section of the PSAT won't ask you to write an essay, you'll definitely do better on this section if you've honed your writing skills. Invest in a handbook that contains the rules of standard written English and, if you come to a place in your writing where you're not sure of grammar or usage, look in the handbook for the answer. (It is a good idea to make sure the book contains a section on style as well.)

Practice

Yes . . . again. Besides writing on your own, do ALL the exercises in this book. And don't forget to read the answer explanations at the end of each test.

Try These Strategies

Following are reminders and suggestions you can use in approaching the Identifying Sentence Errors portion of the PSAT:

Read the entire sentence first. If you do not spot an error after inspecting the sentence carefully and if the sentence "sounds right," check choice (E) and move on.

Chances are, though, there will be an error. Take a look at the following example:

> There was <u>some evidence that</u> the twins had a
>   A
> <u>psychic connection</u> that allowed each one <u>to know</u> what the
>   B   C
> other <u>is thinking.</u> <u>No error.</u>
>   D   E

The correct answer is (D). The error is a shift in tense from past (*had* and *allowed*) to present (*is*). Perhaps the underlined portion sounds off to you when you read it silently. If this were the real test, you would trust your instinct, mark your answer, and continue. Remember: Don't waste time trying to figure out the technical name for the error. Don't waste time considering the non-underlined portions of the sentence, even if you think they could be improved. Assume anything that isn't underlined is correct.

There will be only ONE error per sentence. If you find an error you're sure of, don't squander time looking for more. Remember: You DO NOT have to know the technical name of the error, so don't waste valuable moments trying to pin a label on it. Consider the following:

> <u>During the 1950s,</u> a Hollywood scriptwriter, <u>if accused of</u>
>   A   B
> being a Communist, could be <u>blacklisted, which</u> meant
>   C
> <u>they could not get jobs.</u> <u>No error.</u>
>   D   E

The correct answer is (D). In this sentence, the plural pronoun does not agree with its singular antecedent. You SHOULD know what a pronoun is (a word that stands for a noun—in this case *they*), as well as what an antecedent is (a word or group of words that a pronoun refers to—in this case *scriptwriter*), but you don't HAVE to. Again, for the test, all you have to know is what segment of the sentence the error is in.

Correct answers must follow the rules of standard written English. Look at this sentence.

The button popped off Ilse's suit <u>just as</u> she was <u>fixing to</u>
                                          A   B
leave the house, <u>so she was late for</u> <u>the interview.</u> <u>No error.</u>
                          C   D   E

The correct answer is (B). The phrase *fixing to* is not standard written English; it is a colloquialism for *preparing to*. (Again, don't waste time wondering if *popped off* is standard English. It doesn't matter. That phrase is not underlined.)

Improving Sentences

What to Expect

Improving Sentences questions are designed to test your capacity to identify, from five choices, the sentence that is the:

- Most clear and precise
- Least awkward or ambiguous
- Most effective in expression

(See Directions on the following page.)

How to Approach Improving Sentences Questions

Following are pointers on how to prepare for and deal with Improving Sentences questions.

Read Widely

With this advice, I'm breaking the rule against redundancy. But there is no way around it—if you avoid reading, you're making a huge, life-altering mistake.

For Improving Sentences questions, you will be instructed as follows:

Directions: The sentences below test correctness and effectiveness of expression. When you choose your answers, select the sentence or sentence part that is most clear and correct and that conforms best to the requirements of standard written English.

Each of the following sentences is either underlined or contains an underlined part. Under each sentence, there are five ways of phrasing the underlined portion. Choice (A) repeats the original; the other four options are different. You can assume that the elements that are not underlined are correct.

Choose the answer that best expresses the meaning of the original sentence. If in your opinion the original sentence is the best option, choose it. Your choice should produce the most effective sentence.

Example:

I am going to the store to <u>buy a food item, which is bread</u>.

(A) buy a food item, which is bread
(B) buy a food item, bread
(C) buy bread
(D) buy a food item, which is called bread
(E) buy what is called bread

Sample Answer:

Write Whenever You Get the Chance

Again, write a lot. And, as suggested above, get a good handbook which contains sections on both grammar and style, to help you through the rough spots.

Practice

Do you want to make the rugby team? Then practice. Do you want to learn to play the trombone or bake prize-winning cookies? Then practice. Do you want to do well on the Writing Skills section of the PSAT? The way to accomplish that is obvious.

Try These Strategies

Following are tips and reminders you can use in approaching the Improving Sentences portion of the PSAT.

Examine the original sentence carefully, especially the underlined portion. Speak the sentence silently and listen for clunkiness or strangeness. Try reading this sentence aloud:

> I have a guinea pig, two white mice, and a gerbil for pets, which my mom says I can't name the gerbil after my sister.

Hear it? There's something wrong, or clunky, about the sentence. It's awkward—it just doesn't sound right.

If the sentence sounds odd, identify the problem segment.

Now see if you can identify the awkward segment from among the five choices.

> I have a guinea pig, two white mice, and a gerbil for <u>pets, which my mom says I can't name the gerbil after my sister.</u>

- **(A)** pets, which my mom says I can't name the gerbil after my sister.
- **(B)** pets, which my mom says. I can't name the gerbil after my sister.
- **(C)** pets, which my mom says I can't name the gerbil. After my sister.
- **(D)** pets; my mom says I can't name the gerbil after my sister.
- **(E)** pets, my mom says I can't name the gerbil after my sister.

The correct answer is **(D)**. *Which* is a relative pronoun and must have an antecedent. Is there any noun in the sentence that *which* can logically refer to? No. Therefore, choices (A), (B), and (C) are incorrect. Choice (E) is wrong because it contains a comma splice (two complete sentences joined by a comma).

If the problem is repeated in any of the choices, you can discard those choices as possible answers. In the above example, the phrase *which my mom says* is repeated in choices (A), (B), and (C), so if you recognize the relative pronoun error, these choices are eliminated as possibilities.

Choice (A) always repeats the original sentence. If the original sentence is more clear and effective than any of the other choices, mark (A) and move on. For example:

My cousin is now attending Briggs Community College.

- **(A)** My cousin is now attending Briggs Community College.
- **(B)** Briggs Community College is now being attended by my cousin.
- **(C)** At this point in time, my cousin is attending Briggs Community College.
- **(D)** My cousin is currently attending Briggs Community College at the present time.
- **(E)** Even as we speak, my cousin is presently attending Briggs Community College.

The correct answer is (A). The original sentence is clearer and less wordy than the other four choices.

Also remember: if more than one version is grammatically correct, choose the clearest, most effective version. Choose the best answer from the five choices, even if you can think of a better revision than the ones offered.

Improving Paragraphs

What to Expect

The Improving Paragraphs section is designed to test your ability to make choices that will:

- Improve the logic of a passage in need of revision

- Improve the coherence of a passage in need of revision

- Improve the organization of a passage in need of revision

- Identify faulty sentences within a passage in need of revision

For Improving Paragraphs questions, you will be instructed as follows:

> **Directions:** Read the passage below and answer the questions that come after it. Some of the questions will ask you to improve sentence structure and word choice. Other questions will refer to parts of the essay or to the entire essay and ask you to improve organization and development. Base your decisions on the rules of standard written English, and mark your answer on the corresponding oval on the answer sheet.

How to Approach Improving Paragraphs Questions

Following are tips on how to deal with the Improving Paragraphs questions on the PSAT.

Read Widely
Read essays and nonfiction pieces wherever you can find them to get a feel for the way whole compositions are put together. Pay attention to the way the essays you read are organized and how the author marks transitions from one idea to another in order to achieve overall coherence.

Write Whenever You Can
Again, take every opportunity to write. Letters are good practice. Think about the things you enjoy, whether they be sporting events, the opera, or even just shopping. Write a paragraph or two on the subject. Aim for coherence. Try out different organizational schemes: cause-and-effect, comparison–contrast, chronological order, and so forth. Refer to your handbook of grammar and style.

Practice
If you were planning an audition, you'd practice. Well, in a sense you are—an audition for college. So again, do the exercises in this book, all of them, and pay close attention to the answer explanations at the end of each test.

Try These Strategies
Following are suggestions on how to approach an Improving Paragraphs item.

Read the whole essay quickly to get an overall sense of it. Don't linger over the errors you will find during this first read-through. You'll be asked questions about these.

Here is a very short example of a paragraph with questions, such as you might encounter on the test.

(1) *The lounge was high-ceilinged and oppressive, with dark paneling, faded Oriental carpeting, and outsized leather chairs and couches.* (2) *As I crossed it, I felt strangely disembodied, an observer of myself, alone in a roomful of strangers.* (3) *At the far end, above a fireplace, hung a huge portrait of a round-faced, unsmiling, middle-aged man in black gown and purple-edged doctoral hood.* (4) *In the center of the room stood a long table, which held a coffee urn, a dozen small glasses of orange juice, and an ornate, silver tray of chocolate eclairs and Danish sweet rolls.* (5) *His eyes seemed to follow me as I crossed the room.* (6) *Beside the tray of Danish, a tall man in his early forties, impeccably dressed and sporting a feathery, copper-colored beard, was leaning down close to a woman in a yellow dress, gazing at her and speaking softly.* (7) *The woman, in her mid-forties, with a thin face and wispy blond hair, was watching the tall man through narrowed eyes.* (8) *I had the impression the woman was cogitating on something else at the present time.*

11. The essay as a whole would be more coherent if sentence 5 were placed before

    (**A**)   sentence 2.
    (**B**)   sentence 3.
    (**C**)   sentence 4.
    (**D**)   sentence 7.
    (**E**)   sentence 8.

The correct answer is (C). The man in the picture should be mentioned before the statement *His eyes seemed to follow. . . .* It is true that two men are mentioned, the one in the picture and the one standing beside the table. However, choice (D) is wrong, because the tall man's eyes cannot seem to follow the narrator, as the tall man is looking at the blond woman. Remember, for each question, be sure to take into account the *context* of the segment you're being asked about. Make certain that your revision (if any) makes sense in terms of the whole essay.

Pay attention to the style and tone. Don't just concentrate on the content of the essay. Suppose the second question on the above essay were the following:

2. Which of the following is the clearest, most effective version of sentence 8 (repeated below)?

I had the impression the woman was cogitating on something else at the present time.

(A) I had the impression the woman was cogitating on something else at the present time.
(B) I had the impression the woman was thinking about something else.
(C) I had the impression the woman was cogitating on something else.
(D) I had the impression the woman was thinking about something else at the present time.
(E) I had the impression the woman was thinking about something else at present.

The correct answer is (B). It is the least wordy and eliminates the pretentious word *cogitating*, which does not fit in with the style of the rest of the essay.

Common Grammar and Usage Problems

Here is a list of common grammar and usage problems you may find on the PSAT:

Shifts in tense: *I went to the supermarket and buy some pickle loaf.*

Shifts in number or person: *If one wants to take the PSAT as a sophomore, they can.*

Misuse of prepositions: *I was attentive on my girlfriend, but still she dumped me.* (The correct form here would be *to*.)

248

www.petersons.com

Errors in subject-verb agreement: *The pounding of the drums are giving me a headache.* (The subject here is pounding, not drums, so the correct verb form would be *is*.)

Errors in pronoun-antecedent agreement: *We love our drives into the country, because it gives us a sense of freedom.* (Because the pronoun refers to a plural noun, it should be plural as well. The correct form to refer to *drives* would be *they*.)

Misplaced parts (These will often, though not always, sound humorous): *Frightened to death, Milton's knees buckled.* (It was *Milton* who was frightened, not his *knees*. You might say, *Frightened to death, Milton felt his knees buckle.*)

Misuse of idioms: *Many the man has met that fate.* (The correct idiom would be *Many a man . . .*)

Confusion of adjectives and adverbs: *I did beautiful on the test.* (*Beautiful* is an adjective; it describes a thing. The correct word would be an adverb, *beautifully.*)

Comparison errors: *I have a more busier schedule than you do.* (Don't "double-compare"—the right term is just *busier*.) *Arthur is the fastest of the two.* (Use the correct form for comparing two items, which in this case is *faster*.) *Arthur is the faster of us all.* (Use the correct form for comparison of more than two items, which in this case is *fastest*.)

Errors in parallel structure: *I came, I saw, also definitely I conquered.* (Parallel grammatical form can make a sentence effective and memorable: *I came, I saw, I conquered.*)

Wordiness: *At this point in time, I will most surely go with you.* (*I will go with you* says what it needs to and has more punch.)

Mixed, illogical, or "strange" construction: *When Myra plays the saxophone drives her neighbors crazy.* (This is an adverb clause plus predicate. The sentence should read: *Myra's saxophone playing drives her neighbors crazy.*)

Comma splices and run-on sentences: *Wait a minute while I get my coat, I'll give you a ride.* (This is an example of a comma splice.) *Wait a minute while I get my coat I'll give you a ride.* (This is an example of a run-on sentence.) Correct revisions would be *Wait a minute while I get my coat; I'll give you a ride.* (or) *Wait a minute while I get my coat. I'll give you a ride.*

Sentence fragments: *My sister always studying.* (The main verb is missing. The sentence should read: *My sister is always studying.*)

249

Awkwardness or ambiguity: *An example of poor manners is a dinner guest, especially when she slurps her soup.* (It is *slurping* that is poor manners, not the *guest*. A correct version would be: *An example of poor manners is a guest's slurping her soup.*)

Faulty use of transitions: *Ashur was small, likewise strong.* (*Likewise* indicates that the two elements are similar. To indicate a contrast, write: *Ashur was small but strong.*)

Practice Exercises

Now try the following practice exercises. Answers begin on page 259.

Identifying Sentence Errors

1. If we leave now, we should get to the circus in time to see the
          A   B   C
   elephant march, which is more better than the trapeze artists'
                                     D
   performances. No error.
                   E

2. In the forest, the elves were dancing, yodeling, and
            A   B
   also they were cavorting; however, no one saw them. No error.
               C   D   E

3. When riding a motorcycle, a helmet should be worn, and
                A   B
   one should also be clothed in long trousers. No error.
       C   D   E

4. The only alternative that one can choose is to decide to finish what
             A   B   C
   you started. No error.
     D   E

5. There are several reasons to revise your
         A   B
   essay: it will be shorter, more polished, and they will find it easier to
                                  C   D
   read. No error.
       E

6. The horseback <u>riders</u> in the holiday parade <u>appear</u> on ten parades
              A   B
every year <u>and enjoy</u> the activity <u>very much.</u> <u>No error.</u>
           C   D   E

7. No matter <u>what your age is,</u> <u>our teacher said,</u> <u>you were</u> never too
            A   B   C
<u>old to learn</u> yoga. <u>No error.</u>
      D   E

8. If you <u>invent</u> something new, to prevent <u>its</u> being
        A   B
<u>stolen, registering it</u> with the patent <u>office immediately.</u> <u>No error.</u>
            C   D   E

9. Daytime television dramas <u>are called soap operas</u> because <u>they were</u>
                              A   B
originally sponsored by soap companies and, even

<u>in the beginning, are intended</u> to make selling products <u>easier.</u>
                     C   D
<u>No error.</u>
  E

10. Each of these organizations, <u>while appearing</u> perfectly legitimate <u>on</u>
                                 A   B
the surface, <u>was accused of doctoring</u> <u>their books.</u> <u>No error.</u>
            C   D   E

11. <u>Some critics say</u> that the United States Supreme Court is
          A
<u>unresponsive with</u> the <u>needs of</u> poor people and
         B   C
<u>should be reformed.</u> <u>No error.</u>
        D   E

12. The <u>genius of</u> Albert Einstein <u>is different from</u> Pablo Picasso, but
          A   B
<u>both men</u> are geniuses <u>nonetheless.</u> <u>No error.</u>
      C   D   E

13. <u>In ancient times,</u> the court jester (a kind of early-day comic, usually
        A
male, called the Fool) had <u>license to tell</u> the king any truth
                           B
<u>without fear of punishment,</u> <u>provided they told</u> that truth with
            C   D
humor. <u>No error.</u>
        E

14. The two electrical engineers, Mohammed and Fred, <u>rides to work</u>
A
together <u>every morning</u>, but Mohammed <u>walks home</u> at night <u>for</u>
B   C   D
the exercise. <u>No error.</u>
E

15. I fixed <u>cole-slaw</u>, baked beans, and chicken wings <u>to take</u> to the
A   B
company picnic <u>for my</u> coworkers
C
<u>with spicy barbecue sauce on them.</u> <u>No error.</u>
D   E

16. Every one of the girls <u>in my family</u>, including Linda Sue, <u>has a tin</u>
A   B
ear <u>for music</u>, but the boys sing <u>marvelous</u>. <u>No error.</u>
C   D   E

17. <u>After skiing</u> both the lower, milder slope and Dead Man's Drop,
A
<u>I like it better</u>, so that's <u>where I'm going</u> <u>next Saturday</u>. <u>No error.</u>
B   C   D   E

18. <u>Our</u> American History professor, the renowned Professor Bing,
A
<u>described</u> Joseph McCarthy's persecution <u>of</u> suspected Communists
B   C
<u>in class Wednesday</u>. <u>No error.</u>
D   E

19. <u>Would you like</u> <u>to come</u> to the movies with <u>Ayana and me</u>, and
A   B   C
<u>go to</u> dinner afterward? <u>No error.</u>
D   E

20. <u>Glancing up</u> uneasily, <u>I saw</u> that, close to <u>the tops of the trees</u>,
A   B   C
<u>hanged</u> a fat goblin moon. <u>No error.</u>
D   E

Improving Sentences

21. In Hollywood, all the stars' handprints (including Marilyn Monroe's and Jane Russell's) reside at Mann's Chinese Theater.

(A) In Hollywood, all the stars' handprints (including Marilyn Monroe's and Jane Russell's) reside at Mann's Chinese Theater.

(B) All the stars' handprints are, including Marilyn Monroe's and Jane Russell's, at Mann's Chinese Theater in Hollywood.

(C) Mann's Chinese Theater in Hollywood is the place where all the star's handprints are, including Marilyn Monroe's and Jane Russell's.

(D) Mann's Chinese Theater in Hollywood is the place where all the stars' handprints are.

(E) Mann's Chinese Theater in Hollywood is the place where all the stars' handprints, including Marilyn Monroe's and Jane Russell's, are.

22. When choosing a melon in the produce department of the grocery store, look for one that is slightly soft and not too green.

(A) slightly soft and not too

(B) slightly, soft and not too

(C) slightly soft: and not too

(D) slightly soft; and not too

(E) slightly soft and, not too

23. When preparing for an important test, it is necessary not only to study the material, and to get a good night's sleep the night before.

(A) material, and to get

(B) material, in other words getting

(C) material, meanwhile to get

(D) material, in addition to get

(E) material, but to get

24. For months I received anonymous phone calls, <u>who made strange noises then hung up.</u>

- **(A)** For months I received anonymous phone calls, who made strange noises then hung up.
- **(B)** For months I received an anonymous phone call from someone who made strange noises then hung up.
- **(C)** Someone made strange noises, then hung up, on anonymous phone calls I received for months.
- **(D)** I received an anonymous phone call from someone for months, then hung up after making strange noises.
- **(E)** For months I received anonymous phone calls from someone who made strange noises, then hung up.

25. I do not like codfish as well as my Aunt Rhoda.

- **(A)** I do not like codfish as well as my Aunt Rhoda.
- **(B)** I do not like codfish as well as my Aunt Rhoda does.
- **(C)** Codfish I do not like, as well as my Aunt Rhoda.
- **(D)** I do not like, as well as my Aunt Rhoda, codfish.
- **(E)** Codfish I do not like, my Aunt Rhoda either.

26. Once we start up the mountain, <u>and there will be no turning back.</u>

- **(A)** and there will be no turning back.
- **(B)** there will be no turning back.
- **(C)** so there will be no turning back.
- **(D)** thus there will be no turning back.
- **(E)** but there will be no turning back.

27. <u>Though often glamorized by fans, the lives of film stars are quite hard.</u>

- **(A)** Though often glamorized by fans, the lives of film stars are quite hard.
- **(B)** In reality, the lives of film stars are quite hard; however, it is often glamorized by fans.
- **(C)** Often glamorized by fans is the life of the film star; however, they are quite hard.
- **(D)** In reality quite hard, fans often glamorize the lives of film stars.
- **(E)** Glamorized by fans, in reality quite hard are the lives of film stars.

28. Some people believe that "familiarity breeds contempt"; <u>moreover,</u> it's not necessarily true.

   (A) moreover,
   (B) secondly,
   (C) in addition,
   (D) however,
   (E) furthermore,

29. <u>I had my purse stolen in Kansas City, but did not worry about it. What a great city!</u>

   (A) I had my purse stolen in Kansas City, but did not worry about it. What a great city!
   (B) I had had my purse stolen. In Kansas City. But I did not worry about it, what a great city!
   (C) I had my purse stolen in Kansas City. But did not worry about it. What a great city!
   (D) I had my purse stolen. In Kansas City, but I did not worry about it. What a great city!
   (E) I had my purse stolen. In Kansas City, but I did not worry about it. What a great city!

30. <u>Tell me why did you dress for the concert. Like that?</u>

   (A) Tell me why did you dress for the concert. Like that?
   (B) Tell me why did you dress for the concert like that?
   (C) Tell me. Why did you dress for the concert like that?
   (D) Tell me. Why did you dress for the concert? Like that?
   (E) Tell me. Why did you dress? For the concert? Like that?

31. French philosopher Rene Descartes was a devout <u>Catholic; there-fore, his writings</u> did more to undermine church authority than those of any other philosopher of his day.

   (A) Catholic; therefore, his writings
   (B) Catholic, yet his writings
   (C) Catholic, when his writings
   (D) Catholic, where his writings
   (E) Catholic; meanwhile, his writings

32. Neither Walt Whitman nor Herman Melville <u>were appreciated during their lifetimes.</u>

  (A) were appreciated during their lifetimes.
  (B) was appreciated during their lifetime.
  (C) was appreciated during his lifetime.
  (D) have been appreciated during their lifetime.
  (E) were appreciated during his lifetime.

33. A prophet can expect to be disbelieved <u>when you predict</u> the end of the world.

  (A) when you predict
  (B) when one predicts
  (C) when predicting
  (D) when we predict
  (E) when they predict

34. When not playing football, NFL star Rosie Greer enjoyed doing <u>needlepoint. Which surprised</u> his fans.

  (A) needlepoint. Which surprised
  (B) needlepoint, which surprised
  (C) needlepoint, which he surprised
  (D) needlepoint. Whereas he surprised
  (E) needlepoint, which he surprises

35. <u>What about Serena and I?</u>

  (A) What about Serena and I?
  (B) What about Serena and me?
  (C) What about Serena and myself?
  (D) Myself, what about, and Serena?
  (E) What about I, myself, and Serena?

Improving Paragraphs

Answer questions 36–40 on the basis of the following essay excerpt, which is a draft that needs revision.

(1) I found the room unsettling. (2) It was small and immensely crowded, two of its walls spanned by floor-to-ceiling bookshelves, the other two paneled in dark walnut. (3) Its windows were shuttered. (4) A massive oak desk was laden with notebooks and papers. (5) It dominated the cramped space. (6) The remainder was taken up by several battered metal filing cabinets and an ancient leather chair

256

and sofa. (7) The room had evidently been shut up for some time, permeated as it was by a musty smell; there was another, fainter odor, like an under-taste, which I recognized as the odor of formaldehyde. (8) Over every surface, you could see dust lay like a fine layer of ash.

(9) Against one wall loomed a tall, glass-fronted display case. (10) Harsh interior lights had been activated by the switch beside the door—the case contained birds preserved by taxidermy. (11) There perched a song sparrow on the top shelf, a starling, a jackdaw, a kite, and a large, dark, blunt-winged bird I did not recognize. (12) On a white card beneath this specimen were written the words: Nannopterum harrisi, flightless cormorant, Galapagos Islands. *(13) Birds are fascinating, sometimes exotic creatures, and their scientific study is definitely worthwhile. (14) The right-hand case contained a bird with a slender, curved beak and crimson plumage; its card read* Eudocimus ruber, Scarlet Ibis. *(15) Just beneath the Ibis stood a snowy-feathered bird whose card identified it as a* White Tern, Cap D'Ambre, Madagascar.

(16) The birds were excellently preserved, uncannily lifelike, their eyes watching brightly from behind the glass.

36. Which of the following is the best revision of sentences 4 and 5 (reproduced below)?

A massive oak desk was laden with notebooks and papers. It dominated the cramped space.

- **(A)** A massive oak desk, was laden with: notebooks and papers. It dominated the cramped space.
- **(B)** A massive oak desk, laden with notebooks and papers, dominated the cramped space.
- **(C)** A massive oak desk, laden with notebooks and papers. It dominated the cramped space.
- **(D)** A massive oak desk was laden with, notebooks and papers, dominated the cramped space.
- **(E)** A massive oak desk was laden with notebooks and papers. Dominated the cramped space.

37. Which of the following is the best revision of the underlined portion of sentence 11 (reproduced below), so that there is a smoother transition between sentences 10 and 11?

There perched a song sparrow on the top shelf, a starling, a jackdaw, a kite, and a large, dark, blunt-winged bird I did not recognize.

- **(A)** There perched a song sparrow
- **(B)** Standing on the top shelf, there perched a song sparrow
- **(C)** On the top shelf perched a song sparrow
- **(D)** A song sparrow perched on the top shelf, plus there was a
- **(E)** A song sparrow, perching on the top shelf

38. To improve the coherence of paragraph 2, which of the following sentences should be deleted?

- **(A)** Sentence 11
- **(B)** Sentence 12
- **(C)** Sentence 13
- **(D)** Sentence 14
- **(E)** Sentence 15

39. The organizational pattern of paragraph 2 can best be described as a general statement followed by

- **(A)** cause-and-effect analysis.
- **(B)** comparison–contrast analysis.
- **(C)** chronological order of events.
- **(D)** elements in order of importance.
- **(E)** specific descriptive details.

40. Which of the following revisions of sentence 8 (reproduced below) would make it more consistent with the rest of the passage?

Over every surface, you could see dust lay like a fine layer of ash.

- **(A)** Delete "over every surface."
- **(B)** Delete "you could see."
- **(C)** Delete "dust lay like a fine layer of ash."
- **(D)** Add the word "everywhere" to the end of the sentence.
- **(E)** Change "lay" to "lie."

Explanatory Answers

Identifying Sentence Errors

1. **The correct answer is (D).** The sentence contains faulty comparison. The correct comparative word is simply *better*.

2. **The correct answer is (C).** This sentence would be more effective if it made use of parallel structure: *dancing, yodeling, and cavorting.* (As the phrase is written, it is unnecessarily wordy as well.)

3. **The correct answer is (A).** The error is one of a misplaced modifier: the *helmet* seems to be *riding a motorcycle*, rather than a person.

4. **The correct answer is (D).** The error here is one of shift in person from third (*one*) to second (*you*).

5. **The correct answer is (D).** The pronoun *they* has no antecedent in the sentence.

6. **The correct answer is (B).** The error is one of misuse of a preposition. The phrase should read *appear in*.

7. **The correct answer is (C).** The sentence contains a shift in tense from present (*is*) to past (*were*).

8. **The correct answer is (C).** This sentence has mixed, illogical construction. To correct it, change choice (C) to: *stolen, you should register it.*

9. **The correct answer is (C).** The error is one of shift in tense, from *were* to *are*. Although the first clause is in present tense, the phrase *in the beginning* points to an event in the past.

10. **The correct answer is (D).** This is a pronoun/antecedent error: The plural pronoun (*their*) refers to a singular antecedent (*each*). (Note that the pronoun does NOT refer to *organizations*.)

11. **The correct answer is (B).** The error is one of misuse of the preposition *with*. The correct wording would be *unresponsive to*.

12. **The correct answer is (B).** The error is one of faulty comparison. *The genius of Albert Einstein is different from the genius of Pablo Picasso*, not from Picasso himself.

13. **The correct answer is (D).** The error is a shift in number from one (*the court jester*) to more than one (*they*).

14. **The correct answer is (A).** The error is one of faulty subject-verb agreement—the subject is plural (*The two electrical engineers*) and the verb is singular (*rides*). The correct version would be *The two electrical engineers . . . ride . . .*

15. **The correct answer is (D).** This is a misplaced modifier. The *chicken wings* had *sauce* on them, not (we hope) the *coworkers*. A modifier should not be remote from the thing modified.

16. **The correct answer is (D).** The error here is in the use of an adjective (*marvelous*) instead of an adverb (*marvelously*) to modify the verb *sing*.

17. **The correct answer is (B).** This is an error of vague pronounce reference. It's impossible to tell which ski area the speaker likes better.

18. **The correct answer is (D).** The error is one of misplaced modifier. Ask yourself, "*What* happened in class?"

19. **The correct answer is (E).** The sentence is correctly written.

20. **The correct answer is (D).** The mistake is one of incorrect verb form. The correct form here is *hung*.

Improving Sentences

21. **The correct answer is (C).** Choices (B) and (E) are unnecessarily convoluted. In choice (A), the word *reside* is inexact when applied to handprints. Choice (D) leaves out part of the information.

22. **The correct answer is (A).** The other choices have unnecessary or erroneous punctuation.

23. **The correct answer is (E).** This choice is grammatical and shows a contrast. The other choices are illogically constructed.

24. **The correct answer is (E).** The other choices are unclear because they are awkwardly constructed. Choice (B) is almost right; however, one cannot receive only one anonymous phone call *for months*.

25. **The correct answer is (B).** The other choices are unnecessarily convoluted and also show faulty comparison.

26. **The correct answer is (B).** No connecting word is needed to relate the first half of the sentence to the second. Connecting words between the two halves of the sentence turn the sentence into a fragment.

27. **The correct answer is (A).** This is the only clear answer. In choices (B) and (C), the pronouns *it* and *they* do not agree with the words to which they refer. In choice (D), the first phrase seems to refer to *fans* when it should refer to *the lives of film stars*. Choice (E) is unnecessarily convoluted.

28. **The correct answer is (D).** The word *however* provides the clearest and most logical transition between these two ideas; the other choices are less logical.

29. **The correct answer is (A).** The other choices create sentence fragments.

30. **The correct answer is (C).** Choices (A), (D), and (E) create fragments. Choice (B) is a run-on sentence.

31. **The correct answer is (B).** The word *yet* provides the clearest and most logical transition between these two contrasting sentence elements.

32. **The correct answer is (C).** In this choice, the singular subject (*Neither*) agrees with the singular verb (*is*).

33. **The correct answer is (C).** In this choice, there is no unnecessary shift in person; the other answers contain shifts in person from *prophet* to *you, one,* and *we*. (The only other correct form would be *when he or she predicts*, which is not among the choices.)

34. **The correct answer is (B).** Choices (A) and (D) contain sentence fragments. Choices (C) and (E) are illogically constructed.

35. **The correct answer is (B).** The other choices contain errors in the case of the pronoun *I*.

Improving Paragraphs

36. **The correct answer is (B).** It is correctly written and avoids the choppiness of the original. Choice (A) incorrectly inserts a comma between subject and verb and makes ineffective use of a colon. Choice (C) contains a sentence fragment. Choice (D) improperly inserts a comma between a preposition (*with*) and its object (*notebooks and papers*). Choice (E) contains a sentence fragment.

37. **The correct answer is (C).** This creates the smoothest, most economical transition. Choice (A) leaves out information. Choices (B) and (D) are wordy. Choice (E) is ungrammatical.

38. **The correct answer is** (C). This comment on birds interrupts the flow of the paragraph, which is mainly a listing of the birds in the glass case.

39. **The correct answer is** (E). The birds in the glass cases are simply described. None of the other choices apply to the paragraph.

40. **The correct answer is** (B). The use of second person (*you*) is inconsistent with the point of view of the rest of the essay.

Answer Sheet

SECTION 1 — Critical Reading

1 Ⓐ Ⓑ Ⓒ Ⓓ Ⓔ	8 Ⓐ Ⓑ Ⓒ Ⓓ Ⓔ	15 Ⓐ Ⓑ Ⓒ Ⓓ Ⓔ	22 Ⓐ Ⓑ Ⓒ Ⓓ Ⓔ
2 Ⓐ Ⓑ Ⓒ Ⓓ Ⓔ	9 Ⓐ Ⓑ Ⓒ Ⓓ Ⓔ	16 Ⓐ Ⓑ Ⓒ Ⓓ Ⓔ	23 Ⓐ Ⓑ Ⓒ Ⓓ Ⓔ
3 Ⓐ Ⓑ Ⓒ Ⓓ Ⓔ	10 Ⓐ Ⓑ Ⓒ Ⓓ Ⓔ	17 Ⓐ Ⓑ Ⓒ Ⓓ Ⓔ	24 Ⓐ Ⓑ Ⓒ Ⓓ Ⓔ
4 Ⓐ Ⓑ Ⓒ Ⓓ Ⓔ	11 Ⓐ Ⓑ Ⓒ Ⓓ Ⓔ	18 Ⓐ Ⓑ Ⓒ Ⓓ Ⓔ	25 Ⓐ Ⓑ Ⓒ Ⓓ Ⓔ
5 Ⓐ Ⓑ Ⓒ Ⓓ Ⓔ	12 Ⓐ Ⓑ Ⓒ Ⓓ Ⓔ	19 Ⓐ Ⓑ Ⓒ Ⓓ Ⓔ	
6 Ⓐ Ⓑ Ⓒ Ⓓ Ⓔ	13 Ⓐ Ⓑ Ⓒ Ⓓ Ⓔ	20 Ⓐ Ⓑ Ⓒ Ⓓ Ⓔ	
7 Ⓐ Ⓑ Ⓒ Ⓓ Ⓔ	14 Ⓐ Ⓑ Ⓒ Ⓓ Ⓔ	21 Ⓐ Ⓑ Ⓒ Ⓓ Ⓔ	

SECTION 2 — Math

1 Ⓐ Ⓑ Ⓒ Ⓓ Ⓔ	8 Ⓐ Ⓑ Ⓒ Ⓓ Ⓔ	15 Ⓐ Ⓑ Ⓒ Ⓓ Ⓔ
2 Ⓐ Ⓑ Ⓒ Ⓓ Ⓔ	9 Ⓐ Ⓑ Ⓒ Ⓓ Ⓔ	16 Ⓐ Ⓑ Ⓒ Ⓓ Ⓔ
3 Ⓐ Ⓑ Ⓒ Ⓓ Ⓔ	10 Ⓐ Ⓑ Ⓒ Ⓓ Ⓔ	17 Ⓐ Ⓑ Ⓒ Ⓓ Ⓔ
4 Ⓐ Ⓑ Ⓒ Ⓓ Ⓔ	11 Ⓐ Ⓑ Ⓒ Ⓓ Ⓔ	18 Ⓐ Ⓑ Ⓒ Ⓓ Ⓔ
5 Ⓐ Ⓑ Ⓒ Ⓓ Ⓔ	12 Ⓐ Ⓑ Ⓒ Ⓓ Ⓔ	19 Ⓐ Ⓑ Ⓒ Ⓓ Ⓔ
6 Ⓐ Ⓑ Ⓒ Ⓓ Ⓔ	13 Ⓐ Ⓑ Ⓒ Ⓓ Ⓔ	20 Ⓐ Ⓑ Ⓒ Ⓓ Ⓔ
7 Ⓐ Ⓑ Ⓒ Ⓓ Ⓔ	14 Ⓐ Ⓑ Ⓒ Ⓓ Ⓔ	

SECTION 3 — Critical Reading

1 Ⓐ Ⓑ Ⓒ Ⓓ Ⓔ	9 Ⓐ Ⓑ Ⓒ Ⓓ Ⓔ	17 Ⓐ Ⓑ Ⓒ Ⓓ Ⓔ	25 Ⓐ Ⓑ Ⓒ Ⓓ Ⓔ
2 Ⓐ Ⓑ Ⓒ Ⓓ Ⓔ	10 Ⓐ Ⓑ Ⓒ Ⓓ Ⓔ	18 Ⓐ Ⓑ Ⓒ Ⓓ Ⓔ	26 Ⓐ Ⓑ Ⓒ Ⓓ Ⓔ
3 Ⓐ Ⓑ Ⓒ Ⓓ Ⓔ	11 Ⓐ Ⓑ Ⓒ Ⓓ Ⓔ	19 Ⓐ Ⓑ Ⓒ Ⓓ Ⓔ	27 Ⓐ Ⓑ Ⓒ Ⓓ Ⓔ
4 Ⓐ Ⓑ Ⓒ Ⓓ Ⓔ	12 Ⓐ Ⓑ Ⓒ Ⓓ Ⓔ	20 Ⓐ Ⓑ Ⓒ Ⓓ Ⓔ	
5 Ⓐ Ⓑ Ⓒ Ⓓ Ⓔ	13 Ⓐ Ⓑ Ⓒ Ⓓ Ⓔ	21 Ⓐ Ⓑ Ⓒ Ⓓ Ⓔ	
6 Ⓐ Ⓑ Ⓒ Ⓓ Ⓔ	14 Ⓐ Ⓑ Ⓒ Ⓓ Ⓔ	22 Ⓐ Ⓑ Ⓒ Ⓓ Ⓔ	
7 Ⓐ Ⓑ Ⓒ Ⓓ Ⓔ	15 Ⓐ Ⓑ Ⓒ Ⓓ Ⓔ	23 Ⓐ Ⓑ Ⓒ Ⓓ Ⓔ	
8 Ⓐ Ⓑ Ⓒ Ⓓ Ⓔ	16 Ⓐ Ⓑ Ⓒ Ⓓ Ⓔ	24 Ⓐ Ⓑ Ⓒ Ⓓ Ⓔ	

SECTION 4

Math

1	Ⓐ Ⓑ Ⓒ Ⓓ Ⓔ		5	Ⓐ Ⓑ Ⓒ Ⓓ Ⓔ		8	Ⓐ Ⓑ Ⓒ Ⓓ Ⓔ
2	Ⓐ Ⓑ Ⓒ Ⓓ Ⓔ		6	Ⓐ Ⓑ Ⓒ Ⓓ Ⓔ		9	Ⓐ Ⓑ Ⓒ Ⓓ Ⓔ
3	Ⓐ Ⓑ Ⓒ Ⓓ Ⓔ		7	Ⓐ Ⓑ Ⓒ Ⓓ Ⓔ		10	Ⓐ Ⓑ Ⓒ Ⓓ Ⓔ
4	Ⓐ Ⓑ Ⓒ Ⓓ Ⓔ						

11 12 13 14 15

16 17 18 19 20

SECTION 5

Writing Skills

1	Ⓐ Ⓑ Ⓒ Ⓓ Ⓔ	11	Ⓐ Ⓑ Ⓒ Ⓓ Ⓔ	21	Ⓐ Ⓑ Ⓒ Ⓓ Ⓔ	31	Ⓐ Ⓑ Ⓒ Ⓓ Ⓔ
2	Ⓐ Ⓑ Ⓒ Ⓓ Ⓔ	12	Ⓐ Ⓑ Ⓒ Ⓓ Ⓔ	22	Ⓐ Ⓑ Ⓒ Ⓓ Ⓔ	32	Ⓐ Ⓑ Ⓒ Ⓓ Ⓔ
3	Ⓐ Ⓑ Ⓒ Ⓓ Ⓔ	13	Ⓐ Ⓑ Ⓒ Ⓓ Ⓔ	23	Ⓐ Ⓑ Ⓒ Ⓓ Ⓔ	33	Ⓐ Ⓑ Ⓒ Ⓓ Ⓔ
4	Ⓐ Ⓑ Ⓒ Ⓓ Ⓔ	14	Ⓐ Ⓑ Ⓒ Ⓓ Ⓔ	24	Ⓐ Ⓑ Ⓒ Ⓓ Ⓔ	34	Ⓐ Ⓑ Ⓒ Ⓓ Ⓔ
5	Ⓐ Ⓑ Ⓒ Ⓓ Ⓔ	15	Ⓐ Ⓑ Ⓒ Ⓓ Ⓔ	25	Ⓐ Ⓑ Ⓒ Ⓓ Ⓔ	35	Ⓐ Ⓑ Ⓒ Ⓓ Ⓔ
6	Ⓐ Ⓑ Ⓒ Ⓓ Ⓔ	16	Ⓐ Ⓑ Ⓒ Ⓓ Ⓔ	26	Ⓐ Ⓑ Ⓒ Ⓓ Ⓔ	36	Ⓐ Ⓑ Ⓒ Ⓓ Ⓔ
7	Ⓐ Ⓑ Ⓒ Ⓓ Ⓔ	17	Ⓐ Ⓑ Ⓒ Ⓓ Ⓔ	27	Ⓐ Ⓑ Ⓒ Ⓓ Ⓔ	37	Ⓐ Ⓑ Ⓒ Ⓓ Ⓔ
8	Ⓐ Ⓑ Ⓒ Ⓓ Ⓔ	18	Ⓐ Ⓑ Ⓒ Ⓓ Ⓔ	28	Ⓐ Ⓑ Ⓒ Ⓓ Ⓔ	38	Ⓐ Ⓑ Ⓒ Ⓓ Ⓔ
9	Ⓐ Ⓑ Ⓒ Ⓓ Ⓔ	19	Ⓐ Ⓑ Ⓒ Ⓓ Ⓔ	29	Ⓐ Ⓑ Ⓒ Ⓓ Ⓔ	39	Ⓐ Ⓑ Ⓒ Ⓓ Ⓔ
10	Ⓐ Ⓑ Ⓒ Ⓓ Ⓔ	20	Ⓐ Ⓑ Ⓒ Ⓓ Ⓔ	30	Ⓐ Ⓑ Ⓒ Ⓓ Ⓔ		

Practice Test

1

Section 1—Critical Reading

Time—25 Minutes • 25 Questions

For each question below, choose the best answer from the choices given and fill in the corresponding oval on the answer sheet.

> **Directions:** Each sentence below has either one or two blanks in it and is followed by five choices, labeled (A) through (E). These choices represent words or phrases that have been left out. Choose the word or phrase that, if inserted into the sentence, would best fit the meaning of the sentence as a whole.
>
> **Example:**
>
> Canine massage is a veterinary technique for calming dogs that are extremely _____.
>
> (A) inept
> (B) disciplined
> (C) controlled
> (D) stressed
> (E) restrained   Ⓐ Ⓑ Ⓒ ● Ⓔ

1. While maintaining an outward appearance of religious _____, medieval scholar Peter Abelard revealed, in his writings, hope for the triumph of reason over faith.

   (A) heterodoxy
   (B) orthodoxy
   (C) incredulity
   (D) vacillation
   (E) skepticism

2. My cat Lloyd loves to go for car rides and will jump into the back seat with _____ whenever he is invited.

   (A) devotion
   (B) aggravation
   (C) dedication
   (D) alacrity
   (E) apathy

GO ON TO THE NEXT PAGE

PETERSON'S
getting you there

3. My sister Rose is a/an _____ person, always objecting to everything I want to do, while my brother Jamal is, by contrast, nearly always _____.

   (A) feisty..obedient
   (B) depressed..joyous
   (C) arrogant..disdainful
   (D) pretentious..carefree
   (E) contentious..accommodating

4. The _____ of women in physics and astronomy is cause for concern, because it _____ these sciences of the rich brain power of half the human race.

   (A) paucity..deprives
   (B) celebration..dispossesses
   (C) poverty..preempts
   (D) audacity..relieves
   (E) scarcity..assures

5. The monks of New Skete believe that dogs are often willing to please without hope of reward, that they are able to show a kind of _____ caring.

   (A) refractory
   (B) altruistic
   (C) incautious
   (D) preemptive
   (E) precocious

Directions: Read each of the passages carefully, then answer the questions that come after them. The answer to each question may be stated overtly or only implied. You will not have to use outside knowledge to answer the questions—all the material you will need will be in the passage itself. In some cases, you will be asked to read two related passages and answer questions about their relationship to one another.

Questions 6–7 are based on the following passage.

This passage is from the U.S. State Department Web site.

Line   In 1963, in Moscow, the Treaty Banning Nuclear Weapon Tests (. . .) was signed by the United States, Great Britain, and the Soviet Union. The Test Ban Treaty of
(5)   1963 prohibits nuclear weapons tests "or any other nuclear explosion" in the atmosphere, in outer space, and under water. While not banning tests underground, the Treaty does prohibit nuclear
(10)   explosions in this environment if they cause "radioactive debris to be present outside the territorial limits of the State under whose jurisdiction or control" the explosions were conducted. In accepting
(15)   limitations on testing, the nuclear powers accepted as a common goal "an end to the contamination of . . . [the human] environment by radioactive substances."

6. Which word best describes the Test Ban Treaty of 1963?

(A) Comprehensive
(B) Intensified
(C) Inflated
(D) Limited
(E) Retroactive

7. The passage suggests that the main purpose of the treaty was to prevent global

(A) warfare.
(B) detonation.
(C) pollution.
(D) duplicity.
(E) concession.

Questions 8–9 are based on the following passage.

This passage is based on an e-mail sent to Web site operators by the Federal Trade Commission beginning in November 2001.

Line   Your Web site claims that a product or therapy you sell is effective in the treatment or cure of anthrax, smallpox, or another disease or health hazard that
(5)   may be associated with recent reports about threats of terrorism. We are aware of no scientific basis for such claims. Without competent and reliable scientific evidence to substantiate these claims, the
(10)   claims are illegal under the Federal Trade Commission Act and must be discontinued immediately. Violations of the FTC Act may result in legal action in the form of Federal District Court Injunction or
(15)   Administrative Order. An order also may require that you pay money back to consumers.

8. Which word best describes the purpose of the passage?

(A) Advice
(B) Warning
(C) Opinion
(D) Rejection
(E) Reminder

9. The main purpose of the FTC e-mail is to command Web site owners to

(A) repay consumers.
(B) cease making false claims.
(C) stop making terrorist threats.
(D) find scientific evidence for claims.
(E) inform consumers the claims are false.

Questions 10–11 are based on the following passage.

This passage is adapted from an essay, "When Art and Morality Collide . . . ," by James Swafford (in National Endowment for the Arts magazine Humanities, *July/August, 1997).*

Line   In the 19th century, writer Oscar Wilde produced works that were widely deemed immoral. Of that historical period, 20th century essayist James Swafford writes:
(5)   What purpose do literature and the visual arts serve? What responsibilities must they assume? These were important questions in the last century, as increasing literacy, inexpensive editions, the rise
(10)   of lending libraries, public art exhibitions, and mass-produced prints from steel engravings made the verbal and visual arts available to the masses as never before . . . . Wilde ran afoul of [the
(15)   expectation of moral purpose] on several occasions . . . . "All art is quite useless," announces the last line of the preface to [Wilde's novel], *The Picture of Dorian Gray.*

267

10. According to Swafford, questions about the purpose of art were important in the last century, because art had become increasingly

   (A) admired.
   (B) accessible.
   (C) irresponsible.
   (D) anti-Evangelical.
   (E) nontraditional.

11. What is the meaning of the phrase "ran afoul of" (line 14)?

   (A) Denied the existence of
   (B) Took up the cause of
   (C) Played a part in
   (D) Came in conflict with
   (E) Showed ignorance of

Questions 12–20 are based on the following passage.

This passage discusses the works of Nobel Prize winner Isaac Bashevis Singer.

Line   In Isaac Bashevis Singer's fictional world, seeming dualities—past and present, animate and inanimate, the supernatural and the ordinary world of the senses,
(5)   even life and death—are not set in opposition or even juxtaposed, but rather they are fused, embedded in one another. There is no border between the cosmic and the mundane, because the two are
(10)   not separate countries. In Singer's stories, modes of existence usually thought to be dichotomous have their being on the same plane, and that plane is the world of matter, the world of phenomena.
(15)   In approaching the stories, it is helpful first to divide them into three types.
       Those of the first type are set in the distant past, usually in the 17th or 18th

(20)   century, in the Jewish *shtetls* of Eastern Europe, villages in which the streets are narrow and muddy, and gossip is the important means of gathering and conveying information. The characters
(25)   include all sorts: rabbis, Hasidic scholars, wealthy businesspeople, students, prostitutes, and also supernatural beings, usually demons. Prominent among the characters is the scholar who withdraws
(30)   from the world to read and study the mystical *Cabala*—or attempts unsuccessfully to withdraw, for frequently he (and occasionally she) is distracted from study by sex, or demons, or some violent
(35)   outside force. Included in this group of stories are "The Slaughterer," the story of Yoineh Meir, a ritual slaughterer whose job it is to kill livestock in accordance with religious laws, a man obsessed with
(40)   guilt, who turns to the study of the *Cabala* even though he knows it is forbidden to young men; "Cockadoodle-doo"—somewhat of an exception, since the narrator is a rooster, albeit one who
(45)   wants to understand the nature of God; and "The Black Wedding," which features a demon. Around these stories, there is usually an aura of the folktale or fairy tale.
(50)   Stories of the second type have historical and geographical settings very different from those of the first. They usually take place in post World War II America, and many times are set in New
(55)   York City. As in the first type, the central characters are Jewish, although they are not necessarily orthodox. Like the characters in the first type, they represent all classes, from affluent businesspeople
(60)   and physicians, to writers, to the poor of all sorts. There are some supernatural characters, as well, but the characters in

this type are predominantly human. Prominent among them is a certain kind
(65) of male character who is financially successful, but who is troubled by the ordinary human concerns of love and sex, physical illness, the riddle of death, and the nature of reality. The study of
(70) philosophy—Kant and Spinoza are favorites—replace the study of the sacred books common to the first type of story. Among the stories in this group are "A Wedding in Brownsville" and "The
(75) Cafeteria" (both of which are discussed below), as well as "The Seance," in which it is ambiguous whether the rouged and mascaraed medium, Mrs. Kopitzky, is a fake. She "more than
(80) once" awakes from trances to talk on the phone about "stocks, bonds, and dividends," yet at the end of the story her skeptical boarder, Dr. Kalisher, seems to half-believe she is authentic.

(85) Stories of the third type are confined to no particular time period and to no particular location—sometimes they are set in the ordinary human world and sometimes not. The distinctive feature of
(90) this type is that its central characters are supernatural beings, usually demons but occasionally angels or disembodied souls. No matter how fantastical their natures, however, these creatures, like their
(95) human counterparts in the other story types, often wonder about the nature of God or reality, and they are frequently beset by problems that originate in the human world. Representative of this
(100) group are "Shiddah and Kuziba," in which two demons, mother and son, find that their home, "nine yards inside the earth," is being destroyed by a drill operated by the mysterious humans who
(105) occupy the world above them; and "The

Last Demon," in which a demon declares there are no demons left—"Why demons, when man himself is a demon?" (In the demonic tales, it is frequently unclear
(110) which is more evil, humans or demons.)

The characters, settings, and historical periods in Singer's stories, then, vary widely, yet under the surface there are striking similarities. Everywhere in them,
(115) the reader finds opposites, contraries, ambiguities. In the story "The Slaughterer," the ritual slaughterer develops "an unfamiliar love" for "all that crawls and flies, breeds and swarms." In "The
(120) Cafeteria," the dead of the Nazi holocaust—both perpetrators and victims—come to sit in a cafeteria on Broadway. In "A Wedding in Brownsville," a dead man, not realizing until the end of the
(125) story that he is dead, attends a wedding and sees among the other guests a woman he once loved, who died in the holocaust. (The dead often walk about in Singer's stories, but they are not ethereal
(130) or ghostly; in fact, so substantial a part of the phenomenal world are they that neither the characters in the stories nor the reader can readily identify them.)

So although Singer's fictional realm is
(135) animistic and magical, it seems always to be rooted in the material world. Critic Irving Howe has said of Singer's stories that they "work, or prey, upon the nerves. They leave one unsettled and
(140) anxious, the way a rationalist might feel if, waking at night in the woods, he suddenly found himself surrounded by a swarm of bats."

GO ON TO THE NEXT PAGE

12. The passage is primarily concerned with

(A) the metaphysical world of Singer's stories.
(B) Singer's religious beliefs.
(C) historical aspects of Singer's work.
(D) autobiographical elements in Singer's work.
(E) superstition in Singer's stories.

13. In the context of the passage, which of the following best expresses the meaning of the statement in lines 8 and 9 that, in Singer's fictional world, "There is no border between the cosmic and the mundane"?

(A) The seemingly dualistic elements of Singer's stories are an integral part of one another.
(B) In Singer's stories, both God and demons frequently descend to earth and mingle with human beings.
(C) Singer believes that the dead roam the earth and that sometimes we cannot tell who they are.
(D) In Singer's stories, the characters often wonder about the nature of God and reality.
(E) Singer's stories have many different kinds of settings and characters, yet they all have the same theme.

14. To which of the following does the word "phenomena" (line 14) refer?

(A) Supernatural elements of the physical universe
(B) Startling or incredible aspects of seemingly ordinary things and events
(C) Those parts of the world that appear material and real to the senses
(D) The realm of dead people who do not know they are dead
(E) Obvious truths about the world at large

15. What is the meaning of the word "dichotomous" in line 12?

(A) Subjected to endless debate
(B) Regarded as controversial
(C) Presented in a disjointed fashion
(D) Related to spiritual matters
(E) Divided into two usually contradictory classifications

16. The author most likely divided the stories into three types in order to illustrate the idea that

(A) Singer's stories are too complex to be categorized precisely.
(B) in spite of the many surface differences in the three types of stories, there are important similarities.
(C) some of Singer's stories deal with the ordinary world of people and some with the supernatural.
(D) Singer does not write about a specific ethnic or racial group—his stories are universal.
(E) Singer's stories have orthodox religious underpinnings, in spite of their seemingly strange and unusual themes.

17. The author of the passage uses the story "The Slaughterer" (lines 116–119) to illustrate the fact that Singer's stories often contain

(A) symbolic language.
(B) supernatural elements.
(C) biographical details.
(D) contrary elements.
(E) wanton cruelty.

18. The story "Shiddah and Kuziba" (lines 99–105) demonstrates the author's idea that, in Singer's stories,

(A) demons are usually more sympathetic than human beings.
(B) demons often plague human characters who are searching after God.
(C) demons are written about in the language of folk or fairy tales.
(D) demons are understood to be metaphoric figures.
(E) demons are often beset by problems from the human world.

19. Which of the following elements in the story "Cockadoodledoo" (lines 42–45) is exceptional among Singer's stories?

(A) The setting
(B) The point of view
(C) The historical period
(D) The structure of the story
(E) The central concern of the narrator

20. The final paragraph of the passage indicates that Singer's stories are likely to leave the reader with a feeling of

(A) magic.
(B) dissatisfaction.
(C) inspiration.
(D) uneasiness.
(E) terror.

Questions 21–25 are based on the following passage.

This passage, except for many of the authorial value judgments, is based on Environmental Protection Agency documents on the environmental impact of the pesticide methyl bromide and its planned phase-out.

Line   Although many organizations—especially those connected to the agricultural industries—maintain that the benefits of methyl bromide outweigh its risks,
(5)   methyl bromide is a toxic chemical that will poison, not only the target pests it is used against, but non-target organisms as well. Because it dissipates so rapidly into the atmosphere, this pesticide is most
(10)   dangerous at the actual fumigation site, where human exposure to high concentrations is at a maximum. This exposure can result in central nervous system and respiratory system failure, as well as
(15)   specific and severe deleterious actions on the lungs, eyes, and skin. Exposure of pregnant women may result in fetal defects. Depending upon dose, gross permanent disabilities or death may
(20)   result.
        Assessments made by atmospheric scientists, under the authority of the World Meteorological Organization along with the National Oceanic and
(25)   Atmospheric Administration and the National Aeronautics and Space Administration, indicate that methyl bromide also contributes significantly to the destruction of earth's stratospheric ozone
(30)   layer, which protects life on earth from exposure to dangerous levels of ultraviolet light, a major cause of skin cancer, cataracts, and impaired immune systems. When ozone-degrading chemicals such as
(35)   methyl bromide (whose sources include

271

soil fumigation, as mentioned above, as well as the exhaust of automobiles using leaded gasoline) are emitted, the chlorine and bromine they contain catalyze
(40) destruction of the ozone.

Worldwide, most of the methyl bromide used goes to fumigate soil for preplant purposes. The breakdown is 70 percent to fumigate soil, 16 and 8 percent
(45) to fumigate durable and perishable commodities, respectively, and 6 percent to treat structures. Of all the methyl bromide used, North America uses the most, at 43 percent of the total. Asia uses
(50) 24 percent and Europe 24 percent, while the remaining 9 percent is used by Africa, South America, and Australia. In the United States, growers use 43 million pounds of methyl bromide each year. Of
(55) that, about 35 million pounds go for soil fumigation, 5 million for post-harvest uses, and 3 million for structural fumigation. This means that 81 percent of the chemical used goes to prepare the
(60) soil for vegetables, orchards, nurseries, and other crops—that is, 81 percent actually affects foods we take into our bodies.

Because science has so definitely
(65) fingered methyl bromide as a culprit in destroying the ozone, regulatory actions are needed to control emissions. Under the Clean Air Act, methyl bromide had been scheduled for phase-out in the
(70) United States on January 1, 2001. In spite of its obvious hazards, however, much of the agricultural industry continues to lobby against discontinuing utilization of this pesticide, and Congress
(75) recently signed legislation to extend its use, beginning gradual phase-out by 2005.

21. Which of the following best expresses the main idea of the passage?

(A) Although organizations and political bodies with vested interests support the use of methyl bromide, the facts show that it is too dangerous to go on using.

(B) Congress has been remiss in failing to push for phase-out of methyl bromide by the year 2001.

(C) Although methyl bromide is a dangerous chemical, it does have a number of beneficial uses.

(D) Methyl bromide is hazardous, not only to individual human beings, but to humanity as a whole, since it is depleting the ozone layer.

(E) In today's society, politics and money always take precedence over the well-being of human beings.

22. In the context of the passage, to which of the following does the term "fumigation site" (line 10) refer?

(A) The address of the farm on which the pesticide is being used

(B) The organisms being targeted by the pesticide

(C) The place where the pesticide is actually added to the soil

(D) The location of the company distributing the pesticide

(E) The chemicals that make up the pesticide

23. Readers would probably be more likely to take political action against the use of methyl bromide if the author

- (A) included specific names of corporations and organizations that lobby for the continued use of methyl bromide.
- (B) added a detailed discussion of the scientific designation for ozone—O_3—and how such designations are determined.
- (C) mentioned the exact amount of money saved by the reduction of crop loss through the use of methyl bromide.
- (D) gave the history of the passage of the Clean Air Act.
- (E) deleted mention of the action by Congress from the final paragraph.

24. What is the most likely reason the author included statistics in paragraph 3?

- (A) To reduce the likelihood that the reader will be offended by the final paragraph with its harsh criticism of Congress
- (B) To distract the reader from the fact that there might be fallacies in the central argument of the paper
- (C) To add weight to the central argument by giving concrete proof that methyl bromide is hazardous to humans
- (D) To make the paper and its central argument more persuasive to scientists and other academics
- (E) To demonstrate that North America has less concern than other countries for the harm that big corporations do to its citizens

25. Which of the following does the passage imply is the most important of the "non-target organisms," as the term is used in line 7?

- (A) The bacteria and other organisms, such as worms, that are necessary to the production of food
- (B) The soil itself, into which the pesticide is injected
- (C) Livestock and other domestic animals
- (D) Human beings
- (E) Organisms that lie outside the range of distribution of methyl bromide

S T O P If you finish before time is called, you may check your work on this section only. Do not turn to any other section in the test.

Section 2—Math

Time—25 Minutes • 20 Questions

Solve problems 1–20, then select the best of the choices given for each one and fill in the corresponding oval on the answer sheet. You may use available space on the page for scratchwork.

Notes:

1. You may use a calculator. All of the numbers used are real numbers.

2. You may use the figures that accompany the problems to help you find the solution. Unless the instructions say that a figure is not drawn to scale, assume that it has been drawn accurately. Each figure lies in a plane unless the instructions say otherwise.

Reference Information

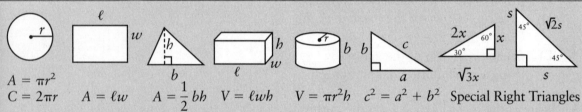

$A = \pi r^2$
$C = 2\pi r$ $A = \ell w$ $A = \dfrac{1}{2}bh$ $V = \ell wh$ $V = \pi r^2 h$ $c^2 = a^2 + b^2$ Special Right Triangles

The number of degrees of arc in a circle is 360.
The measure in degrees of a straight angle is 180.
The sum of the measures in degrees of the angles of a triangle is 180.

1. If $\dfrac{2}{3}$ of the area of a triangle equals 6 square inches, what is its area?

   (A) 2
   (B) 4
   (C) 6
   (D) 9
   (E) 12

2. If $9x + 5 = 23$, what is the numerical value of $18x + 5$?

   (A) 46
   (B) 41
   (C) 36
   (D) 32
   (E) It cannot be determined from the given information.

3. What is the angle measure of α in the figure below?

   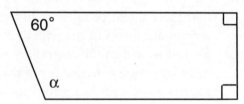

   (A) 90°
   (B) 95°
   (C) 100°
   (D) 110°
   (E) 120°

274

4. The price of admission to a movie theater has increased 15%. If a ticket originally cost 5 dollars, what is the new price?

(A) $4.25
(B) $5.25
(C) $5.75
(D) $6.25
(E) $6.75

5. If $\dfrac{1}{3} - \dfrac{1}{4} + \dfrac{1}{2} - \dfrac{1}{6} = x$, then $\dfrac{1}{x} =$

(A) $\dfrac{12}{5}$

(B) $\dfrac{11}{5}$

(C) $\dfrac{12}{11}$

(D) $\dfrac{-7}{12}$

(E) $\dfrac{-12}{7}$

6. $(x + y) - (x - y) =$

(A) $-2y$
(B) $-2x$
(C) 0
(D) $2x + 2y$
(E) $2y$

7. 40 percent of 50 is four times what number?

(A) 4
(B) 5
(C) 8
(D) 10
(E) 20

8. The net price of a television set is $306 after successive discounts of 15% and 10% off the marked price. What is the marked price?

(A) $234.09
(B) $400
(C) $382.50
(D) $408
(E) None of the above

9. What is the value of x in the figure below?

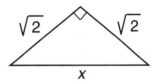

(A) $\sqrt{2}$
(B) $\sqrt{3}$
(C) 1
(D) 2
(E) $2\sqrt{2}$

10. If $x = \sqrt{3 - y}$, then what is y in terms of x?

(A) $x^2 = 3 - y$
(B) $y = 3 - x^2$
(C) $y^2 = 3 - x^2$
(D) $y = 9 - x^2$
(E) $y = x^2 - 9$

11. $(y + 3)(3 + y) =$

(A) $y^2 + 6y + 9$
(B) $9 - y^2$
(C) $y^2 + 9$
(D) $6y$
(E) y^2

275

12. If the area of a square is 36 square meters, what is its perimeter?

    (A) 16 meters
    (B) 18 meters
    (C) 20 meters
    (D) 22 meters
    (E) 24 meters

13. If $\frac{4}{5} < x < \frac{7}{8}$, which of the following could be a value for x?

    (A) $\frac{6}{4}$

    (B) $\frac{2}{3}$

    (C) $\frac{11}{12}$

    (D) $\frac{25}{30}$

    (E) $\frac{28}{30}$

14. A baker's helper earns 9 dollars per hour, including lunch and break time. This week, he works from 4 a.m. to noon on Monday, Tuesday, and Friday and from 5 a.m. to 11 a.m. on Wednesday and Thursday. How much money did the baker's helper earn this week?

    (A) $36
    (B) $216
    (C) $324
    (D) $350
    (E) $369

15. A circle is inscribed in a square. If the area of the circle is 9π in^2, what is the area of the square?

    (A) 3π in^2
    (B) 9π in^2
    (C) 36 in^2
    (D) $(36 - 9\pi)$ in^2
    (E) 9 in^2

16. A cube with a volume of 64 cubic inches is sliced into smaller cubes, each with a side of 1 inch. What dimension is the side of the original cube?

    (A) 4
    (B) 8
    (C) 16
    (D) 32
    (E) 64

17. If $\frac{k}{x} = b$ and $b - 3 = ay$, which of the following correctly expresses y?

    (A) $\dfrac{(ay + 3)}{k}$

    (B) $\dfrac{(ay - 3)}{k}$

    (C) $\dfrac{[(kx - 3)(a)]}{x}$

    (D) $\dfrac{\left(\dfrac{k}{x} + 3\right)}{a}$

    (E) $\dfrac{\left(\dfrac{k}{x} - 3\right)}{a}$

276

18. The length of an arc of a circle equals $\frac{1}{8}$ of the circle's circumference. What is the diameter of the circle if the length of the arc is π?

    (A) 2.83
    (B) 4
    (C) 6.33π
    (D) 8
    (E) 10

19. At Boulder High, $\frac{6}{10}$ of the students are old enough to drive. Of these students, $\frac{1}{3}$ drive their own cars to school each day. What percent of the students at Boulder High drive their own cars to school every day?

    (A) 20%
    (B) 25%
    (C) 33%
    (D) 50%
    (E) 82%

20. If $0 \le a \le 3$ and $5 \le b \le 8$, what is the least possible value of $\frac{16}{b-a}$?

    (A) 0
    (B) 2
    (C) 7
    (D) 8
    (E) 10

S T O P If you finish before time is called, you may check your work on this section only. Do not turn to any other section in the test.

Section 3—Critical Reading

Time—25 Minutes • 27 Questions

For each question below, choose the best answer from the choices given and fill in the corresponding oval on the answer sheet.

> **Directions:** Each sentence below has either one or two blanks in it and is followed by five choices, labeled (A) through (E). These choices represent words or phrases that have been left out. Choose the word or phrase that, if inserted into the sentence, would best fit the meaning of the sentence as a whole.
>
> **Example:**
>
> Canine massage is a veterinary technique for calming dogs that are extremely _____.
>
> (A) inept
> (B) disciplined
> (C) controlled
> (D) stressed
> (E) restrained

1. James Lovelock has posited the theory of *Gaia*, which says that the earth is a single living organism—independent and _____.

   (A) ambivalent
   (B) self-regulating
   (C) indolent
   (D) static
   (E) annihilative

2. With the computer program Windows, you can check for errors on your hard disk, as well as remove unnecessary files, thus _____ the performance of your computer.

   (A) embodying
   (B) adorning
   (C) impeding
   (D) optimizing
   (E) depreciating

3. He was a vile person who lived to _____ wickedness and deceit—he was a/an _____ of lies.

   (A) foment..purveyor
   (B) betray..nullifier
   (C) deliver..disparager
   (D) thwart..embellisher
   (E) decry..proselytizer

4. My cousin Abebi is a/an _____ person—sociable, talkative, and a friend to all.

   (A) obnoxious
   (B) unpalatable
   (C) gregarious
   (D) parsimonious
   (E) reticent

5. At the movies, I could forget myself and the way life really was, settle down in the plush theater seat with my popcorn, and _____ myself in the _____ on the screen.

    (A) emerge..deception
    (B) recuse..fantasy
    (C) importune..emanation
    (D) divulge..exudation
    (E) immerse..illusion

6. In the fall, the chilly wind circles up under the eaves of the house, carrying the first _____ of winter.

    (A) premonition
    (B) spectacle
    (C) meandering
    (D) sighting
    (E) sensation

7. When it became obvious that Ben had _____ money from the petty cash fund, he was fired.

    (A) opportuned
    (B) pilfered
    (C) discounted
    (D) required
    (E) desired

8. Because Mandisa's job was so _____, she had a/an _____ of funds and was able to buy a boat and sail away to Greece.

    (A) lucrative..superfluity
    (B) arduous..penury
    (C) remunerative..audacity
    (D) powerful..mendicancy
    (E) immodest..surfeit

Directions: Read each of the passages carefully and answer the questions that come after them. Base your answers on what is stated or implied, as well as on any introductory material provided.

Questions 9–10 are based on the following passage.

This excerpt is from Sir Thomas More's book, Utopia *(1515).*

Line   There are several sorts of religions [on the island of Utopia], not only in different parts of the island, but even in every town; some worshipping the sun,
(5)   others the moon or one of the planets. . . . Yet the greater and wiser sort of them worship none of these, but adore one eternal, invisible, infinite, and incomprehensible Deity. . . . They differ in this:
(10)   that one thinks the god whom he worships is this Supreme Being, and another thinks that his idol is that god; but they all agree in one principle, that whoever is this Supreme Being . . . is also
(15)   that great essence to whose glory and majesty all honours are ascribed by the consent of all nations.

9. The attitude toward religion on the island of Utopia can best be described as

    (A) atheistic.
    (B) fanatical.
    (C) immature.
    (D) primitive.
    (E) tolerant.

GO ON TO THE NEXT PAGE

PETERSON'S
getting you there

10. The tone of the passage can best be described as

(A) satirical.
(B) awed.
(C) dismissive.
(D) respectful.
(E) skeptical.

Questions 11–13 are based on the following passage.

The following excerpt is from an address by Senator Hillary Rodham Clinton, "New American Strategies for Security and Peace," at the Center for American Progress on October 29, 2003.

Line   Of course in a democracy, there always is tension between the information that the Executive Branch needs to keep secret and the information that must be
(5)   provided to the public to have an informed citizenry. There are no easy answers to striking the right balance. But we must always be vigilant against letting our desire to keep information confiden-
(10)   tial be used as a pretext for classifying information that is more about political embarrassment than national security. Let me be absolutely clear. This is not a propensity that is confined to one party
(15)   or the other. It is a propensity of power that we must guard against.

11. The main purpose of Clinton's address is to advocate an end to

(A) tension between the Executive Branch and the public.
(B) secrets kept by the Executive Branch solely for political reasons.
(C) witholding of information by the political party to which Clinton is opposed.
(D) public insistance on the release of classified information.
(E) false information released by the Executive branch.

12. A main implication of the passage is that, with information, comes

(A) power.
(B) wisdom.
(C) security.
(D) deceit.
(E) confusion.

13. What is the meaning of the word "propensity," as used in the passage?

(A) A right
(B) An entitlement
(C) A decree
(D) An idea
(E) An inclination

Questions 14–15 are based on the following passage.

The following exerpt is from the U.S. Department of Energy archives.

Line
[In 1929, Ernest] Lawrence invented a unique circular particle accelerator, which he referred to as his "proton merry-go-round," but which became
(5) better known as the cyclotron. The first cyclotron was a pie-shaped concoction of glass, sealing wax, and bronze. A kitchen chair and a wire-coiled clothes tree were also enlisted to make the device work.
(10) Despite its Rube Goldberg appearance, the cyclotron proved Lawrence's point: whirling particles around to boost their energies, then casting them toward a target like stones from a slingshot is the
(15) most efficient and effective way to smash open atomic nuclei.

14. In the context of the passage, the phrase "Rube Goldberg" most likely means

(A) impractical.
(B) sophisticated.
(C) technical.
(D) ingenious.
(E) inconspicuous.

15. The colloquial phrase "proton merry-go-round" primarily serves to make the passage more accessible to readers who

(A) are uninterested in technolgy.
(B) lack technical expertise.
(C) plan to become scientists.
(D) understand complex metaphors.
(E) believe technology is dangerous.

Passage 1

From a short story first published in 1891, "The Yellow Wallpaper," by Charlotte Perkins Gilman.

Line
It is very seldom that mere ordinary people like John and myself secure ancestral halls for the summer.
A colonial mansion, a hereditary
(5) estate, I would say a haunted house, all reach the height of romantic felicity—but that would be asking too much of fate!
Still I will proudly declare that there is something queer about it.
(10) Else, why should it be let so cheaply? And why have stood so long untenanted?
John laughs at me, of course, but one expects that in marriage.
John is a physician, and PERHAPS—
(15) (I would not say it to a living soul, of course, but this is dead paper and a great relief to my mind)—PERHAPS that is one reason I do not get well faster.
You see he does not believe I am sick!
(20) And what can one do?
If a physician of high standing, and one's own husband, assures friends and relatives that there is really nothing the matter with one but temporary nervous
(25) depression—a slight hysterical tendency—what is one to do?
My brother is also a physician, and also of high standing, and he says the same thing. . . .
(30) [John] said we came here solely on my account, that I was to have perfect rest and all the air I could get. "Your exercise depends on your strength, my dear," said he, "and your food somewhat
(35) on your appetite; but air you can absorb all the time."
So we took the nursery at the top of the house.

GO ON TO THE NEXT PAGE

PETERSON'S
getting you there

It is a big, airy room, the whole floor
(40) nearly, with windows that look all ways,
and air and sunshine galore. It was
nursery first and then playroom and
gymnasium, I should judge; for the
windows are barred for little children,
(45) and there are rings and things in the
walls.

The paint and paper look as if a
boys' school had used it.

It is stripped off—the paper—in great
(50) patches all around the head of my bed,
about as far as I can reach, and in a great
place on the other side of the room low
down. I never saw a worse paper in my
life.

(55) One of those sprawling flamboyant
patterns committing every artistic sin.

It is dull enough to confuse the eye in
following, pronounced enough to
constantly irritate and provoke study,
(60) and when you follow the lame uncertain
curves for a little distance they suddenly
commit suicide—plunge off at outrageous angles, destroy themselves in
unheard of contradictions.

(65) The color is repellent, almost
revolting; a smoldering unclean yellow,
strangely faded by the slow-turning
sunlight.

It is a dull yet lurid orange in some
(70) places, a sickly sulfur tint in others.

No wonder the children hated it! I
should hate it myself if I had to live in
this room long.

Passage 2

From a short story that first appeared in 1839,
"The Fall of the House of Usher," *by Edgar*
Allen Poe.

Line   During the whole of a dull, dark, and
soundless day in the autumn of the year,
when the clouds hung oppressively low
in the heavens, I had been passing alone,
(5) on horseback, through a singularly
dreary tract of country; and at length
found myself, as the shades of the
evening drew on, within view of the
melancholy House of Usher. I know not
(10) how it was—but, with the first glimpse of
the building, a sense of insufferable
gloom pervaded my spirit. I say insufferable; for the feeling was unrelieved by
any of that half-pleasurable, because
(15) poetic, sentiment, with which the mind
usually receives even the sternest natural
images of the desolate or terrible. I
looked upon the scene before me . . .
with an utter depression of soul which I
(20) can compare to no earthly sensation
more properly than to the after-dream of
the reveler upon opium—the bitter lapse
into everyday life—the hideous dropping
off of the veil. . . .

(25)   Nevertheless, in this mansion of
gloom I now proposed to myself a
sojourn of some weeks. Its proprietor,
Roderick Usher, had been one of my
boon companions in boyhood; but many
(30) years had elapsed since our last meeting.
A letter, however, had lately reached me
in a distant part of the country—a letter
from him—which, in its wildly importunate nature, had admitted of no other
(35) than a personal reply. The MS gave
evidence of nervous agitation. The writer
spoke of acute bodily illness—of a mental
disorder which oppressed him—and of

an earnest desire to see me, as his best,
(40) and indeed his only personal friend, with
a view of attempting, by the cheerfulness
of my society, some alleviation of his
malady. . . .

A servant in waiting took my horse,
(45) and I entered the Gothic archway of the
hall. A valet, of stealthy step, thence
conducted me, in silence, through many
dark and intricate passages in my
progress to the studio of his master.
(50) Much that I encountered on the way
contributed, I know not how, to heighten
the vague sentiments of which I have
already spoken.

16. Which of the following occurs as the
narrator is describing the nursery room in
Passage 1?

(A) The narrator begins to realize she
really is ill.
(B) The narrator resigns herself to
staying in the nursery room.
(C) The narrator grows more terrified.
(D) The narrator's impression shifts from
negative to positive.
(E) The narrator's impression shifts from
positive to negative.

17. Which of the following can be inferred
from Passage 1?

(A) In reality, the narrator is not mentally
disturbed at all.
(B) The narrator's husband understands
and wants to help her.
(C) The narrator's husband has seriously
misjudged the severity of the narrator's illness.
(D) The house that the narrator and her
husband occupy is haunted by the
narrator's ancestors.
(E) The nursery room was previously
occupied by the narrator's own
children.

18. What is the most likely reason the
narrator says the nursery room appears
"as if a boys' school had used it"?

(A) The nursery windows are barred.
(B) The paper on the nursery walls has
been stripped off.
(C) There are rings in the nursery walls.
(D) The nursery walls are a sickly color.
(E) The nursery used to be a playroom
and gymnasium.

19. What can we conclude from the narrator's
description of the wallpaper in lines
49–70?

(A) She believes it was chosen with her in
mind.
(B) She has been obsessively studying it.
(C) She blames John for making her look
at it.
(D) She has begun, in a sick sort of way,
to like it.
(E) It reminds her of something in her
past.

GO ON TO THE NEXT PAGE

20. To whom or what does the phrase "commit suicide" refer in line 62?

(A) The colors in the wallpaper
(B) The pattern of the wallpaper
(C) The previous inhabitant of the room
(D) The narrator in her own imagination
(E) The narrator's brother

21. What does the narrator of Passage 2 mean by the word "insufferable" in line 11?

(A) Maddening
(B) Unrelieved
(C) Insupportable
(D) Immeasurable
(E) Revolting

22. In Passage 2, to what does the phrase "the hideous dropping off of the veil" (lines 23–24) refer?

(A) The unwholesome aspect of the house
(B) The narrator's self-loathing
(C) A return to reality after a drugged state
(D) Repulsive memories from the narrator's past
(E) The narrator's sudden terror

23. What is the meaning of the word "sojourn" in line 27 of Passage 2?

(A) Temporary stay
(B) Journey
(C) Dalliance
(D) Expedition
(E) Appointment

24. In the context of Passage 2, use of the phrase "wildly importunate" (lines 33–34) indicates that, in his letter to the narrator, Roderick Usher

(A) demanded that the narrator visit him.
(B) pleaded with the narrator to visit him.
(C) requested that the narrator visit him.
(D) invited the narrator to visit him.
(E) suggested that the narrator visit him.

25. In the context of the passage, what is the most likely meaning of the phrase "vague sentiments" in line 52?

(A) The welcome that Usher gives the narrator when the narrator arrived at his study
(B) The boyhood friendship that the narrator and Usher shared
(C) The feeling of gloom and depression that the narrator has felt throughout the passage
(D) The cheerfulness of the narrator in contrast to Usher's gloominess
(E) The feeling the narrator has toward Usher's servant and valet

26. A main difference between the *first sentence* of Passage 1 and that of Passage 2 is in the

(A) point of view (first, second, third person).
(B) sex of the narrator.
(C) age of the narrator.
(D) social class of the narrator.
(E) tone it seems to set.

284

27. Which of the following is an important similarity between the narrators of the two passages?

(A) Their state of health
(B) The effect that the stories' settings have on them
(C) The effect that the seasons have on them
(D) Their marital state
(E) Their relationship with the other characters

S T O P If you finish before time is called, you may check your work on this section only. Do not turn to any other section in the test.

Section 4—Math

Time—25 Minutes • 20 Questions

This section is made up of two types of questions, multiple choice—10 questions, and Student-Produced Response—10 questions. You have 25 minutes to complete the section. You may use available space on the page for scratchwork.

Notes:

1. You may use a calculator. All of the numbers used are real numbers.

2. You may use the figures that accompany the problems to help you find the solution. Unless the instructions say that a figure is not drawn to scale, assume that it has been drawn accurately. Each figure lies in a plane unless the instructions say otherwise.

Reference Information

     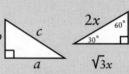

$A = \pi r^2$
$C = 2\pi r$ $\quad A = \ell w \quad A = \dfrac{1}{2}bh \quad V = \ell wh \quad V = \pi r^2 h \quad c^2 = a^2 + b^2$ Special Right Triangles

The number of degrees of arc in a circle is 360.
The measure in degrees of a straight angle is 180.
The sum of the measures in degrees of the angles of a triangle is 180.

---

1. Which linear equation most accurately models the scatter plot diagram shown?

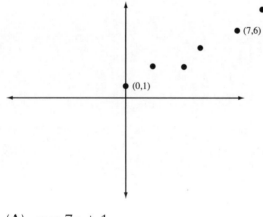

(A) $y = 7x + 1$
(B) $y = 0.7x + 1$
(C) $y = 0.25x + 5$
(D) $y = 1.4x + .5$
(E) $y = -2x + 1$

2. What is the absolute value of the difference between $y^2 + 0.15$ and y^3, given $y = 3$?

(A) -17.85
(B) 17.85
(C) 9.15
(D) -0.15
(E) 0.15

3. Find the product of x and y, given $x = 2^3 + 3^2$ and $y = 3^3 + 2^2$.

(A) 1225
(B) 527
(C) 289
(D) 35
(E) 17

286

4. Given $3c - 4 < 17$ which of the following is NOT a possible value of c?

(A) 7
(B) 6
(C) 0
(D) −7
(E) −17

5. Find x when $y = 1$, given $\dfrac{x}{y} - 7 = 5$.

(A) $\dfrac{1}{12}$

(B) $\dfrac{1}{7}$

(C) 12
(D) 2
(E) 0

6. Given $2\sqrt[3]{x} - 12 = -6$, find x.

(A) 36
(B) 27
(C) 18
(D) 9
(E) 3

7. Given the following diagram with sides x, find β.

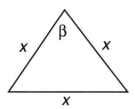

(A) 15°
(B) 30°
(C) 60°
(D) 75°
(E) 90°

8. A year ago, Tom and Al each deposited $1,000 in separate investment accounts. Tom's account earns 5% every year. Al's account earns 2.5% every six months. What is the difference between Tom's and Al's accounts today?

(A) $0
(B) $0.63
(C) $25.63
(D) $25
(E) $50

9. In the figure below, P is the center of a circle with area 9π, points Q and R lie on the circle, and angle α is 45°. What is the length of $\overline{QR}$?

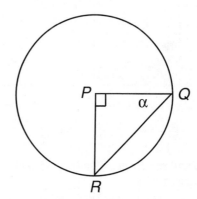

(A) $3\sqrt{2}$
(B) 3
(C) $9\sqrt{2}$
(D) 9
(E) 18

10. Given $f(x) = \dfrac{(196)^{\frac{1}{2}} - x}{x^{\frac{1}{3}} + 1}$, evaluate f for $x = 8$.

(A) 168
(B) 7.33
(C) 3
(D) 2
(E) 1.33

287

Questions 11–20 require you to solve the problems, then enter your answers by marking ovals in the special grid, as shown in the examples below.

Directions for Student-Produced Response Questions

Each of the remaining **10** questions requires you to solve the problem and enter your answer by marking the ovals in the special grid, as shown in the examples below.

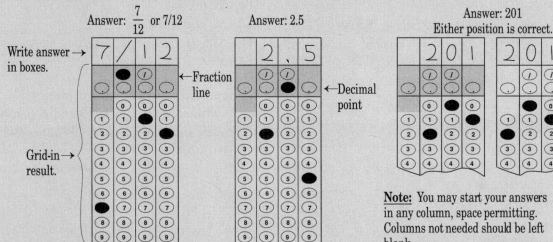

- Mark no more than one oval in any column.
- Because the answer sheet will be machine-scored, **you will receive credit only if the ovals are filled in correctly.**
- Although not required, it is suggested that you write your answer in the boxes at the top of the columns to help you fill in the ovals accurately.
- Some problems may have more than one correct answer. In such cases, grid only one answer.
- No question has a negative answer.
- **Mixed numbers** such as $2\frac{1}{2}$ must be gridded as 2.5 or 5/2. (If [2 1 / 2] is gridded, it will be interpreted as $\frac{21}{2}$, not $2\frac{1}{2}$.)

- **Decimal Accuracy:** If you obtain a decimal answer, **enter the most accurate value the grid will accommodate.** For example, if you obtain an answer such as 0.6666 . . . , you should record the result as .666 or .667. **Less accurate values such as .66 or .67 are not acceptable.**

Acceptable ways to grid $\frac{2}{3}$ = .6666 . . .

11. What area remains when the area of a square with side 3 is subtracted from the area of a circle with radius 2?

12. In the following diagram, find the area of the triangle formed by dropping a perpendicular line from $\overline{AB}$ to Point C, given $x = 4$. Note that $\overline{AB}$ and $\overline{DC}$ are parallel.

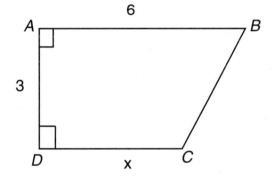

13. In the simple addition problem below, A and B are digits. What must A be?

$$
\begin{array}{r}
0.AB \\
+\,0.BA \\
\hline
0.BB
\end{array}
$$

14. In the figure below, if $AB = \dfrac{1}{2} BC$, then what is the y-coordinate of point B?

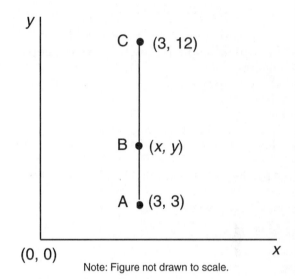

Note: Figure not drawn to scale.

15. How many of the first 100 positive integers contain the digit 7?

16. In the figure below, what is the value of α?

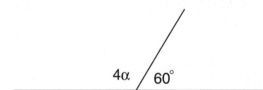

289

17. In order to make enough brownies to serve 1 dozen people, a recipe calls for $\frac{1}{4}$ ounce of cocoa. Using this recipe, how many ounces of cocoa would it take to make enough brownies for 36 people?

18. Let $a \nabla b$ be defined as $\frac{a!}{b!}$. What is the value of $\frac{(3 \nabla 4)}{2}$?

19. Given $x = .25$, what is the length of $\overline{AC}$ in the figure below?

20. In the following addition problems, what is the value of $C - B$?

$$
\begin{array}{r}
5 \\
8 \\
A \\
B \\
+3 \\
\hline
23
\end{array}
\qquad
\begin{array}{r}
1 \\
4 \\
A \\
C \\
+3 \\
\hline
19
\end{array}
$$

S T O P If you finish before time is called, you may check your work on this section only. Do not turn to any other section in the test.

Section 5—Writing Skills

Time—25 Minutes • 39 Questions

For each question below, select the best answer from the choices given and fill in the corresponding oval on the answer sheet.

Directions: The following questions will test your knowledge of grammar, usage, diction, and idiom.

Some sentences are correct.

No sentence contains multiple errors.

In each sentence below, five elements, labeled (A) through (E), are underlined and lettered. One (and ONLY one) of the underlined elements may contain an error. In choosing your answer, be sure to follow the rules of standard written English. You can assume that the parts of the sentences not underlined are correct.

If the sentence has no error, choose ⓔ, "No error."

Example:

My dog Sally and my cat Buster

gets along well with each other, eating
    A   B
and sleeping together, playing quietly,
              C
and sharing their food and treats.
        D
No error.
    E

Sample Answer:

● Ⓑ Ⓒ Ⓓ Ⓔ

1. That Saturday, there was an eclipse, so
        A
   we punch tiny holes in cardboard, so we
     B   C
   could view it directly. No error.
        D   E

2. Looking out over the vast concert hall,
                        A
   Roger's stomach began
        A
   to churn with anxiety, because
            B
   he knew there were talent scouts
            C
   in the audience. No error.
        D   E

GO ON TO THE NEXT PAGE

3. In accordance to the bylaws of the Condo
       A   B

   Association, Ralph Beekerman is

   to remove those plastic ducks
       C

   from his front yard immediately. No error.
       D   E

4. When they were small, Winthrop and
              A

   Nigel Holmes dreamed of emulating
              B

   their famous Uncle Sherlock and becom-
              C

   ing a detective. No error.
       D   E

5. We were sitting in the park, my friend
                   A

   Kameko and me, when I suddenly see a
              B   C

   white squirrel dash up a juniper tree.
              D

   No error.
     E

6. When Roy's dog "Spike"

   won Best in Show at the Westminster, the
       A   B

   American Kennel Club accused him of
             B   C

   forging his pedigree. No error.
          D   E

7. Although Ernest Hemingway identified
              A

   with traditional strongmen types,
     B

   bullfighters, big game hunters, and
              C

   deep-sea fishermen, he died
           C

   alone, a suicide. No error.
         D   E

8. The price of kumquats
         A

   is less than kiwi fruit, so we shall have
          B   C

   kumquats for dessert. No error.
           D   E

9. Keep your skin soft with Tawny Body

   Wash, now containing a special hydrating
     A

   formula that will keep you looking
            B

   refreshed and vibrant, no matter
             C

   how hectic your day! No error.
        D   E

10. The tables and chairs has been set out and
               A

    are ready for the guests, so we have
           B   C

    nothing else to do until the party begins.
                   D

    No error.
      E

11. When my brother and I were teenagers,
                   A

    my favorite sports were

    football, baseball, and soccer, whereas
               B

    his were craps, poker, and
          C

    he also liked pitching pennies. No error.
              D   E

12. If one studies Shakespeare, you will learn
                 A   B

    as much about human relationships
             C

    as about poetry. No error.
         D   E

13. <u>Besides</u> being an Academy Award-winning
　　　A
film, *Rain Man* is an <u>excellent study</u>
　　　　　　　　　B
<u>of autism</u>, <u>starring</u> Dustin Hoffman
　　C　　　　　D
and Tom Cruise. <u>No error.</u>
　　D　　　　　E

14. My mother's diaries, <u>written</u> in the
　　　　　　　　　　A
1920s, <u>are</u> particularly interesting
　　　B
documents, <u>since</u> she worked
　　　　　C
<u>as a fan dancer</u> at that time. <u>No error.</u>
　　D　　　　　　　　E

15. *Consumer Reports*, <u>published by an</u>
　　　　　　　　　　A
<u>independent, nonprofit</u> organization, <u>was</u>
　　　B　　　　　　　　　C
the best guide consumers have today

<u>for finding</u> quality merchandise. <u>No error.</u>
　D　　　　　　　　　　E

16. The genetic code <u>consists of</u> the instruc-
　　　　　　　　A
tions present in living cells <u>that specify</u>
　　　　　　　　　　B
and control the synthesis <u>of polypeptides</u>
　　　　　　　　　C
and proteins <u>from amino acids.</u> <u>No error.</u>
　　　　　D　　　　　　　E

17. Because <u>it's</u> Grandpa's favorite dish, we
　　　A
were <u>planning to</u> have corned beef
　　　B
for supper tonight, but we <u>haven't got no</u>
　　　C　　　　　　　　D
pot to cook it in. <u>No error.</u>
　　　　　　　E

18. In the past, when <u>neurosurgeons had</u> only
　　　　　　　A
low-resolution microscopes <u>to work with,</u>
　　　　　　　　　B
the surgery <u>did</u> on the human brain was
　　　　C
more risky <u>than</u> it is today. <u>No error.</u>
　　　　D　　　　　　　E

19. Because he was absolutely <u>fearless,</u>
　　　　　　　　　A
Chucky was <u>unanimously</u> voted leader <u>to</u>
　　　B　　　C　　　　　　D
the whole gang. <u>No error.</u>
　　　　　E

GO ON TO THE NEXT PAGE

Directions: The sentences below test correctness and effectiveness of expression. When you choose your answers, select the sentence or sentence part that is most clear and correct and that conforms best to the requirements of standard written English.

Each of the following sentences is either underlined or contains an underlined part. Under each sentence, there are five ways of phrasing the underlined portion. Choice (A) repeats the original; the other four options are different. You can assume that the elements that are not underlined are correct.

Choose the answer that best expresses the meaning of the original sentence. If in your opinion the original sentence is the best option, choose it. Your choice should produce the most effective sentence.

Example:

I am going to the store to buy a food item, which is bread.

Sample Answer:

(A) buy a food item, which is bread
(B) buy a food item, bread
(C) buy bread
(D) buy a food item, which is called bread
(E) buy what is called bread

---

20. In point of fact, the book *Being and Nothingness*, written by author Jean-Paul Sartre in 1943, made the philosophy of Existentialism a popular one all over the world.

(A) In point of fact, the book *Being and Nothingness*, written by author Jean-Paul Sartre in 1943, made the philosophy of Existentialism a popular one all over the world.

(B) In point of fact, the book *Being and Nothingness*, written by author Jean-Paul Sartre in 1943, made Existentialism a popular philosophy all over the world.

(C) The book *Being and Nothingness*, written by Jean-Paul Sartre in 1943, made Existentialism popular.

(D) The book *Being and Nothingness*, written by Jean-Paul Sartre in 1943, made the philosophy of Existentialism popular all over the world.

(E) *Being and Nothingness*, written by Jean-Paul Sartre, made Existentialism a popular philosophy all over the world.

21. While running the Boston marathon, a faint feeling suddenly came over me.

(A) marathon, a faint feeling suddenly came over me
(B) marathon, over me came a faint feeling suddenly
(C) marathon, it caused a faint feeling
(D) marathon, I suddenly felt faint
(E) marathon, feeling suddenly faint

22. Too many instructions were given to me by the Head Waiter at once, and I became confused and dropped the bowl of stew in the customer's lap.

    (A) Too many instructions were given to me by the Head Waiter at once
    (B) I was given, by the Head Waiter, too many instructions at once
    (C) The Head Waiter gave me too many instructions at once
    (D) Too many instructions, by the Head Waiter, were given to me
    (E) Instructions were given to me by the Head Waiter, but too many at once

23. Albert Einstein was admired as a scientist throughout the world, but a recent biography suggests that he was unkind to his first wife.

    (A) world, but a recent biography suggests that he was unkind to his first wife.
    (B) world, but it is suggested by a recent biography that he was unkind to his first wife.
    (C) world, but unkindness to his first wife is suggested by a recent biography.
    (D) but was unkind to his first wife, as suggested by a recent biography.
    (E) but, as suggested by a recent biography, unkind he was to his first wife.

24. Verbal phone contact could not be obtained with Mr. Schuler by me, and so I proceeded to his domicile.

    (A) Verbal phone contact could not be obtained with Mr. Schuler by me, and so I proceeded to his domicile.
    (B) I could not reach Mr. Schuler by phone, so I went to his home.
    (C) I could not make verbal contact with Mr. Schuler by phone, so I advanced to his place of residence.
    (D) Verbal phone contact with Mr. Schuler could not be made by me, so I proceeded to his home.
    (E) Phone contact could not verbally be made by me with Mr. Schuler by phone, so I advanced to his domicile.

25. Mr. Pritchard, our trusted bookkeeper and friend of many years, embezzled funds from the supplies account and therefore was busted.

    (A) was busted
    (B) was arrested
    (C) underwent arrestment
    (D) was picked up by the cops
    (E) was detained by the local constable

26. My husband, seeing as how he is an assertive person, requested that we be seated by the window, and the maitre d' complied.

    (A) husband, seeing as how he is an assertive person
    (B) husband, being an assertive person
    (C) husband, for sure an assertive person
    (D) husband, assertive to the max
    (E) husband, a person who is constantly being assertive

GO ON TO THE NEXT PAGE

PETERSON'S
getting you there

27. My boyfriend is <u>as handsome, maybe more handsome than Tiffany's.</u>

    (A) as handsome, maybe more handsome than Tiffany's
    (B) as handsome as, maybe more handsome than, Tiffany's
    (C) way handsome as Tiffany's, maybe even more so
    (D) as handsome over Tiffany's, maybe more handsome
    (E) as handsome, maybe handsomer, than Tiffany's

28. The Komodo dragon, a huge monitor lizard, is <u>native to</u> Indonesia.

    (A) native to
    (B) native by
    (C) native for
    (D) native with
    (E) native in

29. When I was a block from home, my faithful dog Arno <u>coming to meet me</u>, wagging his tail.

    (A) coming to meet me
    (B) comes to meet me
    (C) is coming to meet me
    (D) came to meet me
    (E) come and met me

30. If you sing as well tonight as you did this afternoon, <u>you should win the award.</u>

    (A) you should win the award
    (B) you have won the award
    (C) you will have won the award
    (D) you won the award
    (E) you should be winning the award

31. Treating antisocial patients is particularly difficult, because the therapist cannot assume <u>the existence of a collaborative effort.</u>

    (A) the existence of a collaborative effort
    (B) the effort that exists is a collaborative one on both sides
    (C) that collaboration is truly the name of the game
    (D) that collaboration is the dynamic that is in true existence
    (E) that a collaborative effort is part and parcel of the whole endeavor

32. Why would Uncle Wilhelm change his will when we were so <u>attentive on him</u>?

    (A) attentive on him
    (B) attentive to him
    (C) attentive by him
    (D) attentive for him
    (E) attentive with him

33. We love scary movies, perhaps because <u>it gives us</u> the opportunity to experience the thrill of danger while remaining safe.

    (A) it gives us
    (B) they give us
    (C) we are given
    (D) of their giving
    (E) of its giving

Directions: The following passage is from an essay in its early stages. Some of it may need revision. Read the passage below and answer the questions that come after it. Some of the questions will ask you to improve sentence structure and word choice. Other questions will refer to parts of the essay or to the entire essay and ask you to improve organization and development. Base your decisions on the rules of standard written English, and mark your answer in the corresponding oval on the answer sheet.

Questions 34–39 are based on the following passage.

The following passage is an early draft of an essay about the author's mother. Some parts of the passage need to be revised.

(1) *The meals my mom prepared when I was a child would be a present-day dietitian's nightmare, although I didn't know it then.* (2) *When I was very small, for breakfast we'd have lumpy oatmeal with lots of sugar, or eggs fried in butter, with sausage on the side; for lunch, salami sandwiches with mayonnaise and an iceberg lettuce salad; for dinner, more iceberg (or maybe Jell-O), canned vegetables, round steak rolled in flour and fried within an inch of its life, and store-bought pie with whipped cream for dessert.* (3) *Other kids liked to come to our house for a sugar fix!* (4) *Later on, when I was a teenager and frozen provender became available my mom took to it with perfervidity.* (5) *She gloried in Banquet TV dinners, frozen pot pies, Sara Lee cheesecake that you just had to defrost and dig into.*

(6) *Oh, I'll eat bran muffins and sprouts and soy sandwiches.* (7) *In the dark of night, worrying about my cholesterol, I realize they're good for me.* (8) *In fact, given my childhood eating habits, I'm surprised I've lived this long!* (9) *But before you start feeling sorry for me, thinking I must have been a neglected child, you should know that I still like that kind of food best.* (10) *But I still prefer Wonder Bread to the 6-Grain Sour Dough you buy in the health food store, and I'll still take Mrs. Smith's frozen apple pie with Cool Whip before low-fat yogurt for dessert.*

(11) *So Mom wasn't Suzy Homemaker, or a fiber-gram-counter type, so what?* (12) *It didn't mean she was neglectful or lazy.* (13) *Mealtime was the only time she allowed herself to stop working and sit down.* (14) *Born in the early 1900s to a stoic, Calvinistic family, she grew up laboring on a farm from dawn to dusk.* (15) *That couldn't have been any fun—and she liked to have fun.* (16) *Sometimes I think she must have been a changeling, left on her somber parents' doorstep by mistake.* (17) *Basically she liked leisure and things of the flesh, although she rarely gave in to them.*

(18) *She may not have liked to cook.* (19) *She did like to eat.* (20) *Mealtime was festive at our house.* (21) *We never discussed serious topics at dinner, or bickered and argued at the table like some families do.* (22) *We were too busy talking about how good the food was and asking for seconds!*

34. Sentence 9 would make more sense if it were

(A) placed before sentence 6.
(B) placed before sentence 7.
(C) placed before sentence 8.
(D) placed before sentence 11.
(E) deleted altogether.

297

35. Which of the choices is the best revision of the underlined portion of sentence 4 below?

Later on, when I was a teenager and <u>frozen provender became available my mom took to it with perfervidity.</u>

- **(A)** food that was frozen, which you simply popped into the oven, my mom was only too happy to give over cooking altogether
- **(B)** frozen chow became available my mom took to it with a blithe spirit
- **(C)** frozen foods became available my mom took to them with zeal
- **(D)** frozen victuals became available my mom took to them with a good inclination
- **(E)** frozen fare came along my mom became happy

36. Which of the following would make the best replacement for the underlined phrase, as a transition between sentences 12 and 13?

It didn't mean she was neglectful or <u>lazy. Mealtime</u> was the only time she allowed herself to stop working and sit down.

- **(A)** lazy. Meanwhile, mealtime
- **(B)** lazy. On the contrary, mealtime
- **(C)** lazy. In addition, mealtime
- **(D)** lazy. Nevertheless, mealtime
- **(E)** lazy. Likewise, mealtime

37. In the context of the passage, which of the following topics would most logically be addressed between sentences 15 and 16?

- **(A)** A short list of chores the author's mother had to do on the farm
- **(B)** A description of the physical appearance of the author's mother's parents
- **(C)** A short list of things the author's mother liked to do to have fun
- **(D)** An analysis of the social pressures that caused the author's mother to believe she had to work so hard
- **(E)** A physical description of the author

38. Which of the following is the smoothest and most logical way to revise and combine the underlined portions of sentences 18, 19, and 20 reproduced below?

She may not have liked to <u>cook. She did like to eat. Mealtime</u> was festive at our house.

- **(A)** cook, and she did like to eat, for mealtime
- **(B)** cook, but she did like to eat, so mealtime
- **(C)** cook, and she did like to eat, but mealtime
- **(D)** cook, and she did like to eat, and mealtime
- **(E)** cook, but she did like to eat, yet mealtime

39. Deletion of which of the following sentences would improve the unity of the first paragraph?

- **(A)** Sentence 1
- **(B)** Sentence 2
- **(C)** Sentence 3
- **(D)** Sentence 4
- **(E)** Sentence 5

S T O P If you finish before time is called, you may check your work on this section only. Do not turn to any other section in the test.

Quick Score Answers

Section 1 Critical Reading	Section 2 Math	Section 3 Critical Reading	Section 4 Math	Section 5 Writing Skills
1. B	1. D	1. B	1. B	1. B
2. D	2. B	2. D	2. B	2. A
3. E	3. E	3. A	3. B	3. A
4. A	4. C	4. C	4. A	4. D
5. B	5. A	5. E	5. C	5. C
6. D	6. E	6. A	6. B	6. C
7. C	7. B	7. B	7. C	7. E
8. B	8. B	8. A	8. B	8. B
9. B	9. D	9. E	9. A	9. E
10. B	10. B	10. D	10. D	10. A
11. D	11. A	11. B	11. **3.57**	11. D
12. A	12. E	12. A	12. **3**	12. B
13. A	13. D	13. E	13. **0**	13. D
14. C	14. C	14. A	14. **6**	14. E
15. E	15. C	15. B	15. **19**	15. C
16. B	16. A	16. E	16. **30°**	16. E
17. D	17. E	17. C	17. **.75 ounce**	17. D
18. E	18. D	18. B	**cocoa**	18. C
19. B	19. A	19. B	18. $\frac{1}{8}$	19. D
20. D	20. B	20. B	19. **3**	20. D
21. A		21. B	20. **4**	21. D
22. C		22. C		22. C
23. A		23. A		23. A
24. C		24. B		24. B
25. D		25. C		25. B
		26. E		26. B
		27. B		27. B
				28. A
				29. D
				30. A
				31. A
				32. B
				33. B
				34. A
				35. C
				36. B
				37. C
				38. B
				39. C

Explanatory Answers

Section 1—Critical Reading

1. **The correct answer is (B).** The word *while* indicates that the sentence contains contrasting elements. To find the answer, you must know what the word *orthodoxy* means, and that, chances are, a person who is orthodox believes that faith is more important than reason.

2. **The correct answer is (D).** None of the other choices indicate a *love* of car rides. In fact, you might be able to make the right choice simply by ruling out the wrong ones. But if you have a vocabulary wide enough to encompass the word *alacrity*, which means cheerful willingness or eagerness, you're ahead of the game.

3. **The correct answer is (E).** Again, the word *while* points to a contrast, so you should look for opposites among the answers. Only choices (B) and (E) meet this requirement. Choice (B) is wrong, because a person who is *depressed* does not necessarily object to what another person wants. A person who is *contentious* frequently will.

4. **The correct answer is (A).** The word *because*, as you know, points to a cause-and-effect element in the sentence. Reading closely, you can be pretty sure from the context—and probably from having heard the phrase used this way before—that *half the human race* means women, and that therefore *rich brain power* also refers to women. Now what is it about someone with *rich brain power* that would cause *concern*? Choice (B) can be ruled out immediately, followed by choice (D) (*audacity* might actually help a woman by making her more assertive), so choices (A), (C), and (E) are left. Now move on to the next word. Read closely again, and you'll see that choices (C) and (E) make no sense.

5. **The correct answer is (B).** This is a definition sentence. Ask which choice most clearly indicates a willingness to *please without hope of reward*. If your vocabulary encompasses the word *altruistic*, the answer is clear.

6. **The correct answer is (D).** The treaty does not ban most underground testing. The other choices are not reflected in the passage.

7. **The correct answer is (C).** The treaty states that a common goal is *an end to the contamination of . . . radioactive substances* in the human environment. Choice (B) is incorrect because the treaty allows for underground tests of nuclear weapons, suggesting that the prevention of detonations is not the main purpose of the treaty. The other choices are not supported by the passage.

8. **The correct answer is (B).** The FTC e-mail threatens the Web site owner with legal action for noncompliance, so it is not merely *advice*, *opinion*, or *reminder*—choices (A), (C), or (E). Choice (D) does not make sense in the context of the passage.

9. **The correct answer is (B).** Choice (A) is wrong because the e-mail says only that *if* an order is issued, Web site owners *may* have to pay back money. Choice (D) is wrong because, although the e-mail says that *without . . . scientific evidence* owners must discontinue the claims, it does not order them to find it. Choices (C) and (E) are not supported by the passage.

10. **The correct answer is (B).** The passage states that the questions became important when the arts became *available to the masses as never before* (lines 13–14). The other choices may be true but are not stated in the passage as a main reason.

11. **The correct answer is (D).** The word *afoul* implies conflict. There is no evidence in the passage for the other choices.

12. **The correct answer is (A).** Metaphysics deals with problems of ultimate reality and the structure of the universe. The passage talks mainly about how, in Singer's stories, the supernatural and the ordinary are inextricably fused. Choices (B), (C), and (D) are not mentioned. The supernatural is discussed, but this is not the same thing as superstition, choice (E), which is not mentioned in the passage.

13. **The correct answer is (A).** The statement immediately follows the assertion that in Singer's stories, *dualities are . . . embedded in one another.*

14. **The correct answer is (C).** Lines 13–14 define the term *phenomena* by saying: *. . . that plane is the world of matter, the world of phenomena.* When working on critical reading passages, be sure to look closely at the sentences immediately surrounding the designated lines. It's not an invariable rule that they will be related to the answer, but they're a good place to start.

15. **The correct answer is (E).** Throughout the paragraph, the author discusses opposites: *past and present, animate and inanimate, the supernatural and the ordinary world of the senses, even life and death* (lines 2–5).

16. The correct answer is (B). Immediately following the description of the three types of stories, the passage states that the stories *vary widely, yet under the surface there are striking similarities.* Choices (A) and (E) are not reflected in the passage. Choice (C) is true, but it is a narrower choice than choice (B) and thus not as good. (Remember that in these questions, you are asked to pick the *best* or *most likely* answer, rather than just a possible one.) Choice (D) is incorrect because Singer's stories, as described in the passage, are mostly about Jews.

17. The correct answer is (D). Immediately preceding discussion of "The Slaughterer" in lines 116–119, the passage states that *Everywhere in* [Singer's stories], *the reader finds opposites, contraries, ambiguities.* Choices (A), (C), and (E) are not mentioned in the passage. Choice (B) is not mentioned in connection with this particular story.

18. The correct answer is (E). In "Shiddah and Kuziba," the home of two demons is threatened by a drill operated by humans above them. Choices (B) and (C) are mentioned in the passage but not in particular connection with this story, so choice (E) is still the best choice. Choice (D) is contradicted in the passage—in Singer's stories, demons actually seem to occupy the physical world.

19. The correct answer is (B). The passage calls the story *somewhat of an exception, since the narrator is a rooster.* Choice (D) is not mentioned. The remaining choices are shared by many of Singer's other stories.

20. The correct answer is (D). The final paragraph quotes critic Irving Howe, who maintains that Singer's stories leave one *unsettled and anxious.*

21. The correct answer is (A). It encompasses all the points in the passage, from the dangers of methyl bromide to the reason why it is still being used. Choices (C) and (E) are not mentioned in the passage (though they might be inferred). The other choices are too narrow to be the main idea.

22. The correct answer is (C). Choices (B) and (E) do not describe a *site* (or location). Although toxicity might be high at choices (A) and (D), it makes most sense that the toxicity would be highest at the place where the pesticide is actually added to the soil.

23. **The correct answer is (A).** Knowing the names of such corporations and organizations could fuel readers to write letters to them. Choices (B) and (D) are not so relevant as choice (A) to the dangers of methyl bromide, and choices (C) and (E) might actually make stronger the argument in favor of the pesticide.

24. **The correct answer is (C).** Statistics are widely used tools for backing up claims. There is no evidence in the passage that the author is trying to reassure or distract the reader, choices (A) and (B), or that the author is concerned with an academic audience, choice (D). Although choice (E) is a possible inference, it is not explicitly stated and is not the main thrust of the author's overall argument.

25. **The correct answer is (D).** The term *non-target organism* is followed immediately by a discussion of the effects of exposure on the human body. Choices (A) and (C) are probably based on fact but are not mentioned in the passage. Choice (B) is incorrect, because soil is not an organism. Choice (E) makes no sense.

Section 2—Math

1. **The correct answer is (D).** If $\frac{2}{3}$ Area $= 6$, then the Area $= \left(\frac{3}{2}\right)(6) = 9$ square inches.

2. **The correct answer is (B).** If $9x + 5 = 23$, $9x = 18$, or $x = 2$. Thus, $18x + 5 = 36 + 5 = 41$.

3. **The correct answer is (E).** An easy way to solve this problem is by noticing that the angled side forms a line transecting two parallel lines. The 60° angle equals the angle supplementary to α. Therefore $60° + \alpha = 180°$ or $\alpha = 120°$.

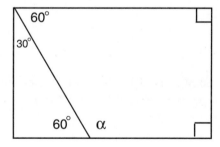

4. **The correct answer is (C).** To solve this one, just add 15% of the original ticket price to the original ticket price.

   New Price $= 5 + 15\%$ of 5
   $$= 5 + (.15)(5)$$
   $$= 5 + .75$$
   $$= 5.75$$

5. **The correct answer is (A).** First, find the common denominator, which is 12, then combine terms, and finally invert the answer to get $\dfrac{1}{x}$. Remember, the question asks for $\dfrac{1}{x}$, NOT x!

   $$x = \frac{1}{3} - \frac{1}{4} + \frac{1}{2} - \frac{1}{6}$$
   $$= \frac{4}{12} - \frac{3}{12} + \frac{6}{12} - \frac{2}{12}$$
   $$= \frac{5}{12}$$

   Now, invert your answer:

   $$\frac{1}{x} = \frac{12}{5}$$

6. **The correct answer is (E).**
   $(x + y) - (x - y) = x + y - x + y = 2y$

7. **The correct answer is (B).** Translate the words into an equation and solve for x.

   "40 percent of 50 is four times what number?" becomes:

   $$(.40)(50) = 4x$$
   $$20 = 4x$$
   $$x = \frac{20}{4}$$
   $$x = 5$$

8. **The correct answer is (B).** If marked price $= m$, first sale price $= .85m$ and net price $= .90\,(.85)m = .765m$.

   $$.765m = 306$$
   $$m = 400$$

   Or work from the answer choices: 15% of \$400 = \$60, making a first sale price of \$340. 10% of this price is \$34, making the net price \$306.

9. **The correct answer is (D).** Did you recognize the triangle as a $45° - 45° - 90°$ triangle, which has sides in the ratio of $1{:}1{:}\sqrt{2}$? You can plug the values given into this ratio.

$1{:}1{:}\sqrt{2}$ becomes $(1)(\sqrt{2}){:}(1)(\sqrt{2}){:}(\sqrt{2})(\sqrt{2})$,

which makes $x = (\sqrt{2})(\sqrt{2}) = 2$.

You can also solve this using the Pythagorean Theorem, which is $a^2 + b^2 = c^2$.

$$\sqrt{2}^2 + \sqrt{2}^2 = x^2$$
$$2 + 2 = x^2$$
$$4 = x^2$$
$$x = 2$$

10. **The correct answer is (B).** Square both sides of the equation to get

$$x^2 = 3 - y$$
$$x^2 - 3 = -y$$
$$y = 3 - x^2$$

11. **The correct answer is (A).** Just multiply out the factors to get the answer to this problem. Did you notice that $(y + 3)(3 + y)$ can also be stated as $(y + 3)^2$?

$$(y + 3)(3 + y) = 3y + 9 + 3y + y^2$$
$$= y^2 + 6y + 9$$

12. **The correct answer is (E).** The formula for the area of a square is $A = s^2$, so $s = \sqrt{36} = 6$. The formula for the perimeter is $P = 4s$, which means the perimeter of the square is $P = (4)(6) = 24$.

13. **The correct answer is (D).** It could be a good idea to use your calculator here. Renaming the inequality from fractions as decimals will make comparison easier and reduce the chances of error. The inequality thus becomes $.800 < x < .875$. Now, you can immediately rule out the first two because choice (A), $\frac{6}{4}$, is obviously much greater than $\frac{7}{8}$, and choice (B), $\frac{2}{3}$, is much less than $\frac{4}{5}$. Here is where it pays to have memorized the most common fractional equivalents in decimals. The last three choices are best tackled with your calculator. After renaming them as decimals, it is easy to spot choice (D), $\frac{25}{30}$ or $.8\overline{33}$, as the answer.

14. **The correct answer is (C).** The helper's hours are:

8 hrs each day on Mon., Tues., and Fri. = (8)(3) = 24 hrs

6 hrs each day on Wed. and Thurs. = (6)(2) = <u>12 hrs</u>

Total hours worked = 36 hrs

This week the helper earned ($9/hr)(36 hrs) = $324

15. **The correct answer is (C).** We can solve this problem in two steps. First, find the radius of the circle. Since it is given that the area of the circle is 9π, we have:

$$A = 9\pi = \pi r^2$$

$$r^2 = \frac{9\pi}{\pi}$$

$$r^2 = 9$$

$$r = 3$$

Second, we must find the length of a side of the square in order to find its area. We know that the radius of a circle is $\frac{1}{2}$ of the diameter of a circle. In this case, the diameter, d, of the circle is also the length of a side, s, of the square. Thus, $d = 2r = (2)(3) = s = 6$. Now it is a simple matter to calculate the area using the formula for the area of a square:

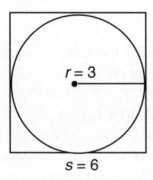

$s = 6$

$$A = s^2$$
$$= 6^2$$
$$= 36 \text{ in}^2$$

16. The correct answer is **(A)**. The only information relevant to the solution of this problem is that the volume of the cube is 64 cubic inches. The other information is given as a logical distraction. To solve this one, just use the formula for the volume of a cube:

$$V = s^3$$
$$64 = s^3$$
$$s = \sqrt[3]{64}$$
$$s = 4$$

17. The correct answer is **(E)**. You can get the answer to this one by first solving for y in the second expression; then plug the first expression into the second to get the answer.

$$ay = b - 3$$
$$y = \frac{(b - 3)}{a}$$

Now replace b in the expression above with $\frac{k}{x}$:

$$y = \frac{\left(\frac{k}{x} - 3\right)}{a}$$

18. The correct answer is **(D)**. Since the length of the arc is π, and this length is $\frac{1}{8}$ of the circumference, the circumference must be 8π. Now, it is easy to find the diameter, d, using the formula for the circumference of a circle.

$$C = 2\pi r = \pi d$$
$$8\pi = \pi d$$
$$d = \frac{8\pi}{\pi}$$
$$d = 8$$

19. The correct answer is **(A)**. You can think of this one as a problem that calculates a percentage of the percentage. To get the answer, you don't even need to know the total number of students at Boulder High, just figure out what $\frac{1}{3}$ of $\frac{6}{10}$ is, and you're all set. First, rename $\frac{6}{10}$ as .6 and $\frac{1}{3}$ as $.3\overline{3}$, then translate the words into an equation:

Percent of students who drive their cars to school $= (.3\overline{3})(.6) \approx .198$, about 20%

20. The correct answer is (B). The least value for the expression is when the denominator is the greatest. This occurs when *b* is greatest, 8, and *a* is least, 0. This means that, within the constraints of the inequality, the least possible value for the given expression is $\frac{16}{8}$, or 2.

Section 3—Reading Skills

1. The correct answer is (B). Living organisms are, by definition, *independent* and *self-regulating*. Choice (A) makes little sense, seeming to apply to a person who has the power of decision-making. Choices (C) and (D) run counter to the idea of life, since both indicate a lack of vitality. Choice (E) means "destructive."

2. The correct answer is (D). This is a definition sentence. Neither choice (A) nor choice (B) makes sense. Choices (C) and (E) are illogical, given the meaning of the rest of the sentence.

3. The correct answer is (A). To make the right choice here, you must be able to define the words, of course, and in the case of choice (A), that demands a fairly big vocabulary. (Look the two words up now—they're the kind of words you're likely to run into on the PSAT.) In the rest of the choices, at least one word runs counter to the meaning of the original statement.

4. The correct answer is (C). To be *gregarious* is to be sociable. Except for choice (E), the other choices denote unpleasant traits. Choice (E) is wrong, because to be *reticent* is to be hesitant or reserved.

5. The correct answer is (E). To *immerse* oneself is to lose oneself, and a movie is an *illusion*. Look up the other words, and you'll find that one or the other of them makes no sense in the context of the sentence.

6. The correct answer is (A). *In the fall*, indicates that it is not yet winter, so the best answer is *premonition*, which means forewarning.

7. The correct answer is (B). Ask yourself, What kind of action, in regard to money, would get one fired? *Stealing* or *embezzling* will probably be the first words that spring to mind. Now look for a synonym of one of these words. Again, your vocabulary must be large enough to contain the word *pilfered*.

8. The correct answer is (A). Look up the other words and you'll find one or the other of them runs counter to the overall meaning of the sentence.

9. **The correct answer is (E).** Utopian citizens are said to *worship* in various ways, which rules out choice (A). The passage does not suggest that emotions run high in Utopia, ruling out choice (B). The passage speaks of the "greater and wiser" citizens of Utopia, so choices (C) and (D) are ruled out.

10. **The correct answer is (D).** The passage expresses only positive opinions, with no evidence of insincerity, ruling out choices (A), (C), and (E). The voice never rises to the elevated level of *awe*, ruling out choice (B).

11. **The correct answer is (B).** Choice (C) is contradicted by the passage, when Clinton says *This [withholding information] is not a propensity that is confined to one party or the other.* Choices (A), (D), and (E) are not supported by the passage.

12. **The correct answer is (A).** Although choice (C) is mentioned in the text, Clinton says security may be used as a pretext for withholding information—not that security comes with information. Choices (B), (D), and (E) may be true, but they are not implied by the passage.

13. **The correct answer is (E).** The other choices do not make sense in the context of the passage.

14. **The correct answer is (A).** It would not make sense to say that the cyclotron was effective despite appearing *sophisticated, technical, or ingenious*—choices (B), (C), and (D). Choice (E) is incorrect because the device is described in a way that makes it seem outlandish in appearance, and therefore conspicuous.

15. **The correct answer is (B).** The passage says that whirling atoms and then casting them at a target is an effective way to *smash open atomic nuclei.* The other choices are not reflected in the passage.

16. **The correct answer is (E).** The initial description of the nursery room is that *It is a big, airy room, the whole floor nearly, with windows that look all ways, and air and sunshine galore.* The final description is that the room's color is *dull yet lurid orange in some places, a sickly sulfur tint in others.* The narrator believes she is ill from the opening of the passage, so choice (A) is wrong. During the description, she seems neither resigned, choice (B), nor terrified, choice (C).

17. **The correct answer is (C).** The narrator's tone is obsessive throughout; her inordinate fascination with the wallpaper hints at mental illness, yet, as she tells us, John does not believe she is ill. This refutes choice (A). Regarding choice (B), the narrator's husband MAY really want to help her, but the content of the passage shows that he does not understand her. Choices (D) and (E) are not in the passage.

18. **The correct answer is (B).** The narrator says that *The paint and paper . . . is stripped off—the paper—in great patches*. This kind of destruction would require strength that only older children would have. In context, the other choices do not indicate anything about the age of the children who used to occupy the room.

19. **The correct answer is (B).** The tone of the description and its close attention to detail seems obsessive; also, the narrator says that the pattern in the wallpaper was *pronounced enough to constantly irritate and provoke study*. None of the other choices is reflected in the passage.

20. **The correct answer is (B).** In the previous two paragraphs, the narrator has been speaking of the wallpaper and of its *flamboyant patterns*. Immediately following, she describes how one can follow its *lame uncertain curves*. She does not speak of herself or other people in this connection, refuting choices (C), (D), and (E).

21. **The correct answer is (B).** In lines 12–14, the narrator says, *I say insufferable; for the feeling was unrelieved. . . .* Again, a good (though not infallible) tactic in answering these questions is to first go to the lines cited, and read the words immediately surrounding them.

22. **The correct answer is (C).** Immediately preceding the phrase, the author has said that he has a sensation like *the after-dream of the reveler upon opium—the bitter lapse into everyday life*.

23. **The correct answer is (A).** A *sojourn* is a limited visit or temporary stay. Even if you do not know the word, the context will give you a clue.

24. **The correct answer is (B).** The description of the letter is followed by the sentence *The MS gave evidence of nervous agitation* and suggests that Roderick needed a visit from the narrator, which logically suggests that the letter had a pleading tone.

25. **The correct answer is (C).** Mention of the *Gothic archway of the hall*; the *valet, of stealthy step*; and *many dark and intricate passages* point to this answer. Also, all the way through the passage, the narrator has been describing the utter depression caused in him by the setting.

26. **The correct answer is (E).** Passage 1 begins with a rather pleased tone; the opening of Passage 2 is decidedly gloomy. Choice (A) is incorrect, because both passages are told from the first-person point of view. Neither the sex, age, nor social class of the narrators is given in the first sentence, which rules out the remaining choices.

27. **The correct answer is (B).** Both stories strongly emphasize the effect of setting on the narrator (even the titles reflect the settings). We cannot know either the state of health or the marital status of the second narrator, ruling out choices (A) and (D). We cannot know the effect of the season on the first narrator, choice (C). In Passage 1, the narrator is married to the other main character, and in Passage 2, the narrator and the other main character are just friends, ruling out choice (E).

Section 4—Math

1. **The correct answer is (B).** A linear equation has the form $y = mx + b$, where m is the slope of the line and b is the y-intercept, which is the point where the line crosses the y-axis. We can see from the diagram that the line crosses the y-axis at point $(0,1)$, which means b is 1. Thus we can immediately eliminate choices (C) and (D). We can also see from the scatter plot that the slope is going to be positive, which eliminates choice (E). But is the slope 7 or 0.7? A line with a slope of 1 makes an angle of 45° with the x-axis. It looks like a line through these dots will make a line that is close to, or a little less than 45°. A line with a slope of 7 means it would be much steeper than 45°. It looks like choice (B) is our answer, but let's make sure; to find m, the slope of the line, use this formula:

$$m = \frac{(y_2 - y_1)}{(x_2 - x_1)}$$

We are given the coordinates for two points in the diagram, $P_1 = (0,1)$ and $P_2 = (7,6)$. We can use these coordinates to approximate the slope:

$$m = \frac{(6 - 1)}{(7 - 0_1)} = \frac{5}{7} \approx 0.7$$

Now we are sure, the correct answer is choice (B).

2. The correct answer is **(B)**. Stated algebraically, we are asked to find $|(y^2 + 0.15) - y^3|$ for $y = 3$, or $|(3^2 + 0.15) - 3^3|$. Simplifying, the expression becomes $|9.15 - 27|$ or $|-17.85|$. Think of a number's absolute value as its distance from the origin. Thus, the point -17.85 on the number line is a distance of 17.85 away from the origin, or $|-17.85| = 17.85$.

3. The correct answer is **(B)**. Solving for both x and y, we have $x = 2^3 + 3^2 = 8 + 9 = 17$ and $y = 3^3 + 2^2 = 27 + 4 = 31$. This means the product of x and y is $x \cdot y = 17 \cdot 31 = 527$.

4. The correct answer is **(A)**. Solving the inequality for c yields:

$$3c - 4 < 17$$
$$3c < 21$$
$$c < 7$$

Now it is clear that possible values of c must be **less than** 7, making choice (A) the correct answer.

5. The correct answer is **(C)**. To decide this one, solve the equation for x:

$$\left(\frac{x}{y}\right) - 7 = 5$$
$$\frac{x}{y} = 5 + 7$$
$$\frac{x}{y} = 12$$
$$x = 12y$$

Substituting $y = 1$ into the equation, we see that $x = 12$.

6. The correct answer is **(B)**. Solve this problem by isolating the unknown (x) on one side of the equation, simplifying the expression, then eliminating the radical sign to find x.

$$2\sqrt[3]{x} - 12 = -6$$
$$2\sqrt[3]{x} = -6 + 12 \qquad \text{Isolate.}$$
$$\sqrt[3]{x} = 3 \qquad \text{Simplify.}$$
$$\left(\sqrt[3]{x}\right)^3 = 3^3 \qquad \text{Eliminate radical.}$$
$$x = 27$$

7. The correct answer is **(C)**. The figure shown is an equilateral triangle. An equilateral triangle is one in which all three sides are equal in length, and all three angles are equal to 60°.

8. **The correct answer is (B).** After one year, Tom has: $1,000 + (.05)(1,000) = $1,050. After one year, Al has: $1,000 + (.025)(1,000) + (.025)(1025) = $1,050.63. This makes the difference between two accounts: $1,050.63 − $1,050 = $0.63.

9. **The correct answer is (A).** To solve this one, we must first find the radius of the circle. Knowing the area of the circle is 9π, we can find the radius using the formula for the area of a circle.

   $$A = \pi r^2 = 9\pi$$
   $$r^2 = 9$$
   $$r = 3$$

   Now, we can proceed to the solution in several different ways. One way is to use the Pythagorean Theorem, $a^2 + b^2 = c^2$.

   $$3^2 + 3^2 = (QR)^2$$
   $$(QR)^2 = 9 + 9 = 18$$
   $$QR = \sqrt{18} = 3\sqrt{2}$$

   Or, you can solve this problem by noticing that the triangle is a 45° - 45° - 90° triangle, which is a special triangle, whose sides have the ratio $1 : 1 : \sqrt{2}$. For the given triangle, this ratio becomes: $3 : 3 : 3\sqrt{2}$, where:

   $$QR = 3\sqrt{2}$$

10. **The correct answer is (D).** Converting rational exponents to their equivalent radical form and simplifying before plugging in $x = 8$, may help you solve this one more easily.

    $$f(x) = \frac{(196)^{\frac{1}{2}} - x}{x^{\frac{1}{3}} + 1} = \frac{\sqrt{196} - x}{\sqrt[3]{x} + 1} = \frac{14 - x}{\sqrt[3]{x} + 1}$$

    for $x = 8$

    $$f(x) = \frac{14 - 8}{\sqrt[3]{8} + 1} = \frac{6}{2 + 1} = \frac{6}{3} = 2$$

313

11. **The correct answer is 3.57.** The area of a circle with radius 2 is:

$A_1 = \pi r^2 = 4\pi = 12.57$ to two decimal places.

The area of a square with side 3 is:

$A_2 = s^2 = 3^2 = 9$

To find the answer, the area remaining, subtract the area of the square from the area of the circle:

$A_1 - A_2 = 12.57 - 9 = 3.57$

12. **The correct answer is 3.** Substituting the values given into the formula for the area of a triangle gives us:

$$\text{Area} = \frac{1}{2}\,\text{Base} \bullet \text{Height} = \left(\frac{1}{2}\right) \bullet (6 - 4) \bullet 3 = \frac{1}{2} \bullet 6 = 3$$

13. **The correct answer is 0.** Any other digit could not produce this result.

14. **The correct answer is 6.** The distance between points A and C is $12 - 3 = 9$.

This means: $AB + BC = 9$. Since $AB = \frac{1}{2}BC$, $BC = 2AB$.

Therefore, $AB + 2AB = 9$

$$3AB = 9$$
$$AB = 3$$

Finally, add 3 to the y coordinate of point A to find the y coordinate of point $B = 3 + 3 = 6$.

15. **The correct answer is 19.** Between 1 and 69, there are 7 integers that contain a digit that is 7. Between 70 and 79, there are 10 integers that contain a digit that is 7. Between 80 and 100, there are 2 integers that contain a digit that is 7. This makes a total of 19 integers in the given range that contain a digit that is 7.

16. **The correct answer is 30°.** 4α and 60° are supplementary angles; therefore,

$$4\alpha + 60° = 180°$$
$$4\alpha = 120°$$
$$\alpha = 30°$$

314

17. **The correct answer is .75 ounce cocoa.** To solve this problem, first convert 36 to 3 (dozen people), then set up the following proportion:

$$\frac{.25}{1} = \frac{x}{3}$$
$$(.25)(3) = x$$
$$x = .75$$

18. **The correct answer is $\frac{1}{8}$.**

$$3 \, \nabla \, 4 = \frac{3!}{4!} = \frac{(3 \times 2 \times 1)}{(4 \times 3 \times 2 \times 1)} = \frac{1}{4}$$

So, the value of $\dfrac{(3 \, \nabla \, 4)}{2} = \dfrac{\left(\frac{1}{4}\right)}{2} = \dfrac{1}{4} \times \dfrac{1}{2} = \dfrac{1}{8}$

19. **The correct answer is 3.** You can find the length of AC by setting up the equation: $AC = AB + BC$. This means that $AC = 7x + 5x = 12x$. Substituting .25 for x yields the solution: $AC = 12x = (12)(.25) = 3$

20. **The correct answer is 4.** In the first column, $A + B = 23 - (5 + 8 + 3) = 7$. In the second column, $A + C = 19 - (1 + 4 + 3) = 11$. Now solve for B and C, respectively.

$A + B = 7$
$A + C = 11$
$B = 7 - A$
$C = 11 - A$

Therefore, $C - B = (11 - A) - (7 - A)$
$$= 11 - A - 7 + A$$
$$= 11 - 7$$
$$= 4$$

Section 5—Writing Skills

1. **The correct answer is (B).** There is a shift in tense from past (*there was*) to present (*we punch*).

2. **The correct answer is (A).** The phrase *looking out over the vast hall* is a misplaced modifier, which should modify Roger, not his stomach.

3. **The correct answer is (A).** The phrase *In accordance to* is the wrong form of the idiom *In accordance with*.

4. **The correct answer is (D).** Noun-number agreement is faulty in this sentence.

315

5. **The correct answer is (C).** The error is a shift in tense from past (*were sitting*) to present (*suddenly see*).

6. **The correct answer is (C).** The error is one of vague pronoun reference.

7. **The correct answer is (E).** The sentence is written in standard English, without errors.

8. **The correct answer is (B).** The error is one of faulty comparison, and it's easy to miss. (*The price of kumquats is less than the price of kiwi fruit.*)

9. **The correct answer is (E).** The sentence is correct as written.

10. **The correct answer is (A).** This is a mistake in subject-verb agreement. The subject (*tables and chairs*) is plural; the verb (*has been*) is singular.

11. **The correct answer is (D).** Type of error: ineffective lack of parallel structure. The series *football, baseball, and soccer,* choice (B), is parallel; however, the phrase *he also liked pitching pennies* is not and makes the sentence wordy. Choice (A) is a correctly written introductory element. Choice (C) is a correctly written noun and verb.

12. **The correct answer is (B).** The error in this sentence is a shift in person from *one* to *you.*

13. **The correct answer is (D).** The sentence order is illogical. The phrase *starring Dustin Hoffman and Tom Cruise* is a misplaced part that should modify the movie title, *Rain Man,* not the word *autism.*

14. **The correct answer is (E).** The sentence is correctly written.

15. **The correct answer is (C).** The sentence error is a shift in tense from past (*was*) to present (*have*).

16. **The correct answer is (E).** The sentence is correctly written.

17. **The correct answer is (D).** The error here is use of a double negative. The phrase should read *have no pots.*

18. **The correct answer is (C).** In this sentence, the use of the verb *did* is ungrammatical. The phrase should read *done on the human brain.*

19. **The correct answer is (D).** Type of error: unidiomatic use of preposition. The correct preposition here would be *of the whole gang.*

20. **The correct answer is (D).** It is clear and contains all the necessary information. The cliché at the very beginning of the original sentence—*In point of fact*—indicates that choice (A) is not the answer, since it's trite and makes the sentence wordy. Choice (B) also contains the cliché and is wordy. Choices (C) and (E) have dropped the cliché and the wordiness, but they have also left out necessary information.

21. **The correct answer is (D).** It is the only choice in which the modifier *While running the Boston marathon* is logically placed so that it modifies the runner.

22. **The correct answer is (C).** The sentence as written makes ineffective use of the passive voice. An approach to this question would be to ask yourself why choice (A) sounds flat. It is because the person committing the action is not in the subject (or active) position in the sentence. The other choices are awkward and unnecessarily convoluted.

23. **The correct answer is (A).** The sentence is fine the way it is. Approach this problem by reading the sentence quickly, "speaking" it silently. You will find it rhythmical and correct. Choices (B) and (C) make ineffective use of the passive voice. Choices (D) and (E) are awkward.

24. **The correct answer is (B).** It is written in the active voice and is the most clear and free of jargon.

25. **The correct answer is (B).** The other choices are inconsistent with the style of the rest of the sentence, being either too formal or too informal.

26. **The correct answer is (B).** It includes a correctly written modifier, and its style is in keeping with the rest of the sentence. Choices (A), (C), and (D) represent a shift in style from formal to informal. Choice (E) is unnecessarily wordy.

27. **The correct answer is (B).** In choice (A), the *as* is missing between *handsome* and *maybe*. Choices (C), (D), and (E) include unidiomatic expressions.

28. **The correct answer is (A).** The other choices make unidiomatic use of a preposition.

29. **The correct answer is (D).** Choice (A) is a fragment. Choices (B) and (C) represent shifts in tense from past to present. Choice (E) is a colloquialism that is too informal for the style of this sentence.

30. **The correct answer is (A).** The sentence is correct as it is. The other choices represent shifts in tense.

31. **The correct answer is (A).** Choice (B) is wordy and redundant. Choices (D) and (E) are wordy, and choice (E) contains the cliché *part and parcel.*

32. **The correct answer is (B).** The other choices make unidiomatic use of prepositions.

33. **The correct answer is (B).** In choices (A) and (E), the pronoun *it* is singular, whereas the noun that the pronoun refers to (*movies*) is plural. Choice (D) is wordy and somewhat convoluted.

34. **The correct answer is (A).** Sentence 9 logically introduces the second paragraph.

35. **The correct answer is (C).** This choice fits best with the style of the rest of the passage. Choice (A) is wordy. The other choices contain words that are either too informal (*chow, victuals*), too formal (*good inclination, fare*), or too pseudo-poetic (*blithe spirit*) to fit the language of the rest of the essay. In addition, choice (E) isn't so active or interesting a sentence as choice (C); also there's no indication that Mom wasn't happy before frozen food came along.

36. **The correct answer is (B).** This choice indicates that the opposite of the previous statement was true.

37. **The correct answer is (C).** This choice would most logically follow the statement . . . *and she liked to have fun.*

38. **The correct answer is (B).** It is the only choice in which the coordinators logically fit the meaning of the sentence as a whole.

39. **The correct answer is (C).** This sentence departs most clearly from the topic of the first paragraph.

Answer Sheet

SECTION

1

Critical Reading

1 Ⓐ Ⓑ Ⓒ Ⓓ Ⓔ
2 Ⓐ Ⓑ Ⓒ Ⓓ Ⓔ
3 Ⓐ Ⓑ Ⓒ Ⓓ Ⓔ
4 Ⓐ Ⓑ Ⓒ Ⓓ Ⓔ
5 Ⓐ Ⓑ Ⓒ Ⓓ Ⓔ
6 Ⓐ Ⓑ Ⓒ Ⓓ Ⓔ
7 Ⓐ Ⓑ Ⓒ Ⓓ Ⓔ

8 Ⓐ Ⓑ Ⓒ Ⓓ Ⓔ
9 Ⓐ Ⓑ Ⓒ Ⓓ Ⓔ
10 Ⓐ Ⓑ Ⓒ Ⓓ Ⓔ
11 Ⓐ Ⓑ Ⓒ Ⓓ Ⓔ
12 Ⓐ Ⓑ Ⓒ Ⓓ Ⓔ
13 Ⓐ Ⓑ Ⓒ Ⓓ Ⓔ
14 Ⓐ Ⓑ Ⓒ Ⓓ Ⓔ

15 Ⓐ Ⓑ Ⓒ Ⓓ Ⓔ
16 Ⓐ Ⓑ Ⓒ Ⓓ Ⓔ
17 Ⓐ Ⓑ Ⓒ Ⓓ Ⓔ
18 Ⓐ Ⓑ Ⓒ Ⓓ Ⓔ
19 Ⓐ Ⓑ Ⓒ Ⓓ Ⓔ
20 Ⓐ Ⓑ Ⓒ Ⓓ Ⓔ
21 Ⓐ Ⓑ Ⓒ Ⓓ Ⓔ

22 Ⓐ Ⓑ Ⓒ Ⓓ Ⓔ
23 Ⓐ Ⓑ Ⓒ Ⓓ Ⓔ
24 Ⓐ Ⓑ Ⓒ Ⓓ Ⓔ
25 Ⓐ Ⓑ Ⓒ Ⓓ Ⓔ

SECTION

2

Math

1 Ⓐ Ⓑ Ⓒ Ⓓ Ⓔ
2 Ⓐ Ⓑ Ⓒ Ⓓ Ⓔ
3 Ⓐ Ⓑ Ⓒ Ⓓ Ⓔ
4 Ⓐ Ⓑ Ⓒ Ⓓ Ⓔ
5 Ⓐ Ⓑ Ⓒ Ⓓ Ⓔ
6 Ⓐ Ⓑ Ⓒ Ⓓ Ⓔ
7 Ⓐ Ⓑ Ⓒ Ⓓ Ⓔ

8 Ⓐ Ⓑ Ⓒ Ⓓ Ⓔ
9 Ⓐ Ⓑ Ⓒ Ⓓ Ⓔ
10 Ⓐ Ⓑ Ⓒ Ⓓ Ⓔ
11 Ⓐ Ⓑ Ⓒ Ⓓ Ⓔ
12 Ⓐ Ⓑ Ⓒ Ⓓ Ⓔ
13 Ⓐ Ⓑ Ⓒ Ⓓ Ⓔ
14 Ⓐ Ⓑ Ⓒ Ⓓ Ⓔ

15 Ⓐ Ⓑ Ⓒ Ⓓ Ⓔ
16 Ⓐ Ⓑ Ⓒ Ⓓ Ⓔ
17 Ⓐ Ⓑ Ⓒ Ⓓ Ⓔ
18 Ⓐ Ⓑ Ⓒ Ⓓ Ⓔ
19 Ⓐ Ⓑ Ⓒ Ⓓ Ⓔ
20 Ⓐ Ⓑ Ⓒ Ⓓ Ⓔ

SECTION

3

Critical Reading

1 Ⓐ Ⓑ Ⓒ Ⓓ Ⓔ
2 Ⓐ Ⓑ Ⓒ Ⓓ Ⓔ
3 Ⓐ Ⓑ Ⓒ Ⓓ Ⓔ
4 Ⓐ Ⓑ Ⓒ Ⓓ Ⓔ
5 Ⓐ Ⓑ Ⓒ Ⓓ Ⓔ
6 Ⓐ Ⓑ Ⓒ Ⓓ Ⓔ
7 Ⓐ Ⓑ Ⓒ Ⓓ Ⓔ
8 Ⓐ Ⓑ Ⓒ Ⓓ Ⓔ

9 Ⓐ Ⓑ Ⓒ Ⓓ Ⓔ
10 Ⓐ Ⓑ Ⓒ Ⓓ Ⓔ
11 Ⓐ Ⓑ Ⓒ Ⓓ Ⓔ
12 Ⓐ Ⓑ Ⓒ Ⓓ Ⓔ
13 Ⓐ Ⓑ Ⓒ Ⓓ Ⓔ
14 Ⓐ Ⓑ Ⓒ Ⓓ Ⓔ
15 Ⓐ Ⓑ Ⓒ Ⓓ Ⓔ
16 Ⓐ Ⓑ Ⓒ Ⓓ Ⓔ

17 Ⓐ Ⓑ Ⓒ Ⓓ Ⓔ
18 Ⓐ Ⓑ Ⓒ Ⓓ Ⓔ
19 Ⓐ Ⓑ Ⓒ Ⓓ Ⓔ
20 Ⓐ Ⓑ Ⓒ Ⓓ Ⓔ
21 Ⓐ Ⓑ Ⓒ Ⓓ Ⓔ
22 Ⓐ Ⓑ Ⓒ Ⓓ Ⓔ
23 Ⓐ Ⓑ Ⓒ Ⓓ Ⓔ
24 Ⓐ Ⓑ Ⓒ Ⓓ Ⓔ

25 Ⓐ Ⓑ Ⓒ Ⓓ Ⓔ
26 Ⓐ Ⓑ Ⓒ Ⓓ Ⓔ
27 Ⓐ Ⓑ Ⓒ Ⓓ Ⓔ

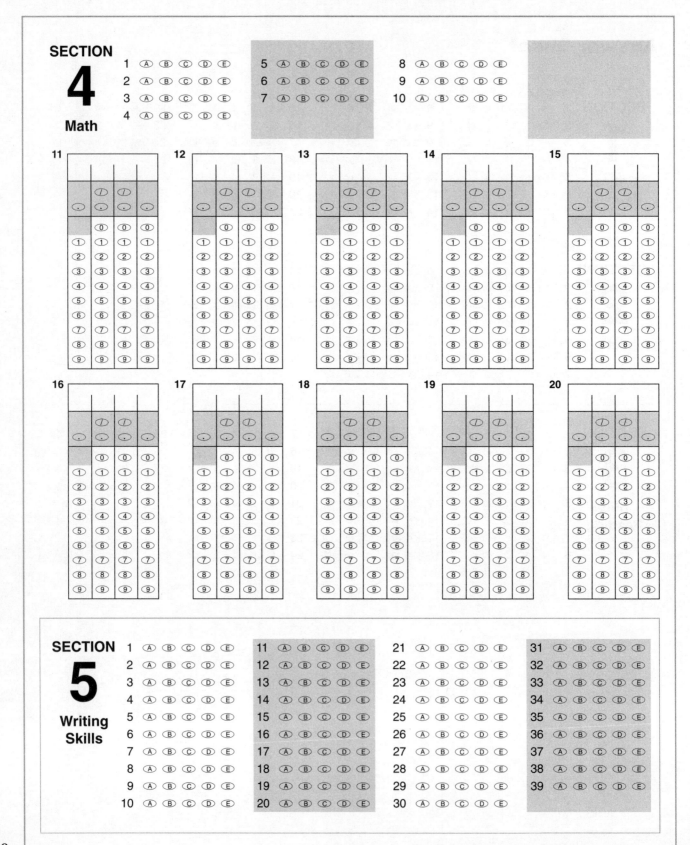

Section 1—Critical Reading

Time—25 Minutes • 25 Questions

For each question below, choose the best answer from the choices given and fill in the corresponding oval on the answer sheet.

> **Directions:** Each sentence below has either one or two blanks in it and is followed by five choices, labeled (A) through (E). These choices represent words or phrases that have been left out. Choose the word or phrase that, if inserted into the sentence, would best fit the meaning of the sentence as a whole.
>
> **Example:**
>
> Canine massage is a veterinary technique for calming dogs that are extremely _____.
>
> (A) inept
> (B) disciplined
> (C) controlled
> (D) stressed
> (E) restrained   Ⓐ Ⓑ Ⓒ ● Ⓔ

1. The professor's lectures were organized, perceptive, and _____, for which the students were deeply grateful and _____ .

   (A) insightful..appreciative
   (B) confusing..indifferent
   (C) patronizing..insulted
   (D) rewarding..incensed
   (E) redundant..perplexed

2. Since excellent writing is precise and clear, a good editor will see to it that a writer remains _____.

   (A) indubitable
   (B) bold
   (C) impeded
   (D) focused
   (E) talented

321

3. Effective mystery stories do not spell everything out for readers, but allow readers to _____ details using their _____.

   (A) dig up..talent
   (B) conjure up..imaginations
   (C) invent..pliability
   (D) guess about..comprehension
   (E) ignore..naiveté

4. Trackers are people who are trained in reading clues along forest trails, in order to find _____ hikers.

   (A) departed
   (B) famished
   (C) wayward
   (D) missing
   (E) obstinate

5. Although they are usually thought of as simply ornamental, many varieties of flowers are _____ and even nutritious.

   (A) fragrant
   (B) noxious
   (C) carnivorous
   (D) robust
   (E) edible

Directions: Read each of the passages carefully, then answer the questions that come after them. The answer to each question may be stated overtly or only implied. You will not have to use outside knowledge to answer the questions—all the material you will need will be in the passage itself. In some cases, you will be asked to read two related passages and answer questions about their relationship to one another.

Questions 6–8 are based on the following passage.

This passage is adapted from an entry in the online encyclopedia Wikipedia.

Line   For I will consider my Cat Jeoffry.
For he is the servant of the Living God duly and daily serving him.
For at the first glance of the glory of God
(5) in the East he worships in his way . . .
Christopher Smart
   The above lines—part of the long poem "Jubilate Agno"—were written in the mid 1700s, when Christopher Smart
(10) was confined to a mental asylum. The poem is a loving and carefully observed depiction of Jeoffry, the poet's cat, as he goes about his daily "devotions" (washing, purring, chasing mice, etc).
(15) Written during the so-called Age of Reason, the poem was considered by many to be the ravings of a lunatic. However, today the poem is seen as an extraordinary—and superbly organized
(20) and complex—meditation on the divine, as revealed through the natural world.

6. The most likely reason the author of the passage includes lines from the poem, "Jubilate Agno" is to

(A) give an example of Smart's ability to portray the link between God and nature.
(B) make the passage less puzzling and incomprehensible to the reader.
(C) show that the author of the passage believes animals are important.
(D) demonstrate that, although intelligent, Smart was mentally ill.
(E) show the depth of Smart's love for his cat, Jeoffry.

7. By using the term *so-called Age of Reason*, rather than simply *Age of Reason*, the author implies that the way Smart was treated was

(A) unfortunate but necessary.
(B) the best judgment of the day.
(C) common in those days.
(D) not based on true reason.
(E) cruel and unusual punishment.

8. The word "devotions," as used in the passage, refers to behaviors that, for Smart, resemble acts of

(A) sacrifice.
(B) defiance.
(C) reverence.
(D) kindness.
(E) intelligence.

Questions 9–11 are based on the following passage.

This passage was taken from an entry in the online encyclopedia Wikipedia.

Line   *Groupthink* is a term coined by psychologist Irving Janis in 1972 to describe one process by which a group can make bad or irrational decisions. In a
(5)   groupthink situation, each member of the group attempts to conform his or her opinions to what they believe to be the consensus of the group. This results in a situation in which the group ultimately
(10)   agrees on an action which each member might normally consider to be unwise. One solution to the pitfall of groupthink is to appoint one group member to play Devil's Advocate—that is, to counter
(15)   each of the group decisions with its opposite, without fear of reprisal.

9. In group decision-making, the role of the Devil's Advocate is mainly to

(A) revile the group's decision.
(B) contradict the group's decision.
(C) agree with the group's decision.
(D) nullify the group's decision.
(E) speed up the group's decision.

10. What is the meaning of "consensus" as used in the passage (line 8)?

(A) Manipulation
(B) Theory
(C) Commandment
(D) Censure
(E) Concurrence

323

11. Based on the passage, which of the following is the best example of groupthink?

(A) A club unanimously elects a treasurer who seems honest and is someone they all like, but who shocks them later by embezzling money.

(B) To avoid hurt feelings, a family goes on vacation together, even though each member secretly wants to stay home; the trip is a disaster.

(C) Soldiers in a squadron dutifully obey their commander's order to take part in a dangerous mission, even though each is secretly terrified.

(D) A corporate officer intimidates employees into working overtime without extra pay, by threatening to outsource their jobs.

(E) A business group considers a new investment. Each member secretly examines the deal, finds it sound, and in the end the group invests.

Questions 12–20 are based on the following passage.

The passage is an essay by George Bernard Shaw, 1925 Nobel Prize winner, entitled "What is a Child?"

Line   An experiment. A fresh attempt to . . . make humanity divine. And you will vitiate the experiment if you make the slightest attempt to abort it into some

(5)   fancy figure of your own: for example, your notion of a good man or a womanly woman. If you treat it as a little wild beast to be tamed, or as a pet to be played with, or even as a means to save

(10)   you trouble and to make money for you (and these are our commonest ways), it may fight its way through in spite of you

and save its soul alive; for all its instincts will resist you, and possibly be strength-

(15)   ened in the resistance; but if you begin with its own holiest aspirations, and suborn them for your own purposes, then there is hardly any limit to the mischief you may do. Swear at a child, throw your

(20)   boots at it, send it flying from the room with a cuff or a kick; and the experience will be as instructive to the child as a difficulty with a short-tempered dog or a bull. Francis Place tells us that his father

(25)   always struck his children when he found one within his reach. The effect on the young Places seems to have been simply to make them keep out of their father's way, which was no doubt what he

(30)   desired, as far as he desired anything at all. Francis records the habit without bitterness, having reason to thank his stars that his father respected the inside of his head whilst cuffing the outside of

(35)   it; and this made it easy for Francis to do yeoman's service to his country as that rare and admirable thing, a Freethinker: the only sort of thinker, I may remark, whose thoughts, and consequently whose

(40)   religious convictions, command any respect.

Now Mr. Place, senior, would be described by many as a bad father; and I do not contend that he was a conspicu-

(45)   ously good one. But as compared with the conventional good father who deliberately imposes himself on his son as a god; who takes advantage of childish credulity and parent worship to persuade

(50)   his son that what he approves of is right and what he disapproves of is wrong; who imposes a corresponding conduct on the child by a system of prohibitions and penalties, rewards and eulogies, for

(55)   which he claims divine sanction: com-

pared to this sort of . . . monster maker, I say, Place appears almost as a Provi-
(60) dence. Not that it is possible to live with children any more than with grown-up people without imposing rules of conduct on them. There is a point at which every person with human nerves has to say to a child "Stop that noise." But suppose the child asks why! There are various
(65) answers in use. The simplest: "Because it irritates me," may fail; for it may strike the child as being rather amusing to irritate you; also the child, having comparatively no nerves, may be unable
(70) to conceive your meaning vividly enough. In any case it may want to make a noise more than to spare your feelings.

You may therefore have to explain that the effect of the irritation will be
(75) that you will do something unpleasant if the noise continues. The something unpleasant may be only a look of suffering to rouse the child's affectionate sympathy (if it has any), or it may run to
(80) forcible expulsion from the room with plenty of unnecessary violence; but the principle is the same: there are no false pretenses involved: the child learns in a straightforward way that it does not pay
(85) to be inconsiderate. Also, perhaps, that Mamma, who made the child learn the Sermon on the Mount, is not really a Christian.

12. The author's main point in the passage is that, when raising a child,

(A) it is wise to use physical punishment, since is the only thing a child understands.
(B) a parent should remember that children are basically wild and need to be tamed, by physical force, if necessary.
(C) a parent should encourage the child's basic nature, since that way the child may grow up to be a freethinker, which will be best for society.
(D) it is better to be straightforward (even physically abusive, though that is not condoned) than to be hypo-critical.
(E) it is all right to use corporal punish-ment as long as it is done with love.

13. What is the meaning of the word "vitiate" as it is used in line 3?

(A) Reiterate
(B) Encourage
(C) Enliven
(D) Spoil
(E) Apply

14. The phrase "its own holiest aspirations" (line 16) refers to the child's

(A) self-love.
(B) love of Jesus.
(C) ambition in life.
(D) secret beliefs.
(E) best instincts.

325

PETERSON'S
getting you there

15. Lines 21–24 state that, if one cuffs or kicks a child, "the experience will be as instructive to the child as a difficulty with a short-tempered dog or a bull." In the context of the rest of the passage, this means that the child will learn

    (A) to be cautious when he or she goes out into the world.
    (B) fear and hatred of the parent.
    (C) a practical lesson—not to do it again.
    (D) respect for the parent.
    (E) to be secretive and devious around the parent

16. In context, the statement that Francis Place "[had] reason to thank his stars that his father respected the inside of his head" (lines 32–34) means that Francis felt lucky to have had a father who, although physically abusive,

    (A) did not try to influence Francis's thinking.
    (B) raised Francis as a freethinker.
    (C) loved Francis deeply.
    (D) gave Francis a good education.
    (E) provided Francis with the basic necessities.

17. Which of the following does the author use to make his point in paragraph 2?

    (A) Objective reporting
    (B) Comparison/contrast
    (C) Appeal to authority
    (D) Sober reasoning
    (E) Bitter sarcasm

18. Which of the following devices does the author use in lines 57–58, when he says that, compared to a father who encourages the child's natural parent-worship, "Place appears almost as a Providence"?

    (A) A concrete example
    (B) Hyperbole (exaggeration)
    (C) A sweeping generalization
    (D) A cliché
    (E) A logical syllogism

19. The last two lines of the essay imply that if a child is misbehaving and you threaten him or her in a straightforward way with unpleasant consequences (even violence), the child will learn that you

    (A) do not love him.
    (B) are a sinner.
    (C) are not perfect.
    (D) know best.
    (E) are a bad parent.

20. It can be inferred from the passage that the author views children with

    (A) distaste.
    (B) respect.
    (C) scorn.
    (D) repugnance.
    (E) indifference.

Questions 21–25 are based on the following passage.

The passage is an excerpt from the Department of Energy's Annual Report of the Council on Environmental Quality *(1993).*

Line   Wetlands and coastal waters, two areas rich in natural resources, have histori-cally been under intense pressure from development, and the pressure is begin-
(5)   ning to show. Of all species currently listed as threatened or endangered, 54 percent are found in wetlands and deepwater habitats.

Wetlands played a prominent role in
(10)   the settlement of the United States, but farmers and settlers, perceiving them as a hindrance to productive land use, routinely drained, filled, or otherwise manipulated bogs, swamps, and marshes
(15)   to produce dry land for agricultural use or homesites. Only recently has society begun to appreciate wetlands and their benefits, but not before half of them were converted to other uses.

(20)   U.S. wetlands range from extensive coastal marshes and inland swamps in the Southeast to bogs and shrub swamps in the North, and from tropical wetland forests in Hawaii to permafrost wetlands
(25)   in Alaska. This diversity reflects regional differences in climate, hydrology, soils, and vegetation. In coastal areas 73 percent of all wetlands are emergent herbaceous wetlands such as marsh,
(30)   whereas inland, only 25 percent are marsh. The remaining inland wetlands are forested (53 percent), shrub (16 percent), and pond (6 percent).

Wetlands provide an array of
(35)   beneficial functions and values. This ecotype plays an integral part in main-taining the quality of human life and

wildlife as well as the vigor of the U.S. economy. Americans also use wetlands
(40)   for recreational activities such as canoeing, fishing, and bird watching.

Wetlands store large amounts of water in organic deposits and basins, providing erosion and flood control, flow
(45)   stabilization, and the recharging of underground aquifers. Effective flood control is the result of a number of factors including the interrelationship of wetlands with streamflow within a
(50)   particular watershed. Recent research finds that flood peaks may be reduced by 80 percent in watersheds with a 30-percent wetland area and by 65 percent if a watershed has only 15 percent of its
(55)   area in wetlands.

. . . As water flows through a wetland system, plants, animals, and sediments absorb, assimilate, or change the chemical form of many contaminants,
(60)   including heavy metals, introduced into the watershed by human activities. Significant amounts of suspended sediments also are removed from the water during the seepage process, and
(65)   thus wetlands serve as natural filtration systems and improve the quality of the water.

Wetlands provide habitats for diverse and abundant fish, wildlife, and plant
(70)   species, many of which are found in the diets of humans. The ecotype produces large amounts of detritus which forms the base of a complex food web that cycles energy and nutrients within the
(75)   wetland environment and exports nutrients into adjacent areas. Half of the species that inhabit wetlands are re-stricted to this land-cover type or choose to frequent it.

(80) Although the rate of wetland losses has declined in recent years, conservation efforts remain essential to protect this ecotype which the nation has come to appreciate.

(85) Recognizing the need to improve federal wetlands policy, the Administration issued a comprehensive package of initiatives that included legislative recommendations and administrative

(90) actions addressing both the Clean Water Act Section 404 program and nonregulatory protection approaches. In addition an array of federal programs were underway to acquire, mitigate, protect,

(95) and restore wetlands.

On August 24, 1993, the Administration announced a package of wetland reforms entitled Protecting America's Wetlands: A Fair, Flexible, and Effective

(100) Approach. The reform package was prepared by the Interagency Working Group on Federal Wetlands Policy convened in June 1993 to formulate a workable policy. Chaired by the White

(105) House Office on Environmental Policy, the group included the EPA, Army Corps of Engineers, Office of Management and Budget, and the departments of Agriculture, Commerce, Energy, Interior, Justice,

(110) and Transportation.

21. Which of the following best expresses the main point of paragraph 2?

(A) Almost too late, society has begun appreciating its wetlands, which it previously nearly destroyed.
(B) Wetlands have been systematically damaged throughout our history.
(C) Wetlands were important to the settlement of the United States.
(D) Earlier farmers and settlers did not appreciate wetlands the way present-day environmentalists do.
(E) Wetlands have always served an important agricultural purpose.

22. As described in paragraph 6, among the services performed by wetlands in their role as *natural filtration systems* (line 65) is

(A) adding important heavy metals for use by humans.
(B) filtering out contaminants such as pesticides.
(C) nourishing plants and animals.
(D) adding rich sediments to the soil.
(E) removing suspended sediments.

23. Paragraph 1 implies that *intense pressure from development* (lines 3–4) is

(A) endangering many species.
(B) causing wetlands to become more widely appreciated.
(C) enabling humans to learn more about wetland history.
(D) causing deepwater habitats to be drained.
(E) enabling developers to profit from wetland use.

24. The statistics reported in paragraph 3 are mainly used to show that wetlands are

(A) being systematically destroyed.
(B) economically important to humans.
(C) geographically diverse.
(D) filled with natural beauty.
(E) becoming more and more heavily populated.

25. The final paragraph deals mainly with wetland

(A) products.
(B) economics.
(C) science.
(D) reform.
(E) manipulation.

S T O P If you finish before time is called, you may check your work on this section only. Do not turn to any other section in the test.

Section 2—Math

Time—25 Minutes • 20 Questions

Solve problems 1–20, then select the best of the choices given for each one and fill in the corresponding oval on the answer sheet. You may use available space on the page for scratchwork.

Notes:

1. You may use a calculator. All of the numbers used are real numbers.

2. You may use the figures that accompany the problems to help you find the solution. Unless the instructions say that a figure is not drawn to scale, assume that it has been drawn accurately. Each figure lies in a plane unless the instructions say otherwise.

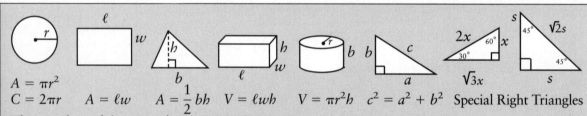

Reference Information

$A = \pi r^2$
$C = 2\pi r$ $A = \ell w$ $A = \dfrac{1}{2}bh$ $V = \ell w h$ $V = \pi r^2 h$ $c^2 = a^2 + b^2$ Special Right Triangles

The number of degrees of arc in a circle is 360.
The measure in degrees of a straight angle is 180.
The sum of the measures in degrees of the angles of a triangle is 180.

---

1. $4 \times (7 + 1) - 6 =$

(A) 7
(B) 8
(C) 21
(D) 23
(E) 26

2. If angle α and obtuse angle β are supplementary angles, which of the following statements is true?

(A) $\alpha < \beta$
(B) $\alpha > \beta$
(C) $\alpha = \beta$
(D) $\alpha = 180°$
(E) $\beta = 90°$

3. If $x + 3y = z$, what is the value of y?

(A) $3(z + x)$

(B) $\dfrac{(xz)}{3}$

(C) $\dfrac{1}{3}(z - x)$

(D) $\dfrac{(x - z)}{3}$

(E) $-3(z - x)$

4. What is the volume, in cubic inches, of a rectangular solid of length 8 inches and width 6 inches if its height is one half its width?

(A) 120
(B) 144
(C) 168
(D) 192
(E) 576

5. What is the wall thickness, in inches, of a tube with an outer diameter of .750 and an inner diameter of .625?

(A) .0625
(B) .125
(C) .625
(D) .6875
(E) .750

6. A pair of pants sells for $6 more than 75% of its price. What is the price of the pants?

(A) $12
(B) $18
(C) $20
(D) $24
(E) $36

7. In the figure below, what is the value of α?

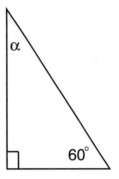

(A) 15°
(B) 20°
(C) 30°
(D) 45°
(E) 90°

8. What % of 5 is 90% of 50?

(A) 2.25
(B) 9
(C) 10
(D) 90
(E) 900

9. For what values of a and b is $(a \times b) < 0$?

(A) $a = 3, b = .0001$
(B) $a = -2, b = -.0001$
(C) $a = 7, b = 0$
(D) $a = -1, b = -19$
(E) $a = -2, b = 3$

10. How tall is a flag pole that casts a 60-foot shadow if a nearby fence post, four feet high, casts a 10-foot shadow?

(A) 40
(B) 36
(C) 30
(D) 24
(E) 15

331

11. What is the value of

$$\left(9x^3 - \frac{z^2}{2}\right)\left(\frac{y}{11}\right)$$

when $x = -1$, $y = 1$, $z = 2$?

(A) $\dfrac{25}{11}$

(B) $\dfrac{1}{11}$

(C) $\dfrac{-1}{11}$

(D) $\dfrac{-7}{11}$

(E) -1

12. In the figure below, if lines l_1 and l_2 are parallel, and l_3 transects l_1 and l_2 at an acute angle, which of the following statements is FALSE? (P, Q, R, S, T, and U are angles.)

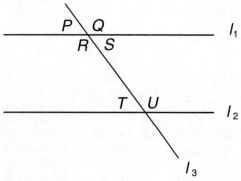

(A) $P = S$
(B) $P = Q$
(C) $T = S$
(D) $T = P$
(E) $R = Q$

13. A woman's coin purse contains 65 cents in 11 coins, all nickels and dimes. How many coins are dimes?

(A) 1
(B) 2
(C) 3
(D) 4
(E) 5

14. What percent of two gallons is a quart?

(A) 12.5%
(B) 25%
(C) 50%
(D) 67%
(E) 75%

15. In the figure below, $\overline{AC}$ and $\overline{BD}$ are chords of a circle that intersect at point E. $\overline{AD}$ is the diameter. If the measure of arc $AB = 40°$ and m$\angle CED = 60°$, what is the measure of $\angle CAD$?

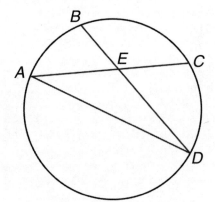

Note: Figure not drawn to scale.

(A) 60°
(B) 45°
(C) 30°
(D) 40°
(E) 15°

16. A shopper obtains a 30% discount on the price of a chair and pays $420. How much was the original price of the chair?

(A) $126
(B) $450
(C) $577
(D) $600
(E) $1,400

17. In triangle ABC, $m\angle C = 2m\angle B$, $m\angle A = 6m\angle B$. What is the measure of $\angle C$?

(A) 5°
(B) 15°
(C) 20°
(D) 30°
(E) 40°

18. If $\begin{matrix} a & b \\ c & d \end{matrix}$ is defined as $ad - cb$, then

$$\begin{matrix} a & b \\ c & d \end{matrix} + \begin{matrix} a & b \\ c & d \end{matrix} + 2cb =$$

(A) $ad - cb$
(B) $-2cb$
(C) 0
(D) $2ad$
(E) $-4cb$

19. If the base of a right triangle is $8\sqrt{2}$ and the hypotenuse is 18, what is the area of the triangle?

(A) 14
(B) $14\sqrt{2}$
(C) $56\sqrt{2}$
(D) 64
(E) $64\sqrt{2}$

20. If $a + b = 27$ and $3c - a = 0$, what does c equal?

(A) $3a$
(B) 27
(C) $27 - b$
(D) $9 - 3b$
(E) $9 - \dfrac{b}{3}$

STOP If you finish before time is called, you may check your work on this section only. Do not turn to any other section in the test.

Section 3—Critical Reading

Time—25 Minutes • 27 Questions

For each question below, choose the best answer from the choices given and fill in the corresponding oval on the answer sheet.

Directions: Each sentence below has either one or two blanks in it and is followed by five choices, labeled (A) through (E). These choices represent words or phrases that have been left out. Choose the word or phrase that, if inserted into the sentence, would <u>best</u> fit the meaning of the sentence as a whole.

Example:

Canine massage is a veterinary technique for calming dogs that are extremely _____.

(A) inept
(B) disciplined
(C) controlled
(D) stressed
(E) restrained

---

1. Studies have shown that breathing exercises can ease _____ during dental work, even without the use of anesthesia, which is good news for patients.

   (A) discomfiture
   (B) discourtesy
   (C) discomfort
   (D) disinterest
   (E) disjunction

2. The airline's brochure reminds passengers that, if they are injured or _____, they may request that an airline _____ meet them at the gate with a wheelchair.

   (A) fatigued..executive
   (B) disabled..escort
   (C) mutilated..paramedic
   (D) disconcerted..paragon
   (E) damaged..handler

3. When we _____ similar beliefs, we identify ourselves as members of the group.

   (A) reform
   (B) espouse
   (C) procure
   (D) enthrall
   (E) remand

4. Dentists say that for effective dental _____, people should brush their teeth for 3 minutes after each meal.

   (A) perquisites
   (B) admonition
   (C) hygiene
   (D) excision
   (E) renovation

5. Parents can use the "V-chip" to ensure that their children do not watch _____ television programs.

   (A) inappropriate
   (B) ineffable
   (C) inconsiderate
   (D) indeterminate
   (E) inexhaustible

6. To ensure patient privacy, the results of certain medical tests are kept _____ by law.

   (A) restrained
   (B) admissible
   (C) legitimate
   (D) confidential
   (E) restorative

7. For people who have allergies to dog and cat hair, the iguana, being _____, makes a/an _____ pet.

   (A) placid..tedious
   (B) surreal..remarkable
   (C) reptilian..grotesque
   (D) unprecedented..engaging
   (E) hairless..lovely

8. Acupuncture, previously thought of as an unorthodox kind of therapy, is now gaining _____ in this country; therefore even some conservative doctors now use it in _____ traditional medical procedures.

   (A) respect..conjunction with
   (B) animosity..spite of
   (C) antipathy..opposition to
   (D) esteem..light of
   (E) disdain..protest to

Directions: Read each of the passages carefully and answer the questions that come after them. Base your answers on what is stated or implied as well as on any introductory material provided.

Questions 9–10 are based on the following passage.

This excerpt is from Jules Verne's Around the World in 80 Days.

Line   Was Phileas Fogg rich? Undoubtedly. But those who knew him best could not imagine how he had made his fortune, and Mr. Fogg was the last person to
(5)   whom to apply for the information. He was not lavish, nor, on the contrary, avaricious; for, whenever he knew that money was needed for a noble, useful, or benevolent purpose, he supplied it quietly
(10)   and sometimes anonymously. He was, in short, the least communicative of men. He talked very little, and seemed all the more mysterious for his taciturn manner. His daily habits were quite open to
(15)   observation; but whatever he did was so exactly the same thing that he had always done before, that the wits of the curious were fairly puzzled.

9. The main purpose of the question that opens the passage is to

   (A) inform the reader.
   (B) goad the reader.
   (C) test the reader.
   (D) intrigue the reader.
   (E) disturb the reader.

335

GO ON TO THE NEXT PAGE

10. In the context of the passage, which is the best meaning of the word "avaricious" (line 7)?

    (A) Bitter

    (B) Cruel

    (C) Greedy

    (D) Dishonest

    (E) Ignorant

Questions 11–13 are based on the following passage.

This excerpt is from Thomas Paine's "The Age of Reason" (1796).

Line   I believe in one God, and no more; and I hope for happiness beyond this life . . . and I believe that religious duties consist in doing justice, loving mercy, and
(5)   endeavoring to make our fellow-creatures happy . . . [But] I do not believe in the creed professed by the Jewish church, by the Roman church, by the Greek church, by the Turkish church, by the Protestant
(10)   church, nor by any church that I know of. My own mind is my own church. All national institutions of churches . . . appear to me no other than human inventions set up to terrify and enslave
(15)   mankind, and monopolize power and profit.

11. In terms of its tone and purpose, the passage can best be described as a(n)

    (A) denunciation.

    (B) investigation.

    (C) meditation.

    (D) summary.

    (E) debate.

12. Which best represents Paine's religious beliefs as expressed in the passage?

    (A) Because I believe in one God, I do not share the beliefs of foreign cultures.

    (B) I do not believe that any organized religion's dogma is divinely inspired.

    (C) The best kind of church is one that believes in a single, all-powerful God.

    (D) Organized religion on a national scale can work for both good and evil.

    (E) My religious beliefs are shared by very few other men and women.

13. In the context of the passage, which word would best replace the word "inventions"?

    (A) Inconsistencies

    (B) Anomalies

    (C) Imitations

    (D) Temptations

    (E) Fabrications

Questions 14–15 are based on the following passage.

The following excerpt is from Wally Lamb's "Why I Write," comments to the National Council on the Arts.

Line   To write a first-person novel is to go on a journey. . . to stow away in the suitcase of some other, imagined person's life. . . . That's how I became a woman in [my
(5)   novel,] *She's Come Undone* and the embittered twin brother of a paranoid schizophrenic in *I Know This Much Is True*. . . . So I do not usually follow the standard rule espoused in creative writing
(10)   classes: write what you know. My impulse, instead, is to write about what I don't know so that I can live the life of "the other" and move beyond the limitations—the benign prison—of my
(15)   own life experiences.

14. The metaphor of stowing away in a suitcase lends to the fiction-writing process an air of

(A) refinement.
(B) adventure.
(C) fraudulence.
(D) sentimentality.
(E) solemnity.

15. The phrase "benign prison. . . of my life experiences" (line 14–15) implies that the writer feels his own life has been

(A) sheltered.
(B) sterile.
(C) insecure.
(D) boring.
(E) depressing.

Passage 1

Passage 1 is comprised of excerpts from an address by Mary Robinson, United Nations High Commissioner for Human Rights, upon her acceptance of the Erasmus Prize on November 9, 1999.

Line   Hard questions are being asked about the gap between the ideals of the human rights movement and the evidence appearing before us daily that shows
(5) how far respect for human rights is from being embedded in society. In this year alone we have witnessed gross human rights violations in Kosovo, East Timor, Sierra Leone and the Great Lakes region,
(10) to mention only some of the worst instances. The placing of human rights centre stage in political life must produce tangible improvements if there is not to be an erosion of credibility and a rise in
(15) cynicism. . . .

  As far as the individual's responsibilities are concerned, champions of human rights have recognized that, just as we possess rights simply by virtue of being
(20) human, so also we have responsibilities to those around us. There is an understandable hesitation to place too much emphasis on responsibilities and duties because unscrupulous regimes have been
(25) known to argue that duties to the State are more important than the rights of the individual. The drafters of the Universal Declaration considered listing parallel responsibilities or duties to match the
(30) rights they proclaimed, but they realized that this might qualify or relativise fundamental rights. So the issue of duties was encapsulated in one article, Article 29. . . .

(35)   The onus on governments to discharge their responsibilities is clear. Governments may have ceded some of their powers to market forces over which they have little control but they retain
(40) far-reaching powers over citizens. The human rights message to governments is: you should rule wisely and respect the rights of the ruled because these rights are not yours to give or take.

(45)   There are three strategies which I would like to emphasize as having a particular role in strengthening the culture of human rights.

  The first is Prevention. Prevention of
(50) human rights violations must become a greater priority than it is at present. Prevention is a normal part of our lives in so many ways but where conflicts are concerned it tends to be honored on
(55) paper but not in practice. We should be alive to the huge advantages of heading off human rights violations before they happen and apply the sophisticated preventive habits we know so well at
(60) home to the field of conflict prevention.

337

The second area is Accountability. Accountability is really a form of prevention since it signals that those who commit gross violations of human rights
(65) will not get away with it. There are encouraging signs that national judicial authorities are taking the position that grave human rights violations must be accounted for, wherever, whenever and
(70) by whomever they were committed. And a major advance has been made with the adoption of the Rome Statute of the International Criminal Court. In that context I would like to pay tribute to the
(75) impressive contribution made over the years by the Netherlands to the development of an effective international criminal justice system.

The third strategy I would support is
(80) greater emphasis on economic, social and cultural rights. This set of rights gets less attention than the better known civil and political rights but I am convinced that an enduring culture of human rights
(85) cannot take root where access to food, to education and even to basic healthcare is denied.

Let me conclude by quoting from Aung San Suu Kyi*, who lives the values
(90) she advocates: "At the root of human responsibility is the concept of perfection, the urge to achieve it, the intelligence to find a path towards it, and the will to follow that path if not to the end at least
(95) the distance needed to rise above individual limitations and environmental impediments. . . . Concepts such as truth,

justice and compassion cannot be dismissed as trite when these are often
(100) the only bulwarks which stand against ruthless power."

Passage 2

Excerpts from the Universal Declaration of Human Rights, *adopted by the United Nations on December 10, 1948.*

Line Now, THE GENERAL ASSEMBLY proclaims THIS UNIVERSAL DECLARATION OF HUMAN RIGHTS as a common standard of achievement for all
(5) peoples and all nations. . . .

Article 1. All human beings are born free and equal in dignity and rights. They are endowed with reason and conscience and should act towards one another in a
(10) spirit of brotherhood.

Article 2. Everyone is entitled to all the rights and freedoms set forth in this Declaration, without distinction of any kind, such as race, colour, sex, language,
(15) religion, political or other opinion, national or social origin, property, birth or other status. Furthermore, no distinction shall be made on the basis of the political, jurisdictional or international
(20) status of the country or territory to which a person belongs, whether it be independent, trust, non-self-governing or under any other limitation of sovereignty.

Article 3. Everyone has the right to
(25) life, liberty and security of person.

Article 4. No one shall be held in slavery or servitude; slavery and the slave trade shall be prohibited in all their forms.

(30) Article 5. No one shall be subjected to torture or to cruel, inhuman or degrading treatment or punishment.

___
* Human rights activist, leader of the prodemocracy movement in Myanmar (formerly called Burma), and winner of the 1991 Nobel Peace Prize, who, in July 1989, was placed under house arrest by the ruling junta for allegedly "endangering the state."

Article 6. Everyone has the right to recognition everywhere as a person (35) before the law.

Article 7. All are equal before the law and are entitled without any discrimination to equal protection of the law. All are entitled to equal protection against (40) any discrimination in violation of this Declaration and against any incitement to such discrimination.

Article 8. Everyone has the right to an effective remedy by the competent (45) national tribunals for acts violating the fundamental rights granted him by the constitution or by law.

Article 9. No one shall be subjected to arbitrary arrest, detention or exile.

(50) Article 10. Everyone is entitled in full equality to a fair and public hearing by an independent and impartial tribunal, in the determination of his rights and obligations and of any criminal charge (55) against him. . . .

Article 16. (1) Men and women of full age, without any limitation due to race, nationality or religion, have the right to marry and to found a family. (60) They are entitled to equal rights as to marriage, during marriage, and at its dissolution. (2) Marriage shall be entered into only with the free and full consent of the intending spouses. (3) The family is (65) the natural and fundamental group unit of society and is entitled to protection by society and the State. . . .

Article 18. Everyone has the right to freedom of thought, conscience, and (70) religion; this right includes freedom to change his religion or belief, and freedom, either alone or in community with others and in public or private, to manifest his religion or belief in teaching, (75) practice, worship, and observance. . . .

Article 29. (1) Everyone has duties to the community in which alone the free and full development of his personality is possible. (2) In the exercise of his rights (80) and freedoms, everyone shall be subject only to such limitations as are determined by law solely for the purpose of securing due recognition and respect for the rights and freedoms of others and of (85) meeting the just requirements of morality, public order and the general welfare in a democratic society. (3) These rights and freedoms may in no case be exercised contrary to the purposes and principles (90) of the United Nations.

16. What device does the author of Passage 1 use for strengthening her argument in the first paragraph?

(A) Irony
(B) Sharp definitions of terms
(C) Real-world examples
(D) Appeal to authority
(E) Statistical data

17. The second paragraph of Passage 1 maintains that the framers of the Declaration decided that, if the responsibilities of citizens were stressed too much in the Declaration,

(A) corrupt governments might use this as an excuse to oppress their citizens even more.
(B) citizens of some countries might reject the Declaration.
(C) corrupt governments might resent being told what their citizens' responsibilities are.
(D) the Declaration might not pass the General Assembly of the United Nations.
(E) citizens would be unfairly burdened by having to act more responsibly.

18. What is the meaning of the word "ceded" in the context of the third paragraph (line 37) of Passage 1?

- **(A)** Perpetuated
- **(B)** Relinquished
- **(C)** Prioritized
- **(D)** Betrayed
- **(E)** Mandated

19. Paragraph 6 of Passage 1 endorses human rights laws that are

- **(A)** clearly written.
- **(B)** fair to both government and citizens.
- **(C)** enforceable.
- **(D)** taken out of national hands and put into international hands.
- **(E)** open-ended.

20. A particular example of the rights that the author feels are NOT emphasized enough would be the right to

- **(A)** free elections.
- **(B)** vote.
- **(C)** learn to read.
- **(D)** hold office.
- **(E)** criticize the government in power.

21. Aung San Suu Kyi, quoted in the final paragraph of Passage 1, is from

- **(A)** Kosovo.
- **(B)** China.
- **(C)** Myanmar.
- **(D)** the United States.
- **(E)** The information is not available in the passage.

22. The Universal Declaration of Human Rights assumes that basic human rights belong to

- **(A)** all citizens of free countries.
- **(B)** all people everywhere.
- **(C)** all governments that treat their citizens fairly.
- **(D)** everyone who has a conscience.
- **(E)** everyone who exercises his or her civil and political responsibilities.

23. In the context of Article 2 of the Declaration, what is the specific meaning of the phrase "without distinction of any kind"?

- **(A)** All citizens of a country should voice their political opinions.
- **(B)** The upper classes shall have a responsibility to take care of the lower classes.
- **(C)** In regard to the granting of equal human rights, there shall be no discrimination of any kind.
- **(D)** All citizens of a country should engage in responsible behavior.
- **(E)** No citizen should be regarded as more distinguished than any other.

24. Articles 8 and 10 of the Declaration deal <u>mainly</u> with

- **(A)** deportation or exile of citizens.
- **(B)** criminal acts by citizens.
- **(C)** family law.
- **(D)** the legal rights of citizens.
- **(E)** the financial rights of citizens.

25. Article 16 of the Declaration specifically grants to each man and woman

    (A) equal human rights, even if he or she is divorced.

    (B) the right to marry regardless of age.

    (C) the right to marry only within one's religion.

    (D) equal rights if he or she is a responsible citizen.

    (E) the right to be protected by his or her family.

26. The passages are alike in regarding human rights as rights that are, first and foremost,

    (A) earned.

    (B) purchased.

    (C) innate.

    (D) relinquishable.

    (E) obscure.

27. Article 16 in Passage 2 relates directly what the author of Passage 1 says in her "three strategies" paragraphs (lines 45–87)—that is,

    (A) prevention.

    (B) accountability.

    (C) economic rights.

    (D) social and cultural rights.

    (E) citizen responsibilities.

STOP   If you finish before time is called, you may check your work on this section only. Do not turn to any other section in the test.

Section 4—Math

Time—25 Minutes • 20 Questions

This section is made up of two types of questions, multiple choice—10 questions, and Student-Produced Response—10 questions. You have 25 minutes to complete the section. You may use available space on the page for scratchwork.

Notes:

1. You may use a calculator. All of the numbers used are real numbers.

2. You may use the figures that accompany the problems to help you find the solution. Unless the instructions say that a figure is not drawn to scale, assume that it has been drawn accurately. Each figure lies in a plane unless the instructions say otherwise.

Reference Information

$A = \pi r^2$
$C = 2\pi r$　　$A = \ell w$　　$A = \dfrac{1}{2} bh$　　$V = \ell wh$　　$V = \pi r^2 h$　　$c^2 = a^2 + b^2$　　Special Right Triangles

The number of degrees of arc in a circle is 360.
The measure in degrees of a straight angle is 180.
The sum of the measures in degrees of the angles of a triangle is 180.

---

1. Simplify $4^{-\frac{3}{2}} + 64^{-\frac{1}{3}}$

- (A) $\dfrac{1}{16}$
- (B) $\dfrac{1}{8}$
- (C) $\dfrac{1}{4}$
- (D) $\dfrac{3}{8}$
- (E) $\dfrac{1}{2}$

2. Given $4x + 3y = 12 + 3y$, find x.

- (A) $3 + \dfrac{3}{2}y$
- (B) $\dfrac{1}{4}$
- (C) $\dfrac{3}{1}$
- (D) $\dfrac{1}{3}$
- (E) $12 + \dfrac{6}{2}y$

3. Suppose a dart is thrown at the target below in such a way that it is as likely to hit one point as another. What is the probability that the dart will land in the inner square?

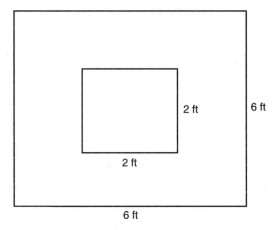

Note: Figure not drawn to scale.

(A) $\dfrac{1}{18}$

(B) $\dfrac{1}{9}$

(C) $\dfrac{1}{3}$

(D) $\dfrac{1}{2}$

(E) $\dfrac{1}{1}$

4. Given the following diagram, find the length of $\overline{PR}$.

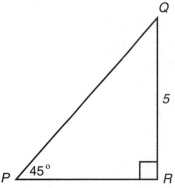

Note: Figure not drawn to scale.

(A) 5
(B) 4
(C) 3
(D) 8
(E) 10

5. For $x = 6$, find $(x^2)^{\frac{1}{2}}$.

(A) 6
(B) 3.460
(C) 2.048
(D) 1.570
(E) 48

6. Given $2y + 4x = 24$, find x when $y = 2$.

(A) 12
(B) 7
(C) 6
(D) 5
(E) 4

343

7. Given the following diagram, find α.

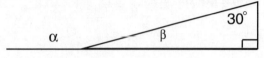

(A) 150°
(B) 120°
(C) 90°
(D) 60°
(E) 30°

8. Find the reciprocal of 0.04.

(A) 25.00
(B) 2.50
(C) 16.00
(D) 0.25
(E) 250.00

9. A car-rental agency will rent you a car for $220 per week plus 40 cents per mile. You have budgeted $400 to spend on car rental. How many miles can you drive without exceeding your budget?

(A) 72
(B) 88
(C) 100
(D) 450
(E) 550

10. If it takes one hour to hike one-third of a three-mile trail, how long does it take to hike one mile?

(A) 20 minutes
(B) 60 minutes
(C) 40 minutes
(D) 200 minutes
(E) 180 minutes

Questions 11–20 require you to solve the problems, then enter your answers by marking ovals in the special grid, as shown in the examples below.

Directions for Student-Produced Response Questions

Each of the remaining 10 questions requires you to solve the problem and enter your answer by marking the ovals in the special grid, as shown in the examples below.

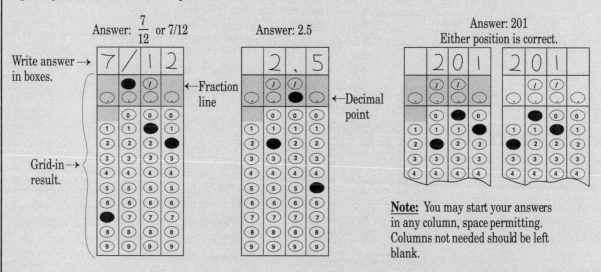

- Mark no more than one oval in any column.
- Because the answer sheet will be machine-scored, **you will receive credit only if the ovals are filled in correctly.**
- Although not required, it is suggested that you write your answer in the boxes at the top of the columns to help you fill in the ovals accurately.
- Some problems may have more than one correct answer. In such cases, grid only one answer.
- No question has a negative answer.
- **Mixed numbers** such as $2\frac{1}{2}$ must be gridded as 2.5 or 5/2. (If [2 1 / 2] is gridded, it will be interpreted as $\frac{21}{2}$, not $2\frac{1}{2}$.)

- **Decimal Accuracy:** If you obtain a decimal answer, **enter the most accurate value the grid will accommodate.** For example, if you obtain an answer such as 0.6666..., you should record the result as .666 or .667. **Less accurate values such as .66 or .67 are not acceptable.**

Acceptable ways to grid $\frac{2}{3}$ = .6666...

GO ON TO THE NEXT PAGE

PETERSON'S
getting you there

11. Given $\frac{2}{10} + \frac{2}{5} + \frac{2}{4} + 8 = x$, find x^2.

16. If a truck can carry a maximum of 1,000 lbs, how many full 60-lb bags of concrete mix can it carry without exceeding 1,000 lbs?

12. Given $x = \sqrt{\frac{1}{64}} + \sqrt{\frac{1}{25}}$, find x to 3 decimal places.

17. If I can travel at a rate of 25 miles in 20 minutes, how many hours will it take me to go 225 miles?

13. 9 is 15% of what number?

18. In the following figure $\overline{AC}$ and $\overline{DB}$ are straight lines, $EB = 16$, $DE = 24$, $BC = 10$. What is the length of AD?

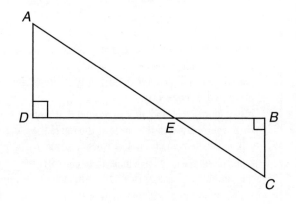

14. The base of a 20-foot ladder is placed nine feet away from a wall. If the ladder is leaned against the wall, how high up the wall will the ladder reach?

15. What decimal does $\dfrac{\frac{3}{5} - \frac{1}{10}}{\frac{1}{3} + \frac{1}{2} - \frac{1}{6}}$ equal?

346

19. What is the difference of $\dfrac{0.64}{8} - \dfrac{0.36}{6}$?

20. A bucket of soil weighs between 12 and 16 pounds. Excluding the container's weight, what is the maximum number of buckets it will take to fill a container to a weight of 240 pounds?

S T O P   If you finish before time is called, you may check your work on this section only. Do not turn to any other section in the test.

Section 5—Writing Skills

Time—25 Minutes • 39 Questions

For each question below, select the best answer from the choices given and fill in the corresponding oval on the answer sheet.

Directions: The following questions will test your knowledge of grammar, usage, diction, and idiom.

Some sentences are correct.

No sentence contains multiple errors.

In each sentence below, five elements, labeled (A) through (E), are underlined and lettered. One (and ONLY one) of the underlined elements may contain an error. In choosing your answer, be sure to follow the rules of standard written English. You can assume that the parts of the sentences not underlined are correct.

If the sentence has no error, choose (E), "No error."

Example:	Sample Answer:
My dog Sally and my cat Buster	● Ⓑ Ⓒ Ⓓ Ⓔ

gets along well with each other, eating
<u> A </u>   <u>   B   </u>
and sleeping <u>together, playing</u> quietly,
                      C
and sharing their food and treats.
          D
<u>No error.</u>
    E

1. The Women's Health Initiative is an

   attempt

   <u>by the National Institutes of Health</u> to
                      A
   correct errors <u>in</u> medical research that
                   B
   results from medications not <u>being tested</u>
         C   D
   on women. <u>No error.</u>
                    E

2. King Arthur was a fine, disciplined

   horse, until he got <u>fed up</u> one day, <u>kicks</u>
   <u> A </u>   B   C
   down the barn door, and attacked

   <u>Bossy, the neighbor's cow.</u> <u>No error.</u>
             D   E

3. I was <u>very frightened</u>, because the
              A
   watchdogs stood <u>in a row</u> and <u>won't</u>
                        B   C
   allow me <u>to enter.</u> <u>No error.</u>
                 D   E

4. One <u>might</u> feel that a health-club member-
A
ship <u>would motivate</u> one <u>to work out</u>
B   C
regularly and get in shape, <u>but you would</u>
D
be sadly mistaken. <u>No error.</u>
E

5. What <u>does</u> <u>either</u> Sam or Josh <u>know</u> about
A   B   C
disease, hunger, or <u>being poor</u>? <u>No error.</u>
D   E

6. <u>Although</u> it is said that democracy means
A
"majority rules," <u>in this country</u> only a
B
<u>minority of eligible voters</u> <u>participate with</u>
C   D
most elections. <u>No error.</u>
E

7. My Great Aunt Ida <u>advises</u> that,
A
when <u>learning to ski, a slope appropriate</u>
B
to one's level of skill is <u>vitally important</u>,
C
and I <u>have learned</u> the hard way that she
D
is right! <u>No error.</u>
E

8. <u>There are</u> war photograph images that
A
<u>we will</u> never forget, because <u>they are</u>
B   C
forever <u>seared onto</u> our collective mind's
D
eye. <u>No error.</u>
E

9. When Roger Baldwin <u>recruited</u>
A
lawyers to <u>defend</u> draft resisters <u>during</u>
B   C
the first world war, he
<u>brought the ACLU into being.</u> <u>No error.</u>
D   E

10. Alice's dogs, Zelda and Max,
<u>do not get fed</u> until 6:00 p.m., but
A
they're frequently <u>whining and begging</u>
B   C
<u>by 4:30</u>. <u>No error.</u>
D   E

11. When arresting <u>loiterers and vagrants</u>,
A
the constitutional <u>right</u> to freedom of
B
assembly <u>must be</u> kept <u>in mind</u> by police.
C   D
<u>No error.</u>
E

12. The teachers, <u>like</u> the students, <u>was sick of</u>
A   B
the strict dress <u>code</u>, even though
C
<u>they knew</u> it was necessary. <u>No error.</u>
D   E

13. John will not bake a pie
for <u>Thanksgiving dinner</u>, because
A
he was mad <u>at Aunt Bette</u> for saying <u>his</u>
B   C
last pie <u>tasted like</u> socks. <u>No error.</u>
D   E

GO ON TO THE NEXT PAGE

14. My dog Taz, a remarkable canine, entered
$\qquad\qquad\qquad$ A
the terrorist's home and immediately sniffs
$\qquad$ B $\qquad\qquad\qquad\qquad$ C
out the explosive device. No error.
$\qquad$ D $\qquad\qquad$ E

15. My boyfriend Bill often orders pizza
$\qquad\qquad\qquad\qquad$ A
for hisself and me, even though I tell him
$\qquad$ B $\qquad\qquad\qquad\qquad$ C
repeatedly that pizza will clog our arteries.
$\qquad\qquad\qquad\qquad\qquad$ D
No error.
$\qquad$ E

16. Carlos was astonished to realize that,
$\qquad$ A $\qquad\qquad$ B
during the marathon, he had drank six
$\qquad\qquad$ C $\qquad\qquad$ D
gallons of water. No error.
$\qquad\qquad\qquad$ E

17. The company president, along with
$\qquad\qquad\qquad\qquad$ A
several other executive officers,
$\qquad$ B
has recently received a
$\qquad$ C
well-deserved bonus. No error.
$\qquad\qquad$ D $\qquad\qquad$ E

18. He pitches the stolen loot into the trunk of
$\qquad\qquad$ A $\qquad\qquad\qquad$ B
his car, covered it with a tarp, and speeds
$\qquad\qquad$ C $\qquad\qquad$ D
away. No error.
$\qquad$ E

19. Although many fans of country music and
$\qquad\qquad$ A
rock-and-roll would disagree, most
$\qquad\qquad$ B
musicologists assert that jazz is
$\qquad\qquad$ C
the only truly American music form.
$\qquad$ D
No error.
$\qquad$ E

Directions: The sentences below test correctness and effectiveness of expression. When you choose your answers, select the sentence or sentence part that is most clear and correct and that conforms best to the requirements of standard written English.

Each of the following sentences is either underlined or contains an underlined part. Under each sentence, there are five ways of phrasing the underlined portion. Choice (A) repeats the original; the other four options are different. You can assume that the elements that are not underlined are correct.

Choose the answer that best expresses the meaning of the original sentence. If in your opinion the original sentence is the best option, choose it. Your choice should produce the most effective sentence.

Example:

I am going to the store to buy a food item, which is bread.

Sample Answer:

(A) buy a food item, which is bread
(B) buy a food item, bread
(C) buy bread
(D) buy a food item, which is called bread
(E) buy what is called bread

20. The sting went off without a hitch, except for a brief moment of hesitation on the part of the victim.

(A) The sting went off without a hitch, except for a brief moment of hesitation on the part of the victim.
(B) The sting went off without a hitch. Except for a brief moment of hesitation on the part of the victim.
(C) The sting went off. Without a hitch, except for a brief moment of hesitation on the part of the victim.
(D) The sting, went off without a hitch, except for a brief moment of hesitation on the part of the victim.
(E) The sting went off without a hitch except, for a brief moment of hesitation on the part of the victim.

21. They finished their supper, retired to the living room, and fall asleep.

(A) fall asleep
(B) falls asleep
(C) fell asleep
(D) falling asleep
(E) falled asleep

351

22. His apartment had been illegally searched, the defendant was convicted.

(A) His apartment had been illegally searched, the defendant was convicted.

(B) Although his apartment had been illegally searched, the defendant was convicted.

(C) Although his apartment has been illegally searched. The defendant was convicted.

(D) His apartment had been illegally searched the defendant was convicted.

(E) Although his apartment, had been improperly gathered, the defendant was convicted.

23. Mr. Arness felt it was time to remarry, but he could not decide whom to ask.

(A) Mr. Arness felt it was time to remarry, but he could not decide whom to ask.

(B) Mr. Arness felt it was time to remarry, he could not decide whom to ask.

(C) Mr. Arness felt it was time to remarry he could not decide whom to ask.

(D) Mr. Arness felt it was time. To remarry, but he could not decide whom to ask.

(E) Mr. Arness felt it was time to remarry he could not decide, whom to ask.

24. John did not think his wife capable to be unfaithful.

(A) think his wife capable to be unfaithful

(B) think his wife capable of being unfaithful

(C) think his wife capable for being unfaithful

(D) think his wife capable as being unfaithful

(E) think his wife capable by being unfaithful

25. Jody's boss ordered him to quit goofing off and return to his desk with an exasperated sigh.

(A) Jody's boss ordered him to quit goofing off and return to his desk with an exasperated sigh.

(B) Jody's boss ordered him to quit goofing off, with an exasperated sigh, and return to his desk.

(C) Jody's boss ordered him with an exasperated sigh. To quit goofing off and return to his desk.

(D) With an exasperated sigh, Jody's boss ordered him to quit goofing off and return to his desk.

(E) Jody's boss ordered him to, with an exasperated sigh, quit goofing off and return to his desk.

26. Sergeant Pepper <u>was the most prettiest horse we ever had, yet he was also the meanest.</u>

- **(A)** was the most prettiest horse we ever had, yet he was also the meanest
- **(B)** was the prettiest horse we ever had, yet he was also the meanest
- **(C)** was the prettiest horse we ever had, yet he was also the most meanly
- **(D)** was the pretty horse we ever had, yet he was also the most mean
- **(E)** was the prettiest horse we ever had, yet he was also the most meaner

27. Raisa thought <u>they should order anchovies on their pizza; moreover, Kyle disagreed.</u>

- **(A)** they should order anchovies on their pizza; moreover, Kyle disagreed.
- **(B)** they should order anchovies on their pizza; meanwhile, Kyle disagreed.
- **(C)** they should order anchovies on their pizza; however, Kyle disagreed.
- **(D)** they should order anchovies on their pizza; furthermore, Kyle disagreed.
- **(E)** they should order pizza, where Kyle disagreed.

28. Because the Academy Awards <u>are based on and around the calendar year, many movie studios speed things up, rushing to release their movies at the end of the year, in December.</u>

- **(A)** are based on and around the calendar year, many movie studios speed things up, rushing to release their movies at the end of the year, in December.
- **(B)** are based on the calendar year, many movie studios rush to release their movies in December.
- **(C)** are based on the calendar year, many film and movie studios hurry things along, rushing to release their movies in December.
- **(D)** have their basis on and around the calendar year, many movie studios rush to release their movies in December.
- **(E)** are based on the 12 months of the calendar year, many movie studios rush to release their movies in December.

GO ON TO THE NEXT PAGE

PETERSON'S
getting you there

29. Ruben wrote a letter to his little brother once a week while he was in Spain.

   (A)   Ruben wrote a letter to his little brother once a week while he was in Spain.
   (B)   When his little brother was in Spain, Ruben wrote a letter to him once a week.
   (C)   When in Spain, a letter was written every day by Ruben to his little brother.
   (D)   His little brother received a letter from Ruben once a week while he was in Spain.
   (E)   Once a week while he was in Spain, a letter was written to his little brother by Ruben.

30. We have several errands to run before we can go to the movie: go to the bank, washing the car, and drop the dog off at the vet.

   (A)   We have several errands to run before we can go to the movie: go to the bank, washing the car, and drop the dog off at the vet.
   (B)   We have several errands to run before we can go to the movie: go to the bank, washing the car, and dropping the dog off at the vet.
   (C)   Several errands have to be run before we can go to the movie: went to the bank, washed the car, and dropped the dog off at the vet.
   (D)   Several errands have to be run before we went to the movie: go to the bank, wash the car, and drop the dog off at the vet.
   (E)   We have several errands to run before we can go to the movie: go to the bank, wash the car, and drop the dog off at the vet.

31. To prevent suffocating, keep plastic bags out of the reach of children.

   (A)   To prevent suffocating, keep plastic bags out of the reach of children.
   (B)   Suffocating can be prevented by keeping plastic bags out of the reach of children.
   (C)   To prevent them from suffocating, plastic bags should be kept out of the reach of children.
   (D)   To prevent children from suffocating, keep plastic bags out of their reach.
   (E)   Plastic bags, to prevent the suffocating of children, should be kept out of reach.

32. Firecrackers in a roomful of children are more dangerous than grownups.

   (A)   than grownups
   (B)   than with grownups
   (C)   than one with grownups
   (D)   than them with grownups
   (E)   than firecrackers in a roomful of grownups

33. The Internet makes communication more convenient where also more risky.

   (A)   where also more risky
   (B)   but also more risky
   (C)   as also more risky
   (D)   because also more risky
   (E)   inasmuch as also more risky

354

Directions: The following passage is from an essay in its early stages. Some of it may need revision. Read the passage below and answer the questions that come after it. Some of the questions will ask you to improve sentence structure and word choice. Other questions will refer to parts of the essay or to the entire essay and ask you to improve organization and development. Base your decisions on the rules of standard written English, and mark your answer in the corresponding oval on the answer sheet.

Questions 34–39 are based on the following passage.

(1) *When an amateur gardener considers using "natural enemy" control of an infestation of aphids (that is, using another insect, rather than a chemical pesticide), chances are that gardener will think first of the ladybug.* (2) *However, there is another natural enemy of the aphid that some gardeners believe is even more effective than the ladybug.* (3) *Ladybugs are cute.* (4) *They are unbuglike to the max in the way they look and appear.* (5) *(The truth is, the ladybug can quite happily become a cannibal if food supplies are scarce.)* (6) *Lacewings also prey on spider mites, whiteflies, moths, leafminers, and small caterpillars.* (7) *This is the green lacewing fly, which is also known as the "aphid lion" because of its skill in hunting down and devouring aphids by the boxcarload!* (8) *In the meantime, they are an important predator of long-tailed mealybugs in greenhouses and interior plantscapes!* (9) *(In fact, some gardeners even regard the lacewing fly as prettier than the ladybug, because of its delicate, filmy wings and huge golden eyes.)*

(10) *Although not as widely known as the ladybug, the green lacewing controls the same pests and is not as prone to fly away from the garden.* (11) *Lacewings can be purchased in the egg stage and will hatch into larvae in 3 to 5 days, or, for faster control, they can be purchased in the larvae stage, which is the stage at which they control pests.* (12) *The lacewing larvae look like tiny, flattened alligators and have hollow mandibles, with which they pierce their prey and suck out body fluids.* (13) *Many other garden predators control pests in the larvae stage.* (14) *After 14 to 21 days the lacewing larvae pupates into a cocoon for about 14 days and emerges as an adult.* (15) *Adults feed on nectar, pollen, and honeydew to stimulate their reproductive process.* (16) *An adult female will lay about 200 eggs, making it easy to get a colony of lacewing going in the garden.* (17) *The larvae will emerge in about 5 days and aggressively devour aphids and other garden pests.*

34. Which of the following is the best way to revise and combine the underlined parts of sentences 3, 4, and 5 reproduced below?

Ladybugs are cute. They are unbuglike to the max in the way they look and appear. (The truth is, the ladybug can quite happily become a cannibal if food supplies are scarce.)

(A) Ladybugs are cute. They are quite unbuglike in the way they look and appear. (Although the truth is

(B) Perhaps this is because ladybugs are cute and quite unbuglike in the way they look and appear (although the truth is

(C) Perhaps this is because ladybugs are cute and quite unbuglike in appearance. (Although the truth is

(D) Perhaps this is because ladybugs are cute and quite unbuglike in appearance (although the truth is

(E) Perhaps this is because ladybugs are cute and quite unbuglike (although the truth is

35. Paragraph 1 of the essay would be more coherent if sentence 7 were placed after

(A) sentence 2.
(B) sentence 3.
(C) sentence 4.
(D) sentence 5.
(E) sentence 6.

36. Which of the following sentences is LEAST relevant to the topic of paragraph 2?

(A) Sentence 10
(B) Sentence 11
(C) Sentence 12
(D) Sentence 13
(E) Sentence 14

37. Which of the following would make the best replacement for the underlined phrase in sentence 8, reproduced below.

In the meantime, they are an important predator of long-tailed mealybugs in greenhouses and interior plantscapes!

(A) In addition, they are
(B) Hence, they are
(C) Conversely, they are
(D) In short, they are
(E) Then, they are

38. Which of the following is the most likely intended audience for the paper?

(A) High school students studying insect anatomy
(B) Biologists performing insect learning experiments
(C) Potential buyers of ladybugs
(D) Potential buyers of lacewings
(E) Naturalists studying the habits of insects

39. Given the overall purpose of the paper, the most likely intent of sentence 5 is to

(A) stimulate interest in the ladybug equal to that of the lacewing.

(B) attract the attention of research entomologists.

(C) attract the attention of amateur naturalists.

(D) make the ladybug less appealing as a competitor of the lacewing.

(E) stimulate the interest of gardeners who might be using pesticides.

S T O P If you finish before time is called, you may check your work on this section only. Do not turn to any other section in the test.

Quick Score Answers

Section 1 Critical Reading	Section 2 Math	Section 3 Critical Reading	Section 4 Math	Section 5 Writing Skills
1. A	1. E	1. C	1. D	1. C
2. D	2. A	2. B	2. C	2. C
3. B	3. C	3. B	3. B	3. C
4. D	4. B	4. C	4. A	4. D
5. E	5. A	5. A	5. A	5. D
6. A	6. D	6. D	6. D	6. D
7. D	7. C	7. E	7. B	7. B
8. C	8. E	8. A	8. A	8. D
9. B	9. E	9. D	9. D	9. D
10. E	10. D	10. C	10. B	10. E
11. B	11. E	11. A	11. 82.81	11. B
12. D	12. B	12. B	12. .325	12. B
13. D	13. B	13. E	13. 60	13. B
14. E	14. A	14. B	14. 17.86 feet	14. C
15. C	15. D	15. A	15. .75	15. B
16. A	16. D	16. C	16. 16 bags	16. D
17. B	17. E	17. A	17. 3 hours	17. E
18. B	18. D	18. B	18. 15	18. C
19. C	19. C	19. C	19. 0.02	19. E
20. B	20. E	20. C	20. 20 buckets	20. A
21. A		21. C		21. C
22. E		22. B		22. B
23. A		23. C		23. A
24. C		24. D		24. B
25. D		25. A		25. D
		26. C		26. B
		27. D		27. C
				28. B
				29. B
				30. E
				31. D
				32. E
				33. B
				34. D
				35. A
				36. D
				37. A
				38. D
				39. D

Explanatory Answers

Section 1—Critical Reading

1. **The correct answer is (A).** This is a definition sentence. Both words in choice (A) are positive words, as are the words in the sentence itself. The words in the other sets contradict one another.

2. **The correct answer is (D).** This is a definition sentence. *Focus* is necessary for *precision* and *clarity* in writing. Choices (A) and (C) make no sense in context and can be discarded immediately. To be *bold*, choice (B), is not necessarily to be *precise* and *clear*. There is no way for an editor to make a writer *talented*, choice (E).

3. **The correct answer is (B).** This is a comparison/contrast sentence. Ask yourself, "What is the opposite of having everything spelled out?" The first words in choices (A), (B), and (C) may all seem plausible, but when you reach the second word in each set, *imagination* will probably catch your eye. To *conjure* is to summon, and it also has the connotation of magic, which fits with the word *imagination*.

4. **The correct answer is (D).** This is a cause-and-effect sentence. Ask yourself, "Among the choices, which is the most logical reason for tracking hikers in a forest?"

5. **The correct answer is (E).** This is a definition sentence. All the other choices may be true of (some) flowers, but in the context of *nutritious*, the word *edible* makes most sense. (Again, remember that you are looking for the best and most logical answer, not just a possible one.)

6. **The correct answer is (A).** The excerpt from the poem expresses the way the *Cat* (representing nature) expresses reverence (*worships*) toward *the Living God*. Choice (B) is incorrect because the author's comments about the poem would still be comprehensible without the lines. Choice (C) is incorrect because the passage is about Smart's feelings, not about the author's. Choice (D) is incorrect because the author's own opinions about Smart's sanity are not directly expressed. Choice (E) is incorrect because, although Smart's love for his cat was probably real, it is not discussed in the passage.

7. **The correct answer is (D).** The phrase *so-called* is commonly used to negate whatever comes after it (e.g., a "so-called good man" probably isn't). The whole passage implies that Smart was an extraordinary poet, not simply a lunatic. The other answers are not reflected in the passage.

359

8. **The correct answer is (C).** The passage calls the poem a *meditation on the divine*, and the poem itself speaks of the cat's *duly and daily serving* God. The other choices are not mentioned in the passage.

9. **The correct answer is (B).** The passage states that the Devil's Advocate's role is to *counter* (that is, to argue against) the group's decision. Choice (A) is wrong because one can argue against something without necessarily reviling it. Choices (C), (D), and (E) are wrong because the passage does not suggest that the Devil's Advocate is there to agree with, nullify, or speed up the group's decision.

10. **The correct answer is (E).** The passage makes it clear that *Groupthink* causes conformity. The other choices are not mentioned in the passage.

11. **The correct answer is (B).** Choice (B) is the only one that satisfies the criteria for groupthink discussed in the passage: Each group member conforms, though secretly disagreeing, and a bad decision results. Choices (A) and (E) are wrong because no one secretly disagrees at the time the decisions are made. Choices (C) and (D) are wrong because the members do not conform out of desire for consensus, but out of duty in the first case, and out of fear in the second.

12. **The correct answer is (D).** Reread the example of Mr. Place. This is a good passage on which to practice making inferences, because, although the message of the passage is serious, it's delivered with humor, and the author doesn't always say directly what he means.

13. **The correct answer is (D).** To *vitiate* is to *spoil*. Note the word *abort* in the same sentence.

14. **The correct answer is (E).** The phrase is used literally here, with *holiest* meaning "highest."

15. **The correct answer is (C).** Remember to look first at the ideas or examples immediately preceding and following the segment in question. In lines 26–29 (which follow the statement), the author gives the example of the Place children's relationship with their father: the children learned (apparently, at least in Francis's case, *without bitterness*) to *keep out of their father's way*.

16. **The correct answer is (A).** The passage makes it clear that Francis's father did not care enough about his children to try to influence their thinking.

17. The correct answer is (B). Note the phrases *But as compared* and *compared to* (lines 45 and 55–56). Also, a careful read-through will rule out the other choices. Choice (E) is wrong because there is no hint of bitterness in the essay.

18. The correct answer is (B). In the context of the entire essay, it is apparent that the author does not believe Mr. Place has the remotest connection with *Providence*. He is exaggerating to make a point.

19. The correct answer is (C). This choice fits in with the light tone of the whole essay, which rules out the sobering choices of (A), (B), and (E). The author doesn't seem, in general, to think parents necessarily *know best*, choice (D), so choice (C) is the most logical choice.

20. The correct answer is (B). Throughout the essay, the author advocates treating children in a straightforward, nonpatronizing manner, which implies that he respects them.

21. The correct answer is (A). Choices (B), (C), and (E) are too narrow to be the main idea. *Environmentalists*, choice (D), are not mentioned in the paragraph.

22. The correct answer is (E). The other choices are either not mentioned or are contradicted in the paragraph

23. The correct answer is (A). See lines 5–8. The other choices are not reflected in paragraph 1.

24. The correct answer is (C). The entire paragraph deals with the geographical diversity of wetlands.

25. The correct answer is (D). See the first sentence of the paragraph.

Section 2—Math

1. The correct answer is (E). If you remember to Please Excuse My Dear Aunt Sally, it will help you perform operations in the right order, which are: Parentheses, Exponents, Multiplication, Division, Addition, and Subtraction. This means we must add the $7 + 1$ first, since they are enclosed within parentheses, then multiply by 4, and finally subtract 6, to get the answer 26.

2. The correct answer is (A). Supplementary angles are those that, when measured together, form a 180° angle. An obtuse angle has an angle measure greater than 90° but less than 180°. Because α and β are supplementary, we know that $\alpha + \beta = 180°$, which means $\alpha = 180° - \beta$. Since $\beta > 90°$, it follows that $180° - \beta < 90°$, or $\alpha < 90°$. Therefore, $\alpha < \beta$.

361

3. The correct answer is (C).

Since $3y = z - x$

$$y = \frac{(z - x)}{3}$$

or

$$y = \frac{1}{3}(z - x)$$

4. The correct answer is (B). The dimensions of the rectangular solid are: Length $(L) = 8$, Width $(W) = 6$, Height $(H) =$ one half its width $= \dfrac{6}{2} = 3$. Now plug these values into the formula for volume of a rectangular solid to find the answer:

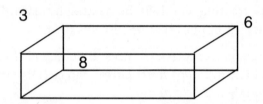

$$V = H \times W \times L = 3 \times 6 \times 8 = 144 \text{ cubic inches}$$

5. The correct answer is (A). As the cross-sectional diagram below shows, the wall thickness is one half of the difference in the two diameters.

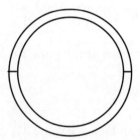

Subtract .625, the inner diameter, from the outer diameter .750, to get the difference in diameters, .125. Remember, .125 is the thickness of both walls. The question asks us to find the thickness of one wall, so you must divide .125 by 2 to get the right answer, .0625.

6. **The correct answer is (D).** To solve this problem, first, translate the words into algebraic form, then solve for the price, P.

The pants sells for $6 more than 75% of the price, which can be restated as:

$$P = 6 + .75P$$
$$P - .75P = 6$$
$$P(1 - .75) = 6$$
$$.25P = 6$$
$$P = \frac{6}{.25}$$
$$P = 24$$

7. **The correct answer is (C).** The sum of the angles of a triangle is 180°. Since we know the measures of two of the angles, we can compute the measure of the third:

$$180° - 60° - 90° = \alpha$$
$$120° - 90° = \alpha$$
$$30° = \alpha$$

8. **The correct answer is (E).** To figure this one out, translate the words into an equation, then solve for x. What % of 5 is 90% of 50 becomes

$$\frac{x}{100}(5) = \frac{90}{100}(50)?$$
$$\frac{5x}{100} = \frac{[(90)(50)]}{100}$$
$$5x = \frac{[(100)(4500)]}{100}$$
$$5x = 4500$$
$$x = 900$$

9. **The correct answer is (E).** For $(a \times b)$ to be less than zero, either a or b (but not both a and b) must be less than zero. All the other choices result in values that are either zero or greater than zero.

10. **The correct answer is (D).** This problem can be solved easily using the method of similar triangles. Both the flag pole and the fence post form a right angle with the surface of the earth and the sun's rays strike both objects at the same angle, therefore we have two similar triangles. To solve a similar triangle problem, set up a proportion.

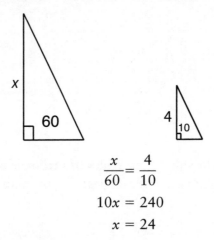

$$\frac{x}{60} = \frac{4}{10}$$

$$10x = 240$$

$$x = 24$$

11. **The correct answer is (E).** To solve this problem, plug in the values for x, y, and z, then simplify.

$$= \left(9x^3 - \frac{z^2}{2}\right)\left(\frac{y}{11}\right)$$

$$= \left((9)(-1)^3 - \frac{2^2}{2}\right)\left(\frac{1}{11}\right)$$

$$= (-9 - 2)\left(\frac{1}{11}\right)$$

$$= \frac{-11}{11}$$

$$= -1$$

12. **The correct answer is (B).** This is false because P and Q are supplementary angles and cannot be equal because they cannot be 90°. The other choices are all true because they are vertical angles, choices (A) and (E), alternate interior angles, choice (C), or corresponding angles, choice (D).

13. The correct answer is **(B)**. Solve this one by translating the word into an algebraic relationship. We know the coins are only nickels or dimes. Of the 11 coins, we are asked to find x, the number of dimes. This means there are x dimes and $(11 - x)$ nickels. Now translate this information into algebraic form:

$.65$ = (value of a dime)(number of dimes) + (value of a nickel)(number of nickels)

$$= (.10)x + (.05)(11 - x)$$
$$= .10x + .55 - .05x$$
$$= (.10 - .05)x + .55$$
$$= .05x + .55$$
$$.05x = .65 - .55$$
$$x = \frac{.10}{.05}$$
$$x = 2$$

14. The correct answer is **(A)**. To solve this one, translate the words into an equation, then solve for x.

What percent of two gallons is a quart or $(x\%)(2 \text{ gallons}) = 1 \text{ quart}$

Next, convert gallons to quarts so the units match:
2 gallons = 8 quarts.

$$(x\%)(8 \text{ quarts}) = 1 \text{ quart}$$
$$\left(\frac{x}{100}\right)(8) = 1$$
$$8x = 100$$
$$x = 12.5$$

15. The correct answer is **(D)**. To solve this problem quickly, recognize that $m\angle CAD = m\angle EAD$, one angle of the triangle AED. If we can find the measure of $\angle ADE$ and $\angle AED$, we can subtract them from $180°$ to find $\angle EAD$. We are given the measure of $\angle ADE$ in another form, as arc $AB = 40°$. To find $m\angle AED$, notice that it is a supplementary angle to $\angle CED = 60°$. This means $m\angle AED = 180° - 60° = 120°$. Now we can solve for $m\angle EAD = m\angle CAD$.

$$m\angle CAD = 180° - 20° - 120°$$
$$m\angle CAD = 40°$$

16. **The correct answer is (D).** First, we must translate the words into an algebraic equation. Since the shopper pays 30% less than the original price (P), the equation is:

$$P - .30P = 420$$
$$(1 - .30)P = 420$$
$$.70P = 420$$
$$P = \frac{420}{.70}$$
$$P = 600$$

17. **The correct answer is (E).** Solve this problem by setting up an equation, solving for $\angle B$, then solving for $\angle C$.

$$m\angle A + m\angle B + m\angle C = 180°$$
$$6m\angle B + m\angle B + 2m\angle B = 180°$$
$$9m\angle B = 180°$$
$$m\angle B = 20°$$

Remember, the question asks us to find $\angle C$!

$$m\angle C = 2m\angle B = (2)(20°) = 40°$$

18. **The correct answer is (D).**

$$\frac{a\ b}{c\ d} + \frac{a\ b}{c\ d} + 2cb = (ad - cb) + (ad - cb) + 2cb$$
$$= ad - cb + ad - cb + 2cb$$
$$= 2ad - 2cb + 2cb$$
$$= 2ad$$

19. **The correct answer is (C).** As the diagram below shows, before we can find the area, we must find the height of the triangle (x).

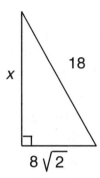

Solve for x using the Pythagorean Theorem:

$$x^2 + (8\sqrt{2})^2 = (18)^2$$
$$x^2 = (18)^2 - (8\sqrt{2})^2$$
$$x^2 = 324 - 128$$
$$x^2 = 196$$
$$x = 14$$

Now, find the area of the triangle using the formula for area of a triangle:

$$A = \frac{1}{2}\ \text{base} \times \text{height}$$
$$= \left(\frac{1}{2}\right)(8\sqrt{2})(14)$$
$$= (7)(8\sqrt{2})$$
$$= 56\sqrt{2}$$

20. **The correct answer is (E).** Solve this problem in two steps. First, solve for a in the first equation:

$$a + b = 27$$
$$a = 27 - b$$

Second, plug this value for a into the second expression:

$$3c - a = 0$$
$$3c - (27 - b) = 0$$
$$3c = 27 - b$$
$$c = 9 - \frac{b}{3}$$

Section 3—Critical Reading

1. **The correct answer is (C).** The purpose of *anesthesia* is to ease *discomfort*. Remember to read all the choices. Be careful not to choose a word that is similar to the one that logically fits, but wrong—in this case, choice (A), *discomfiture*, which means embarrassment. If you're not sure what the other choices mean, it would be a good idea to look them up now.

2. **The correct answer is (B).** In this question, it's likely you can rule out all the wrong choices pretty rapidly! Can you see why?

3. **The correct answer is (B).** This word, which means *to give support to*, is the only choice that makes sense in the context of the sentence.

4. **The correct answer is (C).** Toothbrushing is logically related to *hygiene*. Choices (A) and (B) have nothing to do with tooth care. Choices (D) and (E) are services performed by a dentist but are unrelated to toothbrushing.

5. **The correct answer is (A).** Remembering that the prefix *in-* means "not" may help with this question. Therefore *inappropriate* means "not appropriate."

6. **The correct answer is (D).** This is a definition question. The first segment of the sentence gives you a clue that you are looking for a word closely related to *privacy. Confidential* fits perfectly.

7. **The correct answer is (E).** The other choices, while perhaps true of iguanas, have nothing to do with avoiding pet hair due to allergies. Always make sure you consider the context of the sentence.

8. **The correct answer is (A).** This is a cause-and-effect sentence. Ask yourself, "What would prompt a conservative doctor to use a perhaps unorthodox treatment?" The logical answer to this question rules out choices (B), (C), and (E). Of the two choices left, the combination of words that makes more sense is choice (A).

9. **The correct answer is (D).** The question has the effect of making the reader want to know the answer. Choice (A) is wrong because the question has no information in it. Choices (B) and (E) are wrong because there is nothing unpleasant in the question that would *goad* or *disturb* the reader. Choice (C) is wrong because the question is rhetorical, and therefore not meant to be answered by the reader.

10. **The correct answer is (C).** The passage says that Phileas Fogg was not *avaricious*; this is followed by the suggestion that he was often generous. The other choices are not supported by the passage.

368

11. **The correct answer is (A).** The words *terrify, enslave,* and *monopolize* are harshly accusatory words that denounce organized religion. Choice (C) has a positive connotation; choices (B), (D), and (E) imply a neutral stance.

12. **The correct answer is (B).** Paine considers the teachings of all organized churches *human inventions,* implying that he does not regard any as divinely inspired. Choices (A) and (C) are wrong because he condemns all organized churches, not just those of "foreign" cultures; also he does not discuss other religions in terms of a belief in one god. Choice (D) is wrong because he does not express approval of any national church, implying he sees no *good* in any of them. Choice (E) is wrong because, although Paine implies his own beliefs are private, he does not say they are unique.

13. **The correct answer is (E).** One of the denotations of the word *invention* is *fabrication,* which also has the connotation of *falsehood*—this fits best with the sentiment expressed.

14. **The correct answer is (B).** To stow away in someone else's luggage would be an adventure. Choice (C) is wrong because, although stowing away is illegal, it is not necessarily injurious to another person as fraud would be. The other choices do not make sense in the context.

15. **The correct answer is (A).** *Sheltered* is the only choice that has a positive (*benign*) connotation. The other choices might apply to a prison, but not to a *benign prison.*

16. **The correct answer is (C).** See lines 6–9. The other devices are not used in the paragraph.

17. **The correct answer is (A).** See lines 30–32. The other choices are not in the paragraph.

18. **The correct answer is (B).** Notice the phrase *but they retain* later in the same sentence—you'll be looking for a word that contrasts with that phrase. Choice (B) is the only one.

19. **The correct answer is (C).** This is implied by the word *accountability.* The other choices are not found in this paragraph.

20. **The correct answer is (C).** The others are civil and political rights.

21. **The correct answer is (C).** If there are footnotes with the passage, always be sure to read them.

22. **The correct answer is (B).** This is the meaning of the word "universal." That word is repeated throughout the document. The other choices are restrictions that do not exist in the document.

23. **The correct answer is (C).** Again, the Declaration is intended to deal with *universal* rights and is based on the idea that people have certain rights simply by virtue of being human.

24. **The correct answer is (D).** The point of the two articles is that all people have the right to legal remedy.

25. **The correct answer is (A).** See lines 60–62, which speak of equal rights *as to marriage, during marriage, and at its* <u>dissolution</u>.

26. **The correct answer is (C).** Both passages make it clear that all people, regardless of status, have basic rights by virtue of being human, and that these rights are clear and can be neither bought nor relinquished.

27. **The correct answer is (D).** Article 16 covers various aspects of marriage, which fits under the heading of social and cultural rights.

Section 4—Math

1. **The correct answer is (D).** Tackle this problem by simplifying it one step at a time. First, eliminate the negative exponents, then convert the rational exponents to their equivalent radical forms. Finally, simplify the expression to find the answer.

$$4^{-\frac{3}{2}} + 64^{-\frac{1}{3}} = \frac{1}{4^{\frac{3}{2}}} + \frac{1}{64^{\frac{1}{3}}}$$

$$= \frac{1}{(\sqrt{4})^3} + \frac{1}{\sqrt[3]{64}}$$

$$= \frac{1}{2^3} + \frac{1}{4}$$

$$= \frac{1}{8} + \frac{1}{4}$$

$$= \frac{3}{8}$$

2. **The correct answer is (C).** Figure this one out by solving for x.

$$4x + 3y = 12 + 3y$$
$$4x = 12 + 3y - 3y$$
$$4x = 12$$
$$x = 3$$

Since 3 can also be expressed as $\frac{3}{1}$, choice (C) is the correct answer.

3. **The correct answer is (B).** We find the probability of a successful outcome—that the dart will land inside the inner square—by comparing the area of the inner square to the area of the outer square. The inner square has an area of $2 \times 2 = 4$ sq. ft. The outer square has an area of $6 \times 6 = 36$ sq. ft. So, the probability that the dart will land inside the inner square is $\frac{4}{36}$, or $\frac{1}{9}$.

4. **The correct answer is (A).** Since the total of all angles of the triangle must equal 180°, we know that $\angle PQR + 45° + 90° = 180°$, or $\angle PQR = 180° - 135° = 45°$. This means $\angle PQR = \angle QPR$, and since the sides opposite equal angles have equal lengths, we can conclude that $PR = QR = 5$. This solution can also be derived by identifying the triangle as an isosceles right triangle, in which case the length of the two legs must be of equal length.

5. **The correct answer is (A).** You can solve this by multiplying the exponents together:

$$(x^2)^{\frac{1}{2}} = x^{\left(\frac{2}{1}\right)\left(\frac{1}{2}\right)} = x^{\frac{2}{2}} = x^1 = 6$$

Or, by converting the expression into its equivalent radical expression, you have: $\sqrt{x^2}$. Now it is easy to see that the answer is just $x = 6$.

6. **The correct answer is (D).** Substituting 2 for y, the expression becomes: $4 + 4x = 24$ or $4x = 20$, which simplifies to $x = 5$.

7. **The correct answer is (B).** If you recognize the triangle as a 30°–60°–90° triangle, you know that $\beta = 60°$. Now, α and β are supplementary angles, so $\alpha + \beta = 180°$, or $\alpha = 180° - 60° = 120°$.

8. **The correct answer is (A).** Solve this problem by renaming fractions as decimals.

   This problem is a snap if you use your calculator. Or, you can work it out as follows:

   $$\frac{1}{.04} = \frac{1}{\left(\frac{4}{100}\right)}$$

   $$= 1 \times \left(\frac{100}{4}\right)$$

   $$= 25$$

9. **The correct answer is (D).** Solve this problem by creating a formula, a mathematical model, that uses a variable to represent the unknown quantity. Since we are asked to find the number of miles we can drive, let's make x = number of miles. We know that the total number of dollars we have budgeted for this trip is $400. We also know that the components of this total are $220 for the weekly rental plus 40 cents for every mile we drive. Our next step is to translate these words into a mathematical model, or equation, then solve for x.

   $$220 + 0.40x = 400$$
   $$0.40x = 400 - 220$$
   $$0.40x = 180$$
   $$x = \frac{180}{0.40}$$
   $$x = 450$$

10. **The correct answer is (B).** Since one-third of a three-mile trail is 1 mile, which takes one hour, it takes 1 hour, or 60 minutes, to walk 1 mile.

11. **The correct answer is 82.81.** If you know your decimal equivalences by heart, you can rapidly solve this one by renaming the fractions as decimals:

    $$x = \frac{2}{10} + \frac{2}{5} + \frac{2}{4} + 8$$
    $$= .2 + .4 + .5 + 8$$
    $$= 1.1 + 8$$
    $$= 9.1$$

    But wait, we are asked to find x^2. The correct answer is $(9.1)^2 = 82.81$.

372

12. **The correct answer is .325.** Rewriting the radical expressions and simplifying, we have:

$$x = \sqrt{\frac{1}{64}} + \sqrt{\frac{1}{25}} = \frac{\sqrt{1}}{\sqrt{64}} + \frac{\sqrt{1}}{\sqrt{25}} = \frac{1}{8} + \frac{1}{5} = .125 + .2 = .325$$

13. **The correct answer is 60.** Translating the words into algebraic form gives us the following equation:

$$9 = 15\% \text{ of } x$$

or $9 = .15x$

$$x = \frac{9}{.15}$$
$$x = 60$$

14. **The correct answer is 17.86 feet.** As the following diagram shows, this problem can easily be solved using the Pythagorean Theorem, $a^2 + b^2 = c^2$.

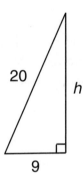

We want to solve for h, and the equation is:

$$h^2 + 9^2 = 20^2$$
$$h^2 = 20^2 - 9^2$$
$$h^2 = 400 - 81$$
$$h^2 = 319$$
$$h = \sqrt{319}$$
$$h = 17.86 \text{ ft.}$$

15. **The correct answer is .75.** The expression is equal to:

$$\frac{\dfrac{6}{10} - \dfrac{1}{10}}{\dfrac{2}{6} + \dfrac{3}{6} - \dfrac{1}{6}} = \frac{\dfrac{5}{10}}{\dfrac{4}{6}} = \frac{\dfrac{1}{2}}{\dfrac{2}{3}} = \left(\frac{1}{2}\right)\left(\frac{3}{2}\right) = \frac{3}{4} = .75$$

16. **The correct answer is 16 bags.** To solve this one, divide the total weight by the unit weight to find the number of units:

$$\frac{1000}{60} \approx 16.67$$

Round down to 16 for your answer because the question asks us to find the number of full bags the truck can carry without going over 1,000 lbs.

17. **The correct answer is 3 hours.** A rate of 25 miles in 20 minutes is equivalent to 75 mph. Use the formula, Distance = Rate × Time, to solve this problem. We know the distance (D) and the Rate (R), and we want to solve for time (T).

$$D = RT$$
$$225 = 75T$$
$$T = \frac{225}{75}$$
$$T = 3 \text{ hours}$$

18. **The correct answer is 15.** Since ∠AED and ∠BEC are vertical angles, they are equal, which means we have similar triangles. Set up a proportion that relates the sides of one triangle to the sides of the other, then solve for length AD.

$$\frac{BE}{DE} = \frac{BC}{AD} \quad \Rightarrow \quad \frac{16}{24} = \frac{10}{AD}$$
$$(16)(AD) = (10)(24)$$
$$AD = \frac{240}{16}$$
$$AD = 15$$

19. **The correct answer is 0.02.** Use your calculator here to speed things up. Or, you can calculate it manually as follows:

$$\frac{0.64}{8} - \frac{0.36}{6} = \frac{(6)(0.64) - (8)(0.36)}{48} = \frac{3.84 - 2.88}{48} = \frac{0.96}{48} = 0.02$$

20. The correct answer is 20 buckets. The number of buckets is at a maximum when the weight per bucket is at a minimum, therefore we should choose 12 pounds as the number to divide into 240. The algebraic relationship is as follows:

$$\text{Total weight} = (\text{bucket weight}) \times (\text{number of buckets})$$
$$240 = 12 \times (\text{number of buckets})$$
$$\frac{240}{12} = \text{number of buckets}$$
$$20 = \text{number of buckets}$$

It will take a maximum of 20 buckets to fill the container to a net weight of 240 pounds.

Section 5—Writing Skills

1. **The correct answer is (C).** This is a subject-verb agreement mistake. The subject (*errors*) is plural; its verb (*results*) is singular.

2. **The correct answer is (C).** The error is one of shift in tense, from past (*was*) to present (*kicks*).

3. **The correct answer is (C).** There is a shift in tense from past (*stood*) to present (*won't*).

4. **The correct answer is (D).** The error is that of a shift in person from third (*one*) to second (*you*).

5. **The correct answer is (D).** Items in a series should be grammatically parallel. A third noun, *poverty*, is needed to balance the nouns *hunger* and *disease*.

6. **The correct answer is (D).** The error is that of faulty use of a preposition (*with*). The correct wording would be *participate in*.

7. **The correct answer is (B).** The error is that of a misplaced modifier. The sentence appears to be saying that *a slope* is *learning to ski*.

8. **The correct answer is (D).** The error is one of misuse of the preposition *onto*. The wording should be *seared into*.

9. **The correct answer is (D).** The sentence has illogical construction. (An adverb clause is mixed with a predicate, but you do not have to know these terms. It is enough to know that "something is wrong" in the sentence and to correctly indicate where.)

10. **The correct answer is (E).** The sentence is written in standard English, with no errors.

11. **The correct answer is (B).** This segment contains a misplaced modifier. The *constitutional right* cannot arrest anyone; that is a job for the police.

12. **The correct answer is (B).** The error is in subject-verb agreement. The verb should be *were*, not *was*, to agree with the plural subject *teachers*.

13. **The correct answer is (B).** The error is one of a shift in tense from future (*will not*) to past (*was mad*).

14. **The correct answer is (C).** The error is a shift in tense from past (*entered*) to present (*sniffs*). The correct form of the verb is *sniffed*.

15. **The correct answer is (B).** The error here is the use of a nonstandard form of the pronoun *himself*.

16. **The correct answer is (D).** The error is in the use of an incorrect verb form (*had drank*). The correct form is *had drunk*.

17. **The correct answer is (E).** The sentence is correctly written. Don't be misled by the plural noun (*officers*) that comes between the singular subject (*The company president*) and the verb (*has*).

18. **The correct answer is (C).** The error here is a shift in tense from present (*pitches* and *speeds*) to past (*covered*).

19. **The correct answer is (E).** The sentence is correctly written.

20. **The correct answer is (A).** Choices (B) and (C) contain sentence fragments. Choice (D) erroneously places a comma between subject (*The sting*) and verb (*went*). Choice (E) erroneously places a comma between the preposition (*except*) and its object (*for a brief moment*).

21. **The correct answer is (C).** The word *fell* is in the past tense, as are *finished* and *retired* in the first part of the sentence. So this is the only sentence among the choices given that uses proper parallel structure. Choice (E) contains a nonstandard form of the verb fall (*falled*), as well.

22. **The correct answer is (B).** Choices (A) and (D) are run-on sentences; choice (C) contains a sentence fragment. Choice (E) improperly places a comma between the subject and verb.

23. **The correct answer is (A).** This is a complete sentence. Choice (B) is a comma splice, choice (C) is a run-on sentence, choice (D) contains a sentence fragment, and choice (E) shows a comma between the verb *decide* and its object *whom*.

24. The correct answer is (B). This is the only choice that uses the correct prepositional phrase (*capable of being*).

25. The correct answer is (D). The modifier *with an exasperated sigh* should be placed next to *Jody's boss*. In addition, choice (C) contains a sentence fragment.

26. The correct answer is (B). This choice is the only one that uses the correct forms of the adjectives *pretty* and *mean*.

27. The correct answer is (C). The word *however* is the clearest and most logical transitional word between the two clauses.

28. The correct answer is (B). It is the least redundant and wordy sentence of the five.

29. The correct answer is (B). In the other choices, the pronoun reference is ambiguous—who's in Spain? Choices (C) and (E) also contain misplaced modifiers: *While he was in Spain*, which seems to refer to *a letter*, rather than a person.

30. The correct answer is (E). It is the clearest and makes effective and consistent use of parallel structure. All the other choices misuse verb tenses.

31. The correct answer is (D). The words in the sentence are in logical order. Choices (A) and (B) are ambiguous—both imply that children might be using plastic bags to suffocate someone. Choice (C) contains a misplaced modifier—the plastic bags seem in danger of suffocating. Choice (E) hints that a person might suffocate children if the plastic bag is not kept out of that person's reach.

32. The correct answer is (E). The error in the other sentences is that of incomplete comparison.

33. The correct answer is (B). This sentence contains the most logical subordinating conjunction, *but*.

34. The correct answer is (D). This version has eliminated the cliché *to the max*, the choppiness and redundancy, and the grammatical error in the parentheses. *Perhaps this is because* also provides a smooth transition.

35. The correct answer is (A). The pronoun *This* most logically refers to *another natural enemy of the aphid . . . more effective than the ladybug*.

36. The correct answer is (D). The characteristics of *other garden predators* are irrelevant to the paragraph, which is all about lacewings.

37. **The correct answer is (A).** Of the choices, this is the only logical transition. The others do not denote an additional function of the lacewing.

38. **The correct answer is (D).** The reader can infer that sentences 2, 6, 8, 16, and 17, in particular, advertise the lacewing as a predator of garden pests.

39. **The correct answer is (D).** The paper appears to be an advertisement in which the ladybug is featured as a competitor of the lacewing.

Going to college?